P9-DYE-674

SAVE IT, FIX IT, KEEP IT, USE IT

1,437 Surprising Ways to Save Cash with Items You Already Have

Publisher's Note

The editors of FC&A have taken careful measures to ensure the accuracy and usefulness of the information in this book. While every attempt has been made to assure accuracy, errors may occur. We advise readers to carefully review and understand the ideas and tips presented and to seek the advice of a qualified professional before attempting to use them. The publisher and editors disclaim all liability (including any injuries, damages or losses) resulting from the use of the information in this book.

The health information in this book is for information only and is not intended to be a medical guide for self-treatment. It does not constitute medical advice and should not be construed as such or used in place of your doctor's medical advice.

"For we walk by faith, not by sight."

— 2 Corinthians 5:7

FC&A Publishing®
103 Clover Green
Peachtree City, GA 30269

Produced by the staff of FC&A

ISBN 978-1-935574-13-2

CONTENTS

In the Kitchen

Let's Eat

Living Spaces

Major Appliances

The Bathroom

Electronics

Your Lawn & Garden

In the Garage

Outside the House

Taking Care of You

Chapter 1

IN THE KITCHEN

Like a carpenter, a cook requires the proper tools. Like a doctor, a cook needs a clean place to operate. Like an artist, a cook should find inspiration in the studio. Make sure your kitchen measures up on all accounts. Discover surprising shortcuts, expert advice, and fun tricks that will help make your kitchen the ideal workspace.

BLENDERS
Puree delight

Clean your blender with ice. Your blender helps make your life easier – until it's time to clean it. Then you struggle to scrub off all the sticky food residue without cutting yourself on the blades. Here's an easier – and safer – way to clean your blender.

Just fill your blender halfway with some lukewarm soapy water, toss in a handful of ice cubes, and run it on high for a minute or two. This trick lets you reach all the blender's nooks and crannies, while also scouring the blades to remove any food buildup.

Prevent disasters with blender basics. Operating a blender is not exactly like operating heavy machinery. But you should still take some commonsense precautions – such as not sticking your hand in it while it's running. Here are some other basic rules for using a blender.

- Don't overdo it. Never let your blender run for too long at one time. For most tasks, the "pulse" setting should do.
- Keep a lid on it. Never run the blender without its lid. Even if you're dealing with just a tiny bit of food, it can make a big mess.
- Stay close. Don't wander too far away from a running blender. In fact, as an extra precaution, you should keep your hand on top of the lid while it's running. Besides keeping the lid on, this also helps make sure the container doesn't come dislodged from the base.
- Come to a full stop. Just like when you're driving and come to a stop sign, make sure your blender comes to a complete

stop before removing the lid or container. You should also let it come to a full stop before switching speed settings.

Turn a Mason jar into a blender. Sick of cleaning out your entire blender after each smoothie you whip up? Try this amazing trick. Swap your regular blender container for a Mason jar. You'll end up with a portable drink in an easy-to-wash container.

Here's how to do it. Most blenders will work with a standard or wide-mouthed Mason jar. Just remove the regular blender container from the base, and screw the base tightly onto your Mason jar full of smoothie fixings. Turn the jar upside down, place it on the blender, and whip up your ingredients.

This trick also works for grinding spices or coffee beans, whipping cream, and making small amounts of things like peanut butter, hummus, or salad dressing. Using a Mason jar for these tasks makes storage a snap. Just screw on the jar's lid and pop the leftovers in your refrigerator. When you need to blend something else, just grab a new Mason jar.

Keep the Mason jar trick in mind for emergencies. If your regular blender container breaks, you can always use a Mason jar until you have time to run out and buy a replacement.

To be safe, don't overfill the Mason jar or use it to blend extremely hot liquids.

COFFEE MAKERS

Singing the brews

Vanquish buildup with vinegar. Your senses will tell you when something isn't right with your coffee maker. Perhaps your coffee pot looks a bit grungy. Maybe your coffee maker makes strange clicking noises – or just makes bad-tasting coffee. When your senses spot trouble, try this sensible solution. Clean your coffee maker with vinegar.

Fill the tank with a mixture of vinegar and water, and put it through a brewing cycle. The vinegar should clear any leftover oils and mineral deposits inside the machine. This buildup can cause clicking noises, affect the taste of your coffee, and impair your coffee maker's performance.

You can also use full-strength vinegar to flush out the machine. As a bonus, vinegar will also help remove any brown film from your coffee pot. When you're finished flushing the coffee maker, dump the pot and wash it with hot, soapy water. Then brew a few pots of plain water to rinse the vinegar from the machine. Your next pot of coffee should be a treat for all of your senses.

Painless way to clean your coffee maker. When heartburn hurts, Alka-Seltzer can help relieve the pain. Cleaning your coffee maker can also be a real pain – until Alka-Seltzer comes to the rescue.

For an easy way to clean your coffee maker, fill the water chamber with water and plop in three or four tablets of Alka-Seltzer. Let the tablets dissolve, then put the coffee maker through the brew cycle. Rinse the chamber with water a few times, then run another brew cycle with plain water to get rid of any residue. Now your coffee maker is clean and ready for brewing.

Blunt bitterness with salt. Sipping coffee shouldn't make you shudder. Try this trick to make your coffee less bitter. Add a pinch of salt. It may sound odd, but salt blocks the taste of bitterness – without making your coffee taste salty. Add about 1/8 of a teaspoon of salt to your coffee grounds before brewing a pot. Or just stir a tiny bit of salt directly into your cup. It will dissolve quickly.

Besides masking bitterness, salt also helps bring out other, more subtle flavors that you may not have noticed before. Instead of shuddering, you will be savoring your new and improved cup of coffee.

COOKWARE

Putting a lid on pots & pans

Banish burned food from pots and pans. Dinner might be ruined, but don't let burned food ruin your cookware, too. Here's how to "fizz" burned-on gunk off your pots and pans. No scrubbing required. Simply fill your pan with warm water, dissolve five or six tablets of Alka-Seltzer in it, and let it sit for an hour or so. What a relief – your pan should be good as new.

Baking soda can also help rescue a burned pan. Cover the bottom of your pan with baking soda, then fill it with water and simmer for about an hour. The burned residue should come right off. You can also pour baking soda onto the bottom of the pan, moisten the baking soda with some water, and let it soak overnight.

Rescue casserole dishes from baked-on food. Covered casserole dishes often collect food splatters and baked-on gunk. Fortunately, you can restore them to their former glory with ease.

Make a paste using equal amounts vinegar and cream of tartar, and spread it on your casserole dish or lid. Let it sit for up to an hour, then wipe it off. The gunk should wash off easily.

4 cheap ways to clean copper. Copper cookware can be expensive. Good thing cleaning it doesn't have to be. These everyday kitchen items can help keep your copper pots and pans shiny for pennies.

- Lemon juice and salt. Cut a lemon in half, sprinkle it with salt, and rub it on your copper cookware to restore its shine.
- Vinegar and baking soda. Mix equal parts vinegar and baking soda into a paste. You can also use a little flour to thicken the paste. With a wet cloth, apply the paste to your pots and gently rub out any tarnish.
- Ketchup. Apply a mixture of ketchup and water to your pans with a soft cloth. Or simply dip a cloth in ketchup and rub your pans with it.
- Yogurt. This tasty snack helps remove spots from your copper pots. Cover the stains with yogurt and let it sit for about five minutes. The stains will disappear.

When you're finished cleaning the copper, rinse your pots and pans thoroughly and dry them with a soft towel. Then stand back and admire your shiny copper cookware.

Get rid of grease with coffee grounds. Your morning coffee can do more than perk you up – it can also help perk up your dirty cookware. Instead of throwing away your used coffee grounds, use them to scour greasy pots and pans. Wet coffee grounds, which are very abrasive and acidic, can help scrub away grease and odors from hard-to-clean dishes.

Clever ways to care for cast iron. Cast iron cookware can be passed down for generations – as long as it's cared for properly. Once you've seasoned your cast iron pots and pans, take care not to ruin the finish. That usually means avoiding soapy water when cleaning them. Here are some handy ways to keep your cast iron clean and rust-free.

- Mesh around. Plastic mesh produce bags come in handy for scrubbing cast iron clean. Wait until the pan cools, then wipe it with the mesh bag. The bag won't harm the seasoning like steel wool, and you can throw it away when you're done.

- Shake on some salt. Coarse salt, like kosher salt, works as an abrasive to remove stuck-on food and rust. Team it with hot water or warm vegetable oil to get rid of debris.

- Scrub with a spud. If your pan has become rusty, try this trick. Slice a potato in half and squirt a little dish detergent on the cut end. Use the potato to rub away rust spots. Rinse, dry thoroughly, and apply a light layer of oil to your cookware when you're finished.

- Simply sponge. For less drastic cleaning, run the still-warm pan under hot water and wipe it with a dishcloth or kitchen sponge.

- Minimize moisture. Dry your cast iron thoroughly so it doesn't rust. You can even set your pan on the stove or in a warm oven for a few minutes to remove any trace of moisture.

- Store safely. Proper storage also helps prevent rust. Remove lids for better air circulation. When stacking pans, line each one with paper towels.

Break out your bundt pan for better chicken. A vertical roaster helps cook chicken evenly, resulting in perfectly crispy skin and juicy meat. But chances are you don't have a vertical roaster in your kitchen. Instead of buying this specialty item, turn to an alternative you probably do have – a bundt pan.

It's easy to turn your bundt pan into a makeshift vertical roaster. Simply slide a whole chicken onto the post in the middle with the legs facing down. This allows the chicken to stand upright and baste in its own juices. As a bonus, the bundt pan can also hold potatoes and veggies, so you can cook a whole meal in one place.

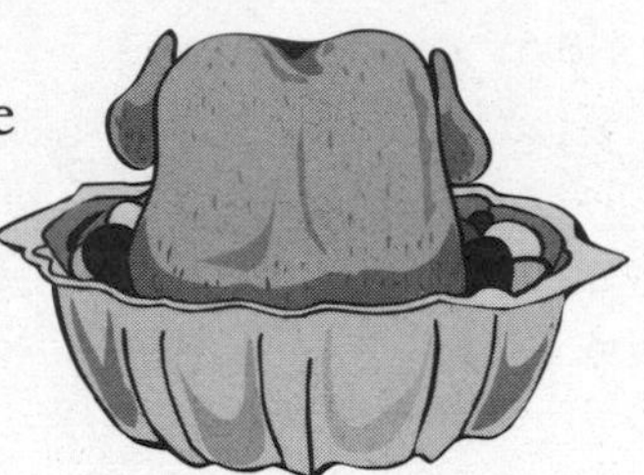

Don't forget to put a baking sheet on the oven rack below your bundt pan, which likely has a hole in the middle. That way, the baking sheet will catch any juices before they drip to the bottom of your oven.

You'll enjoy this new way of cooking chicken – and give your often-neglected bundt pan a new purpose in life.

Trusty way to bust rust. You need to wash your metal pans and baking sheets after you use them – but repeated exposure to water can lead to rust. Dissolve rust from your metal cookware with a combination of lemon juice and salt.

Sprinkle some coarse salt on the rusty spots, then add lemon juice. For an even stronger solution, mix some vinegar with the lemon juice. Let it sit for a little bit – but not too long – then wipe it off, rinse, and dry thoroughly. The rust will be gone, but the fresh citrus smell will remain.

COUNTERTOPS
A surface for every purpose

Zap germs with homemade disinfectants. You need to keep your countertops clean and free of germs – but you don't need to buy expensive commercial cleaning products to do it. Make your own countertop disinfectant with everyday household items.

Put two tablespoons of ammonia, one-half cup of rubbing alcohol, and one-quarter cup of vinegar in a spray bottle. Fill the bottle with water, and spray it on your countertops.

Another option is to mix two teaspoons of borax, four tablespoons of vinegar, and three cups of hot water in a spray bottle. Spray or wipe the mixture onto your counters.

You can also try this two-step process. First, spray your countertops with straight vinegar and wipe them down. Then spray them with hydrogen peroxide and wipe them down again. This combination works as well as any commercial disinfectant on the market.

Try one of these simple disinfecting methods, and you'll clean your countertops without cleaning out your wallet.

Tackle stains with a lemon. Countertop stains can put any cook in a sour mood. Here's a simple way to clean your laminate countertops. Cut a lemon in half, squeeze some of its juice on the counter, and use the lemon to scrub away the stains.

For added scouring power, you can salt the lemon before scrubbing. Let the lemon juice work its magic for a little while, then rinse the surface with water and dry it. Your countertop should be stain-free and lemony fresh.

Fix flaws with a cutting board. Oops! You dropped a heavy jar onto your laminate countertop, and it left a large, ugly gouge. Instead of replacing your entire countertop, try this cutting-edge solution.

Using a router or saber saw, cut out the damaged area of your countertop. Then replace the damaged section with a wooden cutting board – holding it in place with a metal frame.

This trick not only fixes the damage, it also gives you a handy, built-in chopping surface. It's especially convenient if the damage occurred next to your sink or stove, where you're most likely to use a cutting board.

Offbeat way to prevent countertop scratches. Perhaps you protect your hardwood floors by putting self-adhesive felt pads under the legs of your tables and chairs. Use these same little pads to protect your kitchen counters from scratches and scuff marks.

Simply stick a few felt pads under any small appliances you keep on your countertop. You'll be able to easily slide your mixer or coffee maker back and forth on your counter without scratching the surface.

DISHES & CHINA

Tabletop tips

Good guidelines for using good china. Chances are you only break out your good china for special occasions. But if you follow these tips, you should be able to use your china more often. Find out the best ways to store, wash, and use your good china without damaging it.

- Filter out trouble. Coffee filters aren't just for making coffee. The perfect way to protect fragile china is with this item usually used in a kitchen appliance. When storing your china, place a flattened coffee filter between each dish. You'll prevent scuffs and scratches.

- Wrap it up. You can also wrap your china in heavy-duty plastic wrap. This will keep dust out so you won't have to wash it before using it next time.

- Ditch the dishwasher. Wash your china by hand with a mild detergent. Because of the high heat and abrasive detergent, the dishwasher may harm your china. However, if your china was made in the past 30 years, it may be dishwasher-safe. Check to make sure.

- Banish bleach. Don't use bleach, which can damage the finish.

- Nix the knives. Don't use steak knives on china plates.

- Counteract cracking. To prevent cracks in your old china teacups, pour the milk first, then follow with the hot tea. Pouring hot tea over a spoon in the cup should also do the trick.

- Get the facts before microwaving. Don't put antique china in the microwave. Newer china may be microwave-safe, but use caution. Make sure there is no metal banding or decoration on the plate. When in doubt, keep it out. Better safe than sorry.

Discover new uses for coffee filters. Coffee filters can protect your good china during storage. But that's just one of the many things you can do with these cheap and incredibly handy kitchen items. Discover how to fix a busted speaker good-as-new with a coffee filter – and dozens more sneaky household secrets that can save you hundreds of bucks every year. Here's how.

- Make sweet music. To repair a torn speaker cone, make a patch out of a coffee filter. Cut the filter slightly larger than the damaged area, and carefully glue it in place. Rubber cement or plain white glue should do the trick.
- Serve some snacks. Coffee filters make convenient disposable bowls for popcorn, pretzels, chips, and other finger foods.
- Gather ingredients. When baking or cooking, you can measure your dry ingredients into coffee filters for easy access.
- Give it a rest. Use a coffee filter as a spoon rest when cooking.
- Swab spills. Grab a coffee filter to wipe up spills on your kitchen counter.
- Season sauces. For soups and sauces, wrap inedible ingredients like bay leafs or cinnamon sticks in a coffee filter, tie it up, and drop it in the pot. You can easily remove it before serving.
- Pamper your decorations. Wrap your Christmas ornaments in coffee filters for storage.

- Minimize messes. Use a coffee filter to hold a messy sandwich or catch drips from a popsicle.

- Preserve your plants. Line your potted plants with coffee filters so the soil doesn't fall through the drainage holes.

- Wipe out grime. Clean your windows and mirrors with coffee filters. They leave no lint or residue behind.

- Shine your shoes. Apply shoe polish with a balled-up coffee filter.

Foil filmy glasses. Tired of those cloudy drinking glasses? Two household items can get rid of the frustrating film – vinegar and paper towels.

Soak paper towels in white vinegar, then wrap the towels around the inside and outside of your cloudy glasses. Let the vinegar work its magic for a while, then rinse.

You can also soak the glasses in warm white vinegar for about an hour. Then rub them gently with a dishcloth to remove the film. Adding some white vinegar to your dishwasher rinse aid dispenser will also help get rid of any soapy film on your glassware.

Simple way to clean a greasy kitchen. Wipe grease spatters from stovetops with ease. Just use this cheap and simple homemade grease cutter. Mix equal parts vinegar and water in a spray bottle. Spray it on your stovetop, rub it with a paper towel, then wipe the surface dry. You'll be left with no streaks or grease spots.

To remove grease and stains from your dishes or pots and pans, add about a quarter-cup of vinegar to some dish soap and hot water. The same mixture works to wipe down your cabinets, oven, and stovetop.

You can get fancy and concoct a homemade cleaner using citrus peels and vinegar. Just put orange, lemon, and lime peels in a jar, pour vinegar over them, and let it sit for a few weeks. Strain the mixture, and spray it on your stovetop to get rid of grease. Or you could keep things really simple. Full-strength vinegar will also cut through grease.

Snuff out fluff with starch. Had enough of the fluff? Rinse the kitchen towels you use to dry your dishes and glasses in a weak starch solution. This will help prevent fuzzy lint from sticking to them.

Clay makes repairs easier. You may be able to salvage a broken cup or saucer by gluing it back together. But it can be tedious holding the pieces in place while the glue dries. To make this step simpler, use modeling clay as a homemade clamp.

Flatten out the clay, dab glue on the edges of your broken item, fix the pieces in position, and press the item into the clay. The clay will secure the pieces firmly together – leaving your hands free to do something else. When the adhesive sets, just peel off the clay.

HANDY HINT

Colorful trick to mask repairs

How do you hide any evidence that your china has been glued back together? Here's a hint — tint. Mix a dab of paint that matches the color of your china with the epoxy before you apply it.

Add just enough paint to tint the epoxy without thinning it. This tinted glue works just as well as the clear kind — but won't leave a telltale line. Your repair should blend right in with the original color of your china.

Surprising way to mend cracked china. Got milk? If so, you also have the key to repairing slightly cracked china. Place your damaged china in a pot and cover it with milk. Any kind of milk will do – whole, skim, fat-free, or even powdered milk mixed with water.

Bring the milk to a boil, then reduce the heat and simmer for 45 minutes to an hour. Let the milk cool completely before removing the china.

The crack should be gone. That's because the protein in milk can mend most hairline cracks. When heated, this protein expands and fills the crack. As it cools, it bonds with the surface of your china to seal the crack. You can also soak your cracked china in warm milk overnight.

Quick fix for chipped glasses. Don't let a minor chip turn into a major catastrophe. Before you throw out your chipped glass, try this trick. Rub the chip with extra-fine sandpaper to make it smooth. Make sure to sand the rest of the rim, too, so the repair blends in.

One way to do this is to wrap the sandpaper around a small wooden block, then wet the paper. Lay the rim of the glass on the sandpaper and slowly rotate the glass to smooth the rim evenly.

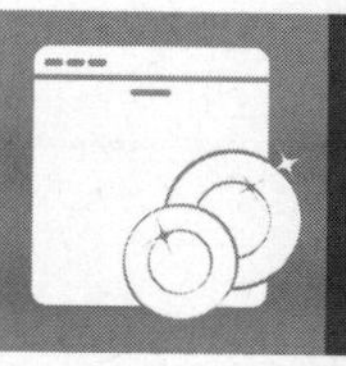

DISHWASHERS

A tough take on grime

Skimp on soap for superior results. Sometimes less is more. You would think that adding more detergent to your dishwasher would get your dishes cleaner. But the opposite is true. To get cleaner dishes for less money, use less detergent.

Chances are you're using too much – not too little – detergent. That's because modern machines use less water, and detergent has become much more concentrated. When you fill the dishwasher's soap cup to the brim, you're just wasting money. Too much soap can also leave a film on your dishes and a soapy residue in your machine. This can lead to mold or mildew buildup.

Putting less soap in your dishwasher's soap cup keeps more money in your pocket. Try cutting back to one teaspoon of liquid or powder detergent. At most, one tablespoon should do the trick.

WARNING

5 things to keep out of your dishwasher.

It may seem easier just to put everything in your dishwasher — but some items should not go in there. Keep these things out of your dishwasher.

- Knives. The blades can become pitted and the wooden handles can crack.
- Nonstick pots and pans. The nonstick surface can become damaged.
- Wooden bowls or utensils. The heat and water can cause wood to split or crack.
- Copper or cast iron cookware. These metals can become damaged and even harm your other dishes.
- Delicate glassware. These items can break in your dishwasher.

Save money with homemade detergent. Stop shelling out big bucks for costly commercial dishwasher detergent. Make your own powerful detergent for pennies. Just mix equal parts borax and baking soda, and store the mixture in a plastic container. Use about two tablespoons of your homemade detergent per load.

Make sure to add some vinegar to your dishwasher's rinse compartment to help prevent residue. Your dishes should come out spot-free.

Flip-free way to wash plastic containers

Plastic containers come in handy for storing leftovers. But when you wash them in the dishwasher, they often flip over and fill with water. To prevent that from happening, put your plastic containers on your dishwasher's upper shelf and place a wire cooling rack on top of them. The wire rack holds your containers in place, while still letting soapy water come through.

Super strategy for silverware. Variety is the spice of life and the key to loading your silverware in the dishwasher. Keeping your utensils organized – forks with forks, spoons with spoons – may make emptying the dishwasher quicker. But it may also leave your silverware less than sparkling clean.

When utensils nest together, food can stick to spoons or fork tines. To prevent this, mix and match. Instead of separating your utensils, stick forks, spoons, and knives in the same basket. Or simply alternate which way the handles face. Put some silverware handle up and others handle down to keep the pieces from nesting.

No matter how you load your silverware, all that bending over and straightening up can be rough on your back. Try this trick. When loading your dishwasher, put the silverware holder in the sink. When it's full, replace it with just one stoop.

Simple steps to maintain your dishwasher. Your dishwasher makes cleanup a breeze. Luckily, dishwasher maintenance is also a snap. Follow these easy tips to keep your dishwasher running smoothly.

- Don't overfill it. You run the risk of blocking the dishwasher's spray arm. Your dishes may not come clean – and they could even become damaged because of the overcrowding.

- Scrape food from dishes. You may not need to rinse your dishes before placing them in the dishwasher, but you should at least scrape the food off them. Too much food could clog the machine.

- Clean the spray arm. The small holes in the spray arm can become clogged with food debris or dried soap. Use a pipe cleaner, awl, or stiff wire to clear these holes. You can also soak the spray arm in warm vinegar or a vinegar and water solution to loosen mineral deposits.

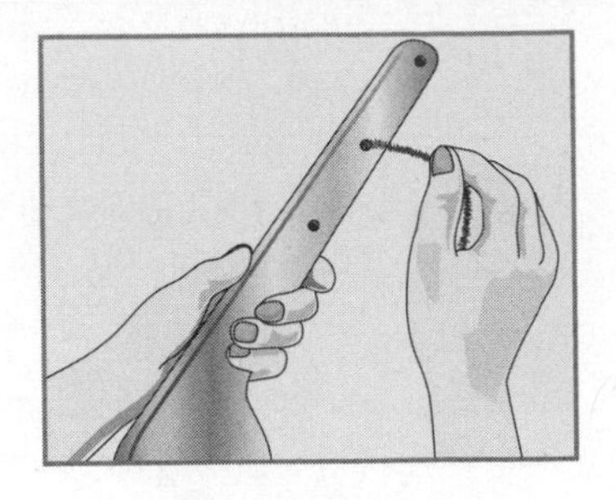

- Clear the trap. The trap at the bottom of your dishwasher catches the food that falls from the dishes. Periodically remove the trap and wash it to get rid of any food or soap particles.

- Run it on empty. Clean and freshen the inside of your dishwasher by running it empty with a cup of baking soda and 1 1/2 cups of vinegar.

- Inspect the gaskets. If water leaks onto your floor in front of your dishwasher, a damaged or worn-out gasket could be to blame. Check the gaskets for cracks or other signs of damage and replace them if necessary. Use a soft brush to clean the gaskets, which can collect food debris.

- Bust the rust. Check your dishwasher rack for nicks or scratches. If the plastic finish wears away and the metal underneath becomes exposed, it can rust – and leave rust on your dishes. You can buy a repair kit to fix this problem.

- Look at the hoses. Check the supply and drain hoses every year for signs of deterioration. Replace them if necessary. Don't wait until they burst and flood your kitchen.

- Keep it level. Make sure your dishwasher is level, so it doesn't leak. You can adjust the feet to raise or lower either side.

- Push the buttons. If you always run your dishwasher on the same setting, the electronic keypad could malfunction when you finally try to use a different setting. To keep your keypad problem-free, push all the buttons at least once a month.

Cheap way to update your kitchen. Tired of looking at your same old kitchen? Give it a makeover. Instead of buying a brand new dishwasher, spruce up your old one with a new paint job.

You can buy appliance paint, which works on dishwashers, refrigerators, washing machines, and cabinets. Follow the instructions, which can vary from brand to brand and by type of paint. But, in general, these tips should work.

- Clean your appliance with soap and water, and let it dry.
- Scrape off any rust with a wire brush or sandpaper. You may also want to apply a treatment on rust spots so the rust doesn't spread or show up through the new paint.
- Get rid of any trace of grease or appliance polish with deglosser.
- Remove or tape any parts, like handles, that you don't want painted.
- Unplug the appliance, and make sure your painting area is well-ventilated.
- Spray on the paint in a steady back-and-forth motion. Slightly overlap each stroke.
- Apply two light coats a few minutes apart, then add another coat within an hour.
- Let it dry completely before moving it back. It should be ready to use again in 24 hours.

GARBAGE DISPOSALS
Make short work of waste

10 little-known disposal troublemakers. Your garbage disposal may seem like a ravenous creature, eager to gobble up anything you feed it. But it's actually quite finicky. Take care not to put the following items down your disposal. They will only cause trouble.

- bones
- sand
- celery
- apple seeds
- twist-ties
- broken glass
- grease
- eggshells
- scouring pads
- drain cleaners

You might have heard that bones, broken glass, or sand will sharpen the disposal's blades, but that's not true. Bones may even clog up the machine. While soft, crisp foods go down the disposal easily, hard or stringy ones – like celery, eggshells, and apple seeds – may cause a jam.

Grease can also gum up the works. If you do happen to get grease down the disposal, some people recommend flushing it with hot water. But this could cause serious problems. The melted grease can run down the drain and coat the pipe. When it cools, it becomes a trap for bits of food and debris, which can form a clog. Flush grease with cold water instead. The grease will harden into clumps and float safely through the pipes instead of sticking to them.

It may seem obvious, but make sure kitchen items like silverware, scouring pads, and twist-ties don't make their way down your disposal. If something does get stuck, turn off the power and pull out the item with needle-nose pliers.

Steer clear of commercial drain cleaners, which can cause permanent damage to your disposal.

Freshen a foul-smelling disposal. Bits of food and debris disappear down your garbage disposal, but the smell lingers. Try these simple tricks to clean and deodorize your stinky disposal.

- Clean blades with cubes. Toss several ice cubes down the disposal. The ice cubes will clean the disposal's cutting blades without nicking them.
- Clear the air with citrus. For a fresh scent, cut citrus fruits like lemons, limes, oranges, and grapefruits into bite-size pieces and put them down the disposal with the ice cubes. The rinds of these fruits will also freshen your disposal.
- Brush up on cleanliness. Use an old toothbrush and warm, soapy water to clean under the flaps of the disposal's black rubber cover. Sometimes bits of food get trapped under these flaps, leading to unpleasant odors. If the cover pops off, remove it and thoroughly wash it with soapy water.
- Banish odors with baking soda. Pour a half-cup of baking soda down the drain, followed by a cup of vinegar. Stop up the drain and let the mixture fizz for a while. Flush it with a kettle of boiling water. Similarly, you can toss a handful of baking soda and half a lemon down the disposal while running cold water.
- Reach for some bleach. Add a tablespoon of liquid bleach to a gallon of water, and slowly pour it down the drain. Let it sit for a few minutes, then flush with cold, running water.
- Salt away smells. Dump a strong salt brine down the drain to get rid of odors and grease.

"Handle" jams with a broomstick. You don't need fancy tools to fix a jammed garbage disposal – just grab a broomstick. After making sure the disposal is turned off at the fuse box, stick your broom handle down into the disposal. Push the handle against one of the blades and crank in a circular motion. Then crank in the opposite direction. Push firmly, but not too hard – you don't want to disconnect the disposal unit from the sink and drain line.

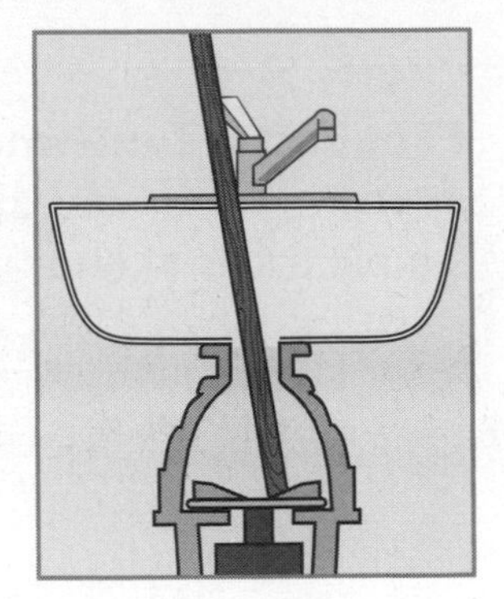

Once the blades are turning freely, remove the broomstick and turn the disposal back on. Your garbage disposal should be working perfectly again.

HANDY HINT

Reset button to the rescue

Garbage disposal not working? The solution may be as simple as one push of a button. Before resorting to drastic measures, look for your disposal's reset button. Most units come with a red or black reset button, which is usually located on the bottom of the disposal under the sink.

Sticky trick to keep track of an important tool. Even the handiest tool doesn't do you any good if you can't find it when you need it. Your garbage disposal probably came with an Allen wrench, the L-shaped kind with a six-sided head. Keep this wrench taped to the side of your disposal unit with masking or duct tape. That way, if you need to unstick a jam, you'll have easy access to it.

Here's how to use the wrench to get a stuck garbage disposal working again. Make sure the disposal is turned off. Then locate the hole underneath the unit. Insert the wrench and turn it back and forth. This should help clear the motor shaft. Once you can feel the unit turning freely, remove the wrench and turn the disposal back on.

That should solve the problem. Just don't forget to tape the wrench to the side of the unit again.

KITCHEN TOOLS
Handy & jim-dandy gadgets

Sharp ideas for storing knives. To chop, slice, and dice your food, you need to keep your kitchen knives sharp. You also need to store them safely. Just tossing loose knives in a drawer is asking for trouble. Not only do you risk damaging the blades, you also risk injury when you rummage through the drawer.

You could buy a butcher-block knife holder, a magnetic wall strip, or individual knife guards to store your knives. Or you can try one of these low-cost, homemade solutions.

- File it away. Transform a manila folder into a knife sheath. Cut the folder into a rectangle using the folded edge as one side. Use your knife blade as a guide to determine how big to make the sheath. Be sure to leave a little room around the blade. Staple the top and side of the rectangle shut, leaving the bottom open to slide your knife in and out. Heavy-duty construction paper also works.

- Try a tube. Turn your empty paper towel tube into a sheath. Flatten the cardboard tube, fold over one end, and either staple or tape it shut. Then slide your knife into the other end. For smaller knives, you can use the same trick with empty toilet paper tubes.

- Box it up. Similarly, you can turn an empty cereal or cracker box into a homemade knife sheath. Cut or tear a section of the box so it's a little longer than the knife blade and more than twice as wide. Lay the knife across the box and fold the cardboard over the blade. Use tape to bind the sheath shut.

- Put a cork in it. Here's a handy way to recycle your wine corks. Glue several corks together, side by side, to form a knife holder. Place the strip of corks in your drawer and rest your knives blade-side down in the slits between the corks.

ALTERNATE USES

Cutting-edge uses for pizza cutters

Your pizza cutter doesn't have to cut only pizza. The sharp wheel comes in handy for several other kitchen tasks. Use your pizza cutter to separate waffle segments, slice a grilled cheese sandwich, cut strips of dough for a lattice pie crust, slice bar cookies and fudge, cut a sheet cake into perfect pieces, mill herbs, make a chopped salad, and cut through puff pastry or quesadillas.

Reduce the "strain" of making stock. You can always buy chicken stock at the grocery store. But you end up with more flavor when you make your own. Of course, you also end up with more of a mess. Make cleanup easier with this simple trick.

Put a pasta insert in your stockpot. Then toss in the chicken, carrots, onion, celery, and other ingredients. Fill the pot with water and let it simmer all day. When your stock is done, simply lift out the pasta insert to get rid of the bones and veggies. You may still need to strain the remaining liquid, but it will be much easier with all of the big, messy stuff out of the way.

Cut cleanly with dental floss. Sometimes soft foods are hard to cut. To make neater slices, skip the knife and reach for some dental floss. Hold the floss taut and press down, applying even pressure. This trick works well for soft desserts, like layer cakes, and soft cheeses, like goat cheese. You'll end up with perfect slices without making a mess.

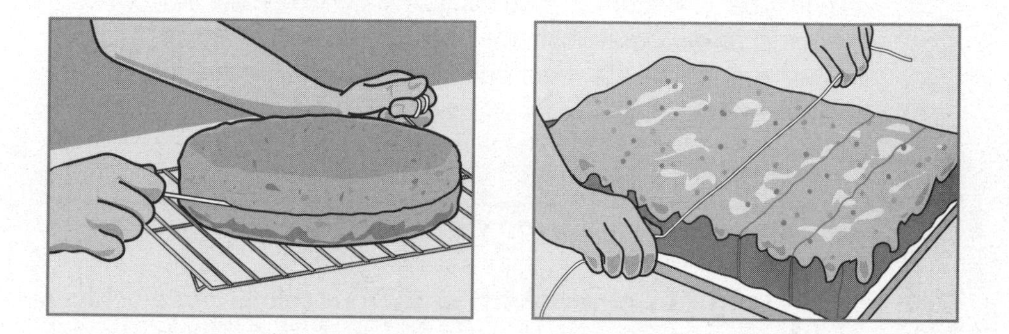

Great ways to clean your grater. It's not always easy to make your cheese grater less cheesy. Stubborn bits of cheese often cling to the grater's holes, resulting in much soaking and scrubbing. Try these tactics to make cleanup less of a hassle.

- Spray it away. Spray nonstick cooking spray on the cheese grater before you even grate any cheese. You'll spend less time scrubbing it later. You'll also have an easier time grating the cheese.
- Fight food with food. Grate a raw potato, apple, or lemon after you grate the cheese. These foods help remove the cheesy residue left on the grater.
- Freeze the cheese. Pop the grater in the freezer for a few hours. The frozen bits of cheese should be easier to scrape off.

- Brush away the bits. Use a toothbrush to scrub your cheese grater. Keep one in your kitchen just for this purpose.

Surprising uses for an egg slicer

With an egg slicer, you can easily cut hard-boiled eggs. But don't let this handy kitchen tool collect dust between batches of egg salad. Hatch up fun, new ways to use your egg slicer. For example, you can use it to slice olives, mushrooms, strawberries, bananas, beets, and soft cheeses, like fresh mozzarella. Your egg slicer will cut these foods neatly, without dirtying a cutting board.

Rub your rolling pin clean with salt. Your rolling pin quickly rolls out dough – but it may not be so quick to part with it. Try this super trick for quicker cleanup. Before you wash and dry your rolling pin, sprinkle it with salt. Then rub it with your hand to loosen any bits of pastry stuck to it. Now your rolling pin should be easier to clean.

Take the "stink" out of wooden utensils. Wooden utensils have a tendency to absorb food odors. But you can take steps to keep your wooden spoons smelling fresh. To prevent new wooden utensils from picking up food odors, soak them overnight in cider or white vinegar before you use them.

To remove food odors from an older wooden spoon or cutting board, scrub it with a mixture of baking soda and water. Baking soda will help neutralize strong smells from foods like garlic, onions, peppers, and seafood.

Make hard-to-read numbers easier to read. Instead of throwing out your old measuring cups, give them a touch of glamour. Use brightly colored nail polish to make the faded markings and numbers more legible. This trick also works for tiny, hard-to-read plastic medicine cups. As a bonus, you can use up the nail polish you don't wear anymore.

ALTERNATE USES

Mesh bags provide dishwasher safety net

Those mesh bags that hold onions and other produce also do a good job of holding things in place in your dishwasher. To prevent skinny items from slipping through the bottom of your dishwasher's silverware basket, line the bottom of the tray with mesh bags. This trick keeps silverware in, but still lets water out.

The bags also work to hold tiny items together. Just place any items that are too small for the shelf in the bag, twist it closed, and hook it over one of the posts on the top shelf. The netting allows water to clean the items, but also keeps them from falling through to the bottom.

Quick trick to clean up a dropped egg. Splat! You dropped a raw egg on your kitchen floor. Instead of trying to wipe it up with a towel, which will only smear it, try this timesaving trick. Suck up the dropped egg with a turkey baster. Then squirt the broken egg into the trash. Your mess will be gone in a flash.

Turn a milk jug into a funnel. Funnels come in handy for pouring things like sauces, gravies, or cooking grease into containers. But you don't need to buy funnels from a fancy kitchen store. Make your own funnels for free. Just cut off the tops of your empty plastic milk jugs or soda bottles. Turn the tops upside down, and pour in your liquids.

Rack up perfect bread slices. Having trouble slicing bread evenly? Your oven rack makes a helpful slicing tool. Just open your oven door, slide the rack out, and put your loaf of bread on it. Place a towel on the open oven door to catch any crumbs. Then slice the bread, using the spaces in the rack as your guide. You'll end up with perfectly neat bread slices.

Find a hidden treasure in your cereal box. Get more out of your cereal box than a sugary breakfast. Save the empty plastic liners from cereal boxes and use them as wax paper.

Stop steel wool from rusting. Make sure your steel wool pads stay rust-free. Keep them in a jar of soapy water or wrap them in aluminum foil. You can also store soapy steel wool pads in your freezer. They thaw quickly and will not rust.

ALTERNATE USES

Can-do method to open plastic packaging

Merchants use rigid "clamshell" packaging to protect their products from shoplifters — but this pesky packaging can be a real pain to open. Stop struggling with scissors or risking injury to your hands. Use a manual can opener instead.

Just turn the package face down, insert the corner of the package between the blade and the clamp, and turn. The sharp wheels of the can opener will cut through the thick plastic without harming your fingers. Cut around the package's edges until you can open it all the way.

Salvage a soggy salad. Your salad spinner helps clean your greens before you make a salad. But it can also come in handy if you accidentally overdress your salad. Just pop the soggy salad back in the spinner and give it a whirl. The excess dressing should fly off. You can even dump the extra dressing back in the jar to use later.

MICROWAVES
Heating things up in a hurry

Mop up microwave messes in minutes. Your microwave lets you cook or reheat food in a flash. But it can also accumulate splatters and gunk at a rapid rate. Luckily, cleaning your microwave can be just as quick and easy as cooking in it. Just follow these tips.

- Warm some water. Put a mixture of water and vinegar in a bowl and zap it for a few minutes. Leave the microwave door shut for about 15 minutes. The moisture and steam from the heated water will help loosen any gunk, and you should be able to wipe it off easily with a moist cloth. Water with a few teaspoons of baking soda also works.

- Freshen the air. You can deodorize while you clean by adding some lemon or lime slices to the bowl of water. A tablespoon of vanilla extract will also do the trick. As the water boils, the pleasant scents will penetrate your microwave and get rid of any lingering odors.

- Soak a sponge. Instead of using a bowl of water, you can soak a sponge in very hot water and vinegar and place it in your microwave. Let the steam work its magic, then wipe the inside of your microwave with the sponge. Wear rubber gloves because the sponge will be hot.

- Take "charge." Scrape off stubborn crud with a credit card. Avoid using anything too sharp, like a razor, or you could scratch the walls of your microwave.

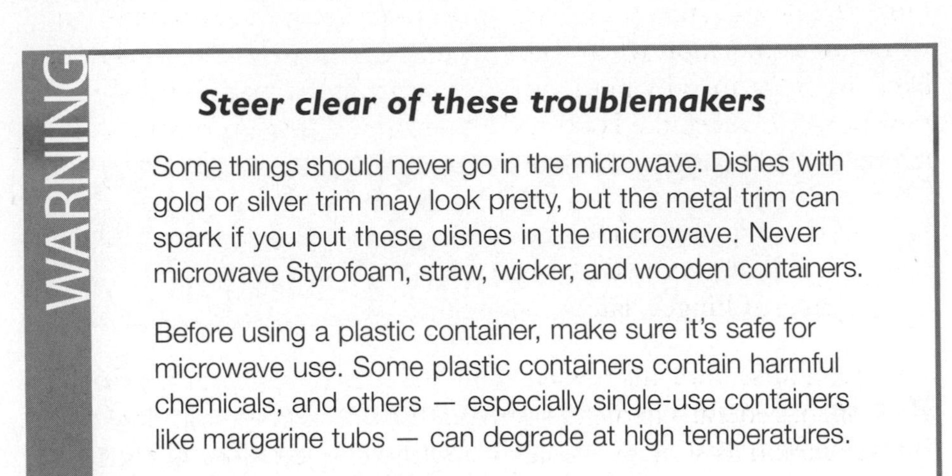

WARNING

Steer clear of these troublemakers

Some things should never go in the microwave. Dishes with gold or silver trim may look pretty, but the metal trim can spark if you put these dishes in the microwave. Never microwave Styrofoam, straw, wicker, and wooden containers.

Before using a plastic container, make sure it's safe for microwave use. Some plastic containers contain harmful chemicals, and others — especially single-use containers like margarine tubs — can degrade at high temperatures.

Filter out food splatters. Here's an easy way to prevent splatters when reheating leftovers in the microwave. Just cover your dish or bowl with a paper coffee filter. You can reuse the same filter a few times, making it a good alternative to plastic wrap.

Quick trick to test dishes for safety. Not sure if a dish is microwave-safe? Put it to the test. Place a cup of water on top of the dish and put it in the microwave at full power for one minute. If the dish remains cool and the water gets warm, then the dish is safe to use. But if the dish becomes warm and the water stays cool, don't use the dish. A warm dish means the dish is absorbing the microwave rays rather than letting them pass through to cook your food.

In general, glass and porcelain are safe for microwave use. So is wax paper. Follow manufacturers' recommendations for pottery, clay, earthenware, and china. Make sure other items – including plastic wrap, plastic containers, and paper products – have been approved for microwave use. Even some aluminum foil or metals may be OK for microwaving, but make sure to check first.

Simple steps to stay safe. Microwave ovens use radiation to heat food. While this may sound scary, you don't have to worry about exposure to radiation when using your microwave. You're much more likely to be harmed by hot food, splattering grease, or steam than by radiation. However, the Food and Drug Administration recommends taking the following precautions.

- Don't use your microwave if the door does not close firmly or if it is bent, warped, or damaged. Radiation could leak from damaged hinges, latches, or seals.
- Don't use your microwave if it continues to run with the door open. Federal standards stipulate that ovens must stop producing radiation as soon as the latch is released or the door is opened.
- Don't lean directly against a microwave for long periods of time while it is in use. Make sure your children avoid doing this as well.
- Don't heat water or other liquids in the microwave for too long. The water could become "superheated," or heated past its boiling temperature. This superheated water, which does not appear to be boiling, can erupt out of the cup and scald your hands or face.
- Put something in it. Some microwaves should not be turned on when empty. Check your instruction manual, and follow all recommended procedures.

Unconventional uses for your microwave. You probably use your microwave mainly to reheat leftovers or pop popcorn. But this handy appliance can do so much more. Here are just a few of the surprising things you can do.

- Sterilize a wooden cutting board. Just zap it for five minutes in your microwave.

- Coax more juice from citrus fruits. Pop a lemon or lime in your microwave for 15 seconds before juicing it. You'll squeeze out more juice.
- Soothe your pain. Fill a cotton sock or small, cotton pillowcase with dry rice and sew it shut. Warm your homemade heating pad in your microwave for a minute or two and use it to ease aches and pains.
- Peel potatoes promptly. Wash your spuds, pierce them with a fork in several places, microwave for 10 minutes, and let cool. The skins will become wrinkled, and you'll be able to pull them off easily under cold water. You can also peel garlic cloves easily by zapping them in your microwave for about 15 seconds.
- Flatten playing cards. All that shuffling has left your playing cards bent. Deal with this problem by quickly zapping the deck to straighten out the cards.

OVENS & COOKTOPS

Keeping it red hot & new

3 clever ways to clean your oven. Yummy casseroles, succulent roasts, and delicious desserts may come out of your oven. But what stays behind – grease, grime, and caked-on food – makes cleaning your oven a daunting task. Stop dreading this unpleasant but necessary job. You don't even need to buy costly oven cleaners or wear yourself out scrubbing. Clean your oven the easy way with these everyday household items.

- Salt and cinnamon. Oh, no! A spill in the oven doesn't have to mean scrubbing. Simply treat it with these two pantry items, and the mess will lift right out. Sprinkle the salt and cinnamon on spills while the oven is still hot. Once everything dries, use a stiff brush or cloth to get rid of the salty spots. As a bonus, this makes your house smell great, too.

- Baking soda and water. Make your own no-scrub oven cleaner – without toxic fumes. This overnight "oven soak" formula softens the worst grime. And it's made from ingredients you have in your pantry. Mix baking soda and water into a paste, then spread it on the sides and bottom of your oven. Let it sit overnight, then wipe your oven clean. You can also try slight variations by adding some dishwashing liquid, washing soda, or salt to the baking soda and water paste.

- Ammonia. Hidden in your garage, you'll find an easy way to clean your oven! Full-strength ammonia loosens baked-on grease and burned-on food. Another trick is to warm up your oven, then turn it off. Place a bowl or pan of ammonia in your oven overnight. The next day, wipe down the oven. Grease and grime should disappear in no time. Don't try this tip if you have a continuous-clean or self-cleaning oven. If you have an older model gas oven with a continuously lit pilot light, extinguish the pilot light before setting the bowl of ammonia in the oven.

Vanquish stovetop grime with vinegar. Your meal looks wonderful – but now your stove looks like a disaster. Luckily, you don't have to spend a lot of time or money to clean it. A greasy, grimy stove is no match for this inexpensive, green formula you make at home. Just spray, wait, and wipe – no elbow grease necessary.

The secret ingredient is vinegar. That's because the acid in vinegar cuts through the grease and germs on your stove and countertops. Simply dilute vinegar with water and use it as a safe and effective kitchen cleaner. For really tough jobs, just use full-strength vinegar.

Unlike harsh chemical cleaners, vinegar is environmentally friendly. It's also much cheaper than commercial products. You won't breathe toxic fumes while cleaning, and it's safe to use around children.

Want to leave your clean kitchen with a pleasant scent? Make your own citrus cleaner with citrus peels and vinegar. Put peels from oranges, lemons, or limes in a jar and pour white vinegar over them. Let it sit for a few weeks, then strain and dilute it with water in a spray bottle.

'Foil' heat damage

It may seem like a good idea to line the bottom of your oven with aluminum foil to guard against drips and spills. But this can actually cause heat damage to your oven.

Instead, put a sheet of aluminum foil on the oven rack below what you're cooking. Make the sheet only a few inches larger than your baking pan, so heat can still circulate properly. The foil should catch any drips before they reach the oven floor.

Scrub away stains with toothpaste. Brush up on kitchen hygiene without busting your budget. Instead of buying expensive ceramic cooktop cleaners, try using toothpaste. Apply nongel toothpaste with a soft cloth or an old toothbrush to remove stains and burned-on food. Your ceramic cooktop will sparkle – just like your smile when you realize how much money you saved.

Super suggestions for self-cleaning ovens. Self-cleaning ovens are convenient – but they're not magical. You still need to do your part to keep your oven clean. Follow these tips to keep your self-cleaning oven in tip-top shape.

- Wipe up spills promptly. Pie fillings and other sugary messes may smoke or become baked on during the cleaning cycle, which uses extremely high heat to burn off residue. They could even damage your oven's porcelain enamel glaze.

- Save on energy costs. Make the most of your already warm oven by running the self-cleaning cycle right after baking.

- Consider the consequences. Your manual may recommend leaving the oven racks in during the cleaning cycle. But they can become discolored, less shiny, and harder to slide in and out. It may be smarter to clean the racks by hand. Similarly, you may be able to put your broiler pan in the oven during the cleaning cycle – but make sure to wipe off any grease first so it doesn't catch fire.

- Protect your pets. You may want to keep your pets out of the area during the self-cleaning cycle. Odorless fumes have reportedly killed birds.

- Steer clear of chemical cleaners. When cleaning up messes, don't use chemical oven cleaners. Any residue left behind may damage the porcelain enamel when exposed to the high heat of the self-cleaning cycle.

REFRIGERATORS
Cooler ways to chill

Keep your fridge running smoothly. All good things must come to an end – even brand new appliances. But how quickly that end comes for your refrigerator is largely up to you. Make your new refrigerator last almost forever. Just follow these simple maintenance tips.

- Clean the condenser coils. Usually located underneath or in back of your refrigerator, these coils can collect dust and pet hair. Dust-covered coils force your fridge to work harder, boosting your energy costs and shortening the life of the unit. Find out where your coils are located. If they're in the back, unplug your fridge and pull it away from the wall. If your coils are underneath, you can remove a panel at the bottom front of your fridge to access them. Vacuum or brush the coils to clean them. You should do this at least once a year, ideally every three months.

- Clear the drain hole. Your refrigerator likely has a drain hole and drip pan to catch condensation. Remove any food particles or mineral deposits from the drain hole, and scrub the drip pan in soapy water to get rid of any odors.

- Change the filter. If your refrigerator has an automatic ice maker or chilled water dispenser, it probably also has a water filter. Change this filter every six months or as recommended by your manual. Water passing through a dirty filter could be even dirtier than unfiltered water.

- Check the gaskets. Gaskets on your refrigerator and freezer doors should seal cold air in and keep warm air out. Examine your door gaskets for cracks or damages. Then try the dollar bill test. Shut a dollar bill in the door, then try to pull it out. If it comes out too easily, that means cold air probably does, too. Replace your gaskets if they fail these inspections. Otherwise, you'll be losing much more than a dollar.

- Correct the balance. Make sure your refrigerator is level. If not, the doors may not close on their own, or they may not close as tightly as they should. This wastes energy. Adjust the support feet until your refrigerator stands level.

Refer to your owner's manual for any additional maintenance duties. Keep up with these tasks, and your refrigerator should keep working for you.

Make mildew disappear. Your refrigerator should be a clean, safe place to store food and beverages – not a breeding ground for mildew. Keep the fridge mildew away with this quick, helpful hint. Just wipe the inside of your refrigerator with vinegar. The acetic acid in vinegar kills mildew fungus. It also absorbs odors, so your fridge will smell fresh.

Instead of sponging, you could fill a spray bottle with a mixture of vinegar and water and zap any sign of mildew. Lemon juice, another acidic liquid, should also do the trick.

WARNING

Stymie floods with shutoff valve

Yikes! You come home to find your refrigerator standing in a growing puddle of water. Chances are the line for your ice maker has sprung a leak. Make sure you know where the shutoff valve is. Usually, you can find it under the sink. It may also be in the basement, beneath the refrigerator. Getting to this valve quickly could be the difference between a slight mess and a flooded kitchen.

Safely sponge smudges from stainless steel. "Stainless" doesn't mean spotless. Here's how to remove dirt, streaks, and fingerprints from your stainless steel refrigerator and other appliances.

Begin by wiping the surface with a cloth soaked in warm water or a mixture of warm water and mild liquid dish detergent. Dry with a clean towel right away to prevent spots.

To get rid of stubborn fingerprints, use a spray glass cleaner. Rubbing alcohol – or an equal mix of rubbing alcohol and water – also helps remove fingerprints.

A dab of olive oil or mineral oil should help restore the shine, while club soda does a good job of removing streaks. You can also polish your stainless steel appliances with vinegar.

When applying any of these substances, make sure to wipe along the grain with a lint-free cloth. Steer clear of abrasive cleaning products or scrubbers, like bleach and steel wool, which can damage the finish.

Great ways to save your gaskets. A tisket, a tasket, don't neglect your gasket. If you're not careful, mildew can form on your refrigerator door gaskets. Besides unpleasant odors, this can also cause these important seals to become brittle and crack.

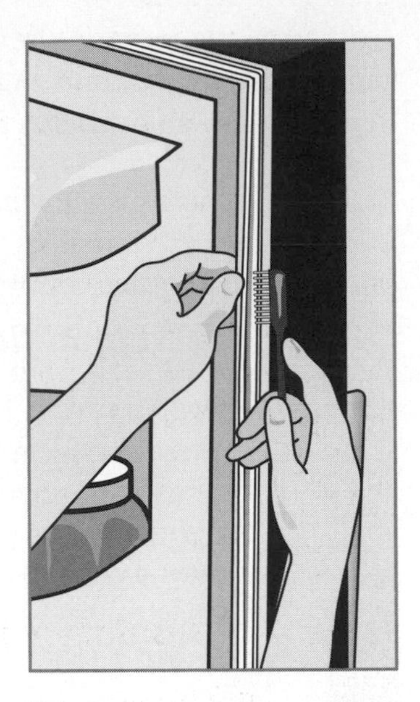

Keep your gaskets clean and lubricated. To clean them, try a solution of warm water and baking soda or water and dish soap. Hydrogen peroxide, WD-40, or vinegar should also get the job done. Use a soft cloth for cleaning. To get at the nooks and crannies, use a cotton swab or an old toothbrush.

Don't let your gaskets get too dry. For lubrication, apply a layer of petroleum jelly with a cotton swab. This should help keep your gaskets supple. Other options include lemon oil and mineral oil.

Handle a sticky situation. You enjoy your stainless steel refrigerator, but something's missing – like your grandchildren's artwork on display. Magnets often do not stick to stainless steel, so it's not as easy to hang drawings, photos, to-do lists, and other items on your fridge. But, with a little ingenuity, you can turn your refrigerator into an art gallery again.

- See double. Double-sided tape will let you stick things to your stainless steel refrigerator.
- Seek out specialty products. You can find products specifically designed to stick to stainless steel. For example, Happeez makes handy clips, as well as list pads, note pads, whiteboards, and picture frames that adhere to stainless steel without leaving any residue. Browse their inventory and order online at *www.mayfairlane.com* or call toll-free 888-408-4352.

- Get on board. Kitchen supply stores sell all sorts of adhesive-backed magnetic boards. Hang them on your refrigerator and stick your magnets to it, just like the old days.

Another solution is to paint a wall in your kitchen with magnetic paint. This way, you'll have an area to display artwork and photos – without messing with your refrigerator. Rust-Oleum makes magnetic primer that you can buy at Ace Hardware, The Home Depot, and many other stores. Apply two to four coats, then cover with your own paint color.

Insulate your ice chest for peanuts

Put those annoying leftover packing peanuts to good use. Shove them in plastic bags, then put the bags in your ice chest. You can line the bottom of your ice chest with the peanut-filled bags or place them on top of the ice, food, and drinks. Either way, the peanuts act as insulation. The ice won't melt as quickly, and everything will stay cold longer. It's a perfect trick for parties and picnics.

Snuff out sour smells. Tired of having to hold your nose when opening your refrigerator? Try these simple steps for a sweeter smelling fridge.

Keep an open box of baking soda in your refrigerator to absorb odors. Replace it with a new one every three months. A lidless plastic container filled with charcoal briquettes will serve the same purpose. Simply throw away the container when the smell has vanished.

You can also soak up unpleasant smells with a bowl of dry cat litter or some newspaper. For strong odors, a dish of fresh coffee grounds should do the trick. A few drops of vanilla extract on a cotton ball can keep your fridge smelling great, too.

These natural deodorizers will freshen your fridge – and make it safe for you to breathe deeply again.

Banish odors with bread. Fresh bread can help freshen a foul-smelling freezer. Just put a loaf or two of fresh bread in your freezer. Leave the bread in there for three or four days. The bread should absorb any unpleasant odors.

Juicy way to clean your fridge. You don't need an arsenal of cleaning products to make your refrigerator sparkle. All you need is a lemon. Cut a lemon and squeeze out the juice. Then mix the lemon juice with an equal amount of water. This cheap solution will clean and deodorize your fridge for a fraction of the cost of commercial products. And it will leave your refrigerator with a pleasing, lemony fresh scent.

Red flags that require a repairman. Most of the time, you can keep your refrigerator running with a few simple, do-it-yourself solutions. But sometimes you need to call in a professional repairman to tackle a serious problem. According to *Popular Mechanics*, watch out for these warning signs.

- Slight hissing noise, with the refrigerator not cooling as efficiently as usual.
- Oily residue on the freezer compartment floor.
- Condenser coils damaged by an accident.
- Refrigerator leaks lots of water, and you can't pinpoint the source of the leak.
- Outer shell of the refrigerator is "sweating."
- Refrigerator continues to cycle on and off, even though the condenser coils are clean.

Chapter 2

LET'S EAT

You are what you eat — so make sure you eat well. Learn the best ways to store, prepare, and enjoy your favorite foods. Make the most of fruits and vegetables, herbs and spices, pizza and burgers, and snacks and desserts. Discover surprising strategies, timesaving tactics, and unusual uses for everyday kitchen items. Your food will be bursting with freshness, flavor, and flair. Bon appetit!

COOKING & BAKING

Feeling potlucky?

Freshen the air when frying. Keep your house from smelling like a "greasy spoon" when you fry food. Just use these handy tips to counteract cooking odors. Keep a bowl of white vinegar near your skillet, either on your counter or stove, while you're cooking. It should get rid of the smell of grease.

You can also microwave vanilla extract in a bowl and set it in your kitchen to dispel lingering food odors. Another good way to absorb odors is to place several bowls of coffee grounds around the room. Leave them there for a few days, then throw them out.

HANDY HINT

Dynamic duo improves frying

Get the best of both worlds when you fry or sauté. Use both butter and olive oil in your skillet. The combination gives you the rich taste of butter and the higher temperature range of oil. Just a little bit of olive oil keeps the butter from burning. As a bonus, olive oil also provides monounsaturated fat — a healthier alternative to butter.

Quick fix for sweet or salty dishes. Oops! You went a little overboard with your seasoning while cooking. Let vinegar come to the rescue. Salvage a recipe that's too sweet or too salty with just a bit of this everyday miracle product. A splash of vinegar will cut the saltiness or sweetness – without making your food taste vinegary.

WARNING

Watch out for warm refrigerators

You think of your refrigerator as a safe storage spot for food — but is it? Not if the temperature is too high. Then it's the one place in the kitchen you should never store your food.

If your refrigerator is too warm, even by just a few degrees, your food will spoil sooner. One red flag is if your milk sours before its sell-by date. A refrigerator that is warmer than 40 degrees Fahrenheit puts your food in the danger zone for bacteria. To be safe, set your fridge for 37 degrees and your freezer for 0 degrees.

To further prevent spoilage, make sure any lids or caps fit tightly, and squeeze all the air out of plastic storage bags. Avoid oversized containers that leave too much space between your food and the lid. That extra space will also speed up spoilage.

Perfect way to reheat pizza. Leftover pizza makes a tasty meal – but only if you reheat it properly. Forget the microwave. It warms the cheese and toppings but leaves the crust soggy and chewy. For a crispier crust, try this trick.

Set your oven to 400 degrees. Line a baking sheet with parchment paper and place your pizza on it, then put it in the oven for five to 10 minutes. The parchment paper, unlike aluminum foil, will absorb moisture from the crust so it doesn't become soggy. Of course, you can sidestep the whole reheating issue by eating your leftover pizza cold, right out of the refrigerator.

Juicy tips for juicier burgers. A good burger should require plenty of napkins. Follow these surefire tips to make your burgers nice and moist every time.

- Fatten up. Start with the right kind of meat – and that means fattier meat. Buy ground beef that's about 15 percent fat, or 85 percent lean.
- Handle with care. Don't overwork your meat when mixing it with other ingredients or forming patties. Be gentle.
- Come out of the cold. Let your patties reach room temperature before cooking them.
- Don't press your luck. Never push down on the patty with your spatula while it's cooking. It might make a neat sizzling noise, but it will also squeeze out the meat's juices.
- Forget about frequent flipping. Turn your burgers only once.
- Give it a rest. Once your burgers are cooked, let them rest for about five minutes before cutting into them.

Sweet way to freeze burgers. You want to stick your extra hamburger patties in the freezer – but you don't want them to stick together. Dip into your baking supplies for the perfect solution. Use flattened cupcake liners to separate the patties. These dainty paper holders are just the right size for the job, so you don't have to waste time cutting plastic wrap into the right shape. Just put a cupcake liner between each patty, and place the whole stack of patties in a large freezer bag.

Stop broiler flare-ups. Broiling meat can be messy – and potentially dangerous. Before you begin, put a few slices of bread in your broiler pan. The bread will soak up any grease that drips, cutting down on smoke and the risk of a grease fire. It also makes cleanup easier. Simply toss the greasy bread in the garbage when you're done.

Tenderize tough meat for easy savings. Meat costs money. Swapping it for vegetarian alternatives, like beans, can help you save at the supermarket. Another way to save money is to buy cheaper – and sometimes tougher – cuts of meat. Then use one of these natural meat tenderizers so you don't need a saw to cut through it.

- Baking soda. Sprinkle some on your meat, rub it in, and let it sit in the refrigerator for a half hour to a couple of hours. Rinse it off completely and pat dry before cooking. This trick, used by some Chinese restaurants, helps make your meat fork-tender.

- Vinegar. Add a tablespoon or two of vinegar to your marinade or cooking liquid. The acid in vinegar breaks down meat fibers to make them more tender. Your stew meat and roasts will melt in your mouth.

- Tea. Try marinating or cooking your meat in tea. The tannins in tea work as a tenderizer to make it tasty and delicious.

- Lime juice. The acids in citrus juices make them effective meat tenderizers and a tangy part of any marinade.

- Mango. Add some of this tasty fruit to your marinade. Not only will it help tenderize your meat and make it tastier, it may also aid in digestion.

- Papaya. Thanks to the enzyme papain, which breaks down tough meat fibers, this tropical fruit makes a great meat tenderizer. In fact, papain is an ingredient in some commercial powdered meat tenderizers.

- Pineapple. The flesh and stems of fresh pineapples contain an enzyme called bromelain that helps break down protein. Enjoy your meat with a tropical twist.

- Kiwi. This exotic green fruit contains the enzyme actinidin, which works great on tough meat and lends an interesting flavor.

Salty bath yields better beans. When soaking your dried beans overnight, add plenty of salt to the water. The brine helps season your beans and soften their skins. It may even speed cooking time and help prevent gas. For best results, use three tablespoons of salt per gallon of water. Make sure to drain and rinse the beans thoroughly before cooking them.

Egg-cellent advice for easy-to-peel eggs. You don't need to be a hard-boiled detective to discover the best tips for making and peeling hard-boiled eggs. Just follow these helpful clues.

- Add a tablespoon of vinegar to the boiling water. It will keep the egg white from leaking if a shell cracks.

- Put some salt in the water, too. This helps the shells come off easily when it's time to peel the eggs.

- Submerge the boiled eggs in ice water. They will be easier to peel that way.

- If hard-boiled eggs have been sitting in your refrigerator for a day or two, dunk them in hot water first, then put them in ice water for easier shell removal.

Dye eggs the natural way. Coloring eggs isn't just for Easter. It's also a good way to tell hard-boiled eggs from raw ones. You don't even need to buy food coloring to tint your eggs. These foods make great natural dyes. Just add them to a mixture of vinegar and water.

Beet juice turns your eggs pink while red cabbage turns them blue. For yellow, choose turmeric. For red, try paprika. Spinach works for green, and blueberries work for purple. Brewed coffee will turn your eggs brown.

Experiment with nature's rainbow. You'll find plenty of colorful foods right in your own kitchen.

New approach to poached eggs. You enjoy poached eggs, but rarely take the time to make them at home. Luckily, you can poach an egg quickly right in your microwave.

Fill a microwave-safe liquid measuring cup, mug, or dessert bowl about halfway to the top with water. Add a splash of vinegar. Crack an egg into the vessel, taking care not to break the yolk. Cover loosely with plastic wrap and put it in your microwave. Set it for about a minute – depending on the wattage and type of microwave, your cooking time could vary. Listen for popping noises, which will let you know it's done. Remove the egg with a slotted spoon and dig in.

Create crispier cookies. Seeking crispier oatmeal cookies? Try using both baking soda and baking powder in your recipe. Thanks to the extra leavening agents, your cookies will end up flatter, with a pleasant snap. Here are some other tricks that help your cookies crisp up.

- Bake your cookies a few minutes longer. Or leave them on the baking sheet a little longer before setting them on a wire rack to cool.
- Replace eggs with milk.
- Add more liquid to the batter. This lets your cookies spread more.
- Opt for white sugar rather than brown sugar. You can also substitute one tablespoon of corn syrup for one tablespoon of sugar.
- Bake with butter – not oil or margarine.

Release stuck cakes with low flame. Wait too long to take your cake out of the pan, and you could have a problem. That's because the grease in the bottom of the pan cools and hardens, leaving your cake stuck and in danger of breaking apart if you try to force it out.

Coax your cake out with this simple trick. Turn a stovetop burner to low, and put the cake pan on it for a few seconds. The heat should melt the hardened grease, letting you pop the cake out of the pan with ease.

Keep some dough in the freezer. Some people stash their cash in the freezer. But your freezer works even better for storing another kind of dough – pie crust dough. Next time you bake a pie, consider making some extra dough and freezing it for future baked goods. It should last at least three months.

Just roll out your pie dough until it's the right size, then sandwich it between squares of wax paper and roll it back up. Wrap the roll of dough in plastic wrap and put it in a freezer bag. You could also press your dough into a cake pan so it freezes in a nice round shape. Then transfer the circle of dough to a freezer bag. This cuts down on the time it takes to thaw and roll the dough later.

To make things even easier, you can freeze the dough in the shape of a pie crust. Just put the dough in a pie plate as if you were baking the pie. Cover the pie pan, and place it in the freezer for about an hour. The pie crust should take the shape of the pie pan. Remove the shell from the pan and put it in a large freezer bag, or wrap it in foil or freezer paper.

When you want to bake a pie, simply take out a frozen shell, put it in a pie pan, and fill it. Your baking experience really will be "easy as pie."

Take the cake with no mistakes. You've baked and frosted a cake – now you just have to bring it to the party. With this trick, transporting a frosted cake is truly a "piece of cake." Cap several toothpicks with miniature marshmallows or gumdrops, and insert them into the top and sides of your cake. Then gently wrap the cake in plastic wrap. The toothpicks help form a tent so the plastic wrap doesn't smear the frosting, while the marshmallows or gumdrops prevent the toothpicks from poking through the plastic wrap.

Get the scoop on smooth ice cream. We all scream for ice cream. But no one is crazy about those ice crystals that form once the carton has been opened and returned to the freezer. To prevent ice crystals from forming on your ice cream, cover the surface of the ice cream with plastic wrap before closing the lid. Better yet, wrap the entire container in plastic wrap before popping it back in the freezer.

Shop for groceries at home. The weather outside is frightful, but your pantry is so delightful. Don't risk a trip to the supermarket in dangerous conditions. Just do your grocery shopping in your own kitchen. It's not only safer – it's also cheaper.

That's why this strategy makes sense even when the weather is fine. Instead of making frequent trips to the store, occasionally make meals using just the canned and frozen foods you have on hand. Chances are you can whip up something delicious using pantry staples like pasta, rice, beans, canned and frozen vegetables, chicken and vegetable stock, potatoes, garlic, onions, and condiments.

Of course, it helps if you have a well-stocked pantry. When you do go grocery shopping, take advantage of sales and coupons to stock up on nonperishable items. Just don't forget to use them.

When you "shop" at home, you save money on both groceries and gas. You also save time because you're making fewer runs to the store. You're being less wasteful, since you're using up the food you already have. And, when the weather is bad, you're much safer indoors. As Dorothy from "The Wizard of Oz" would say, "There's no place like home."

Easy fix for hardened honey. It's a tough task getting out that last bit of honey in the bottom of the jar – especially when it has crystallized. Don't throw the whole thing away. Just put it in a hot-water bath to liquify the honey again. Crack open the jar and set it in a pan of hot, but not boiling, water. The bath should melt the crystals so you can pour out the honey. You can use the same trick to unstick the last of the molasses, as well.

Simple substitutions

Don't make an extra trip to the store — or scrap your recipe completely — just because you ran out of one ingredient. Check this handy list of possible substitutions.

Ingredient	Amount	Substitution
allspice	1 teaspoon	1/2 teaspoon cinnamon and 1/2 teaspoon ground cloves
apple pie spice	1 teaspoon	1/2 teaspoon cinnamon, 1/4 teaspoon nutmeg, and 1/8 teaspoon cardamom
arrowroot	1 1/2 teaspoons	1 tablespoon flour or 1 1/2 teaspoons cornstarch
baking powder	1 tablespoon	1 teaspoon baking soda and 1 teaspoon cream of tartar
baking powder	1 teaspoon	1/4 teaspoon baking soda and 1/2 teaspoon cream of tartar
balsamic vinegar	1 tablespoon	1 tablespoon red wine vinegar plus 1/2 teaspoon sugar
bergamot		mint
brown sugar	1 cup	1 cup white sugar and 1 1/2 tablespoons molasses
buttermilk	1 cup	1 cup plain yogurt
buttermilk	1 cup	1 tablespoon lemon juice or vinegar plus enough regular milk to make 1 cup. Let stand five minutes.
catsup (for cooking)	1 cup	1 cup tomato sauce, 1/2 cup sugar, and 2 tablespoons vinegar
chili sauce	1 cup	1 cup tomato sauce, 1/4 cup brown sugar, 2 tablespoons vinegar, 1/4 teaspoon cinnamon, dash of ground cloves, dash of allspice
chocolate chips	1 ounce	1 ounce sweet cooking chocolate

Ingredient	Amount	Substitution
chocolate, semisweet	1 2/3 ounces	1 ounce unsweetened chocolate and 4 teaspoons sugar
chocolate, semisweet chips, melted	6-ounce package	2 squares unsweetened chocolate, 2 tablespoons shortening, and 1/2 cup sugar
chocolate, unsweetened	1 ounce	3 tablespoons cocoa plus 1 tablespoon butter, margarine, or vegetable oil
cilantro		parsley (for color)
coconut cream	1 cup	1 cup whipping cream
coconut milk	1 cup	1 cup whole or 2 percent milk
corn syrup	1 cup	1 cup honey
corn syrup	1 cup	1 cup sugar and 1/4 cup water or other liquid
cornstarch	1 tablespoon	2 tablespoons all-purpose flour or granular tapioca
cracker crumbs	3/4 cup	1 cup dry bread crumbs
cream, half and half	1 cup	1 cup evaporated milk
cream, half and half	1 cup	3/4 cup milk and 1/2 tablespoon melted butter
cream, heavy	1 cup	3/4 cup milk and 1/3 cup melted butter
cream of tartar	1/2 teaspoon	1 1/2 teaspoon lemon juice or vinegar
cream, whipped	2 cups	1 cup chilled evaporated milk and 1/2 teaspoon lemon juice, whipped until stiff
egg	1 whole	2 tablespoons oil and 1 teaspoon water
egg	1 whole	2 tablespoons mayonnaise

Ingredient	Amount	Substitution
flour, all-purpose	1 cup	1 cup plus 2 tablespoons cake flour
flour, all-purpose	1 cup	1 1/2 cups bread crumbs
flour, all-purpose	1 cup	1 1/3 cup rolled oats
flour, cake	1 cup	1 cup minus 2 tablespoons all-purpose flour
flour, self-rising	1 cup	1 cup minus 2 teaspoons all-purpose flour, 1 1/2 teaspoons baking powder, 1/2 teaspoon salt
garlic	1 clove	1/8 teaspoon garlic powder
garlic	1 clove	1/2 to 1 teaspoon garlic salt (reduce amount of salt called for in recipe)
gelatin, flavored	3-ounce package	1 tablespoon plain gelatin and 2 cups fruit juice
herbs, fresh	1 tablespoon	1 teaspoon dried herbs
honey	1 cup	1 cup sugar and 1 cup water
Italian seasoning		equal parts basil, marjoram, oregano, rosemary, sage, and thyme
lemon grass	2 stalks	zest from 1 lemon
lemon juice	1 teaspoon	1 teaspoon vinegar
limes or lime juice		lemons or lemon juice
marshmallows, miniature	1 cup	10 large marshmallows
mascarpone	1 cup	3 tablespoons heavy cream, 3/4 cup cream cheese, and 4 tablespoons butter
mayonnaise (for salads)	1 cup	1 cup yogurt
mayonnaise (for salads)	1 cup	1 cup sour cream
mayonnaise (for salads)	1 cup	1 cup cottage cheese, pureed

Ingredient	Amount	Substitution
milk, whole	1 cup	1 cup fruit juice
milk, whole	1 cup	1 cup potato water
milk, whole	1 cup	1/2 cup evaporated milk and 1/2 cup water
molasses	1 cup	1 cup honey
mustard, dry	1 teaspoon	1 tablespoon prepared mustard
Neufchatel		cream cheese
onion	1 small	1 1/3 teaspoons onion salt
pimento	2 table-spoons	3 tablespoons fresh red bell pepper, chopped
pumpkin pie spice	1 teaspoon	1/2 teaspoon cinnamon, 1/4 teaspoon ginger, 1/8 teaspoon allspice, and 1/8 teaspoon nutmeg
red peppers		pimientos
Romano cheese		Parmesan cheese
saffron		turmeric (for color)
shallots		red or Spanish onions
shortening, melted	1 cup	1 cup cooking oil
shrimp paste		anchovy paste
sour cream	1 cup	1 cup plain yogurt
sour cream	1 cup	3/4 cup buttermilk
sour cream	1 cup	1 cup evaporated milk and 1 table-spoon vinegar. Let stand 5 minutes.
sour cream	1 cup	3/4 cup milk, 1 tablespoon lemon juice, and 2 tablespoons butter or margarine
sugar, brown	1 cup	1 cup granulated sugar plus 1/4 cup molasses

Ingredient	Amount	Substitution
sugar, powdered	1 cup	1 cup granulated sugar and 1 tablespoon cornstarch. Blend in food processor until powdery.
sugar, white	1 cup	1 cup brown sugar, packed
sugar, white	1 cup	1 cup corn syrup (decrease liquid in recipe by 1/3 cup)
sugar, white	1 cup	1 cup honey (decrease liquid in recipe by 1/4 cup)
sugar, white	1 cup	1 3/4 cups powdered sugar
tamarind juice		5 parts ketchup to 1 part vinegar
tomato juice	1 cup	1/2 cup tomato sauce and 1/2 cup water
vanilla bean	1/2 bean	1 tablespoon vanilla extract
Worcestershire sauce	1 teaspoon	1 teaspoon steak sauce
yogurt	1 cup	1 cup buttermilk
yogurt	1 cup	1 cup sour cream

Waste no paste. Tomato paste helps thicken your pasta sauce. But it also sticks, through thick and thin, to the inside of the can. To scrape out every last bit of tomato paste, use your can opener to open both ends of the can. Then use one lid to push the paste through the can, like a snowplow clearing a tunnel. To avoid this problem completely, you can also buy tomato paste in a tube.

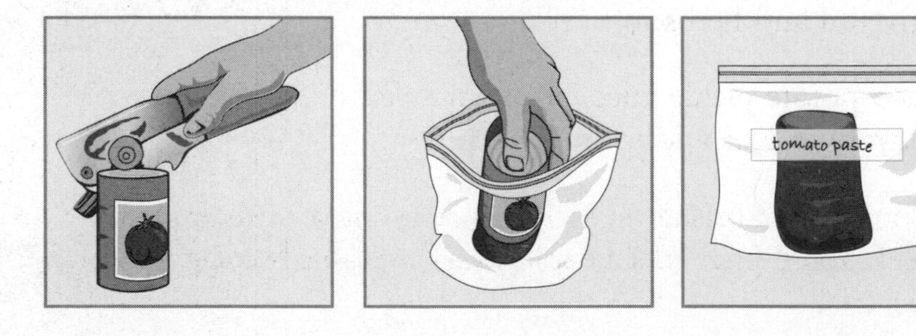

Savvy way to dress your salad. Oil's well that ends well. You may not be able to get the last few drops of olive oil out of the bottle, but that doesn't mean you should let it go to waste. Make a salad dressing right in the olive oil bottle. Just add some vinegar, herbs, salt, and pepper. Shake it up, and pour it on your salad.

Coax out more creamy dressing. Bottled salad dressing can be expensive, so you don't want to waste a drop of it. To use the last bits of a creamy salad dressing, add a little half-and-half or buttermilk to the bottle. Put the cap on and shake it up. You'll dislodge the remnants stuck to the side of the bottle and get one last serving out of it.

Peculiar uses for pickle juice. You enjoy snacking on crunchy pickles – but when you eat the last one, you might find yourself in a bit of a pickle. After all, what do you do with all that pickle juice left in the jar? Don't dump it. Find fun and tasty ways to use it instead.

For example, you can make more pickles. Cut up some cucumbers, put them in the pickle juice, and let them cure for several weeks in your refrigerator. The same trick works to make other pickled veggies, too. Try it with onions, cauliflower, broccoli, carrots, beets, green beans, okra, or celery. You can even pickle eggs.

Here are a few more surprising uses for pickle juice that might tickle your fancy.

- Jazz up your potato salad, egg salad, coleslaw, or pasta salad with a few teaspoons of pickle juice.
- Marinate meat, chicken, or shrimp. Just mix pickle juice with olive oil and herbs for a zesty marinade.
- Incorporate pickle juice into your salad dressings. Mix it with mayonnaise or add it to vinaigrettes.
- Cook a beef brisket in pickle juice to make your own corned beef. You'll have to save a few jars' worth of pickle juice for this trick.

- Add some pickle juice to your barbecue sauce for an added kick.
- Stir pickle juice into yogurt or sour cream to create a tangy dip for chips and veggies.
- Drizzle some pickle juice into cold soups like gazpacho or borscht.
- Doctor your deviled eggs by mixing pickle juice with your mayonnaise.
- Settle an upset stomach. A tablespoon of pickle juice may soothe your aching tummy.
- Just drink it. Pickle juice makes a good alternative to sports drinks. Athletes often drink some after a workout to replenish their electrolytes. And while some people drink it simply because they enjoy the taste, you'll want to watch the sodium content.

Tips for brewing tastier tea

For more flavorful tea, use whole tea leaves. Put them in a large strainer, rather than a tiny tea ball, so they have some room to stretch out. Do not use boiling water, which may burn the tea leaves. Remove the strainer after about three minutes. More delicate teas can steep for up to seven minutes. Add milk, sugar, or lemon if you wish — or just enjoy a plain cup of delicious tea.

Quick trick to unstick sticky ingredients. Overcome a sticky situation when using ingredients like honey, molasses, corn syrup, or peanut butter. Dunk your measuring spoon in a glass of hot water, then use the heated spoon to measure your sticky substance. You can also run very hot water from the tap over the spoon before using it. Either way, the heat prevents the substance from sticking to the spoon, so it ends up in your mixing bowl where it belongs.

Surefire strategy to measure shortening. Stop coming up short when measuring shortening. Solid fats, like shortening, often stick to measuring cups or spoons, making it tough to tell if you used the right amount. Here's a helpful trick to overcome this problem. Say your recipe calls for one-half cup of shortening. Fill a liquid measuring cup with one-half cup of cold water. Then add shortening until the water level reaches one cup. Simply pour out the water and use the shortening. This measuring method, called displacement, also works for other sticky solids, like peanut butter.

Simple way to skin almonds. Don't drive yourself nuts trying to remove the skin from whole almonds. Just use this easy technique. Put the almonds in a bowl and pour boiling water over them. Let them sit for a couple of minutes, then drain and rinse them with cold water. You should be able to slip the skin off by squeezing the almonds between your thumb and index finger. Then let the almonds dry. Or dry and toast them on a baking sheet in an oven set at 325 to 350 degrees Fahrenheit for about 10 minutes.

Super spot for rising dough

Looking for a warm place to let your bread dough rise? Try your slow cooker. Turn it to its lowest setting so it gets warm. Then unplug it. Grease the slow cooker's ceramic liner or spray it with nonstick cooking spray. Put your ball of dough inside and cover it with the lid. The warm, enclosed area works perfectly — and the glass lid lets you keep an eye on your dough so you know when it has risen enough.

Alternatives to alcohol

Your recipe calls for alcohol, but you don't have a drop in the house. Try these clever substitutions instead.

Alcohol	*Alternatives*
beer	chicken broth, beef broth, or ginger ale
bourbon	vanilla extract
rum	vanilla extract, pineapple juice, water, grape juice, apple juice, or apple cider
vodka	water or apple cider mixed with lime juice
sherry	apple cider, vanilla extract, coffee, orange juice, or pineapple juice
champagne	ginger ale, sparkling apple cider, or sparkling white grape juice
red wine	grape juice, chicken broth, beef broth, vegetable broth, cranberry juice, apple juice, or tomato juice
white wine	white grape juice, apple cider, apple juice, vegetable stock, water, chicken broth, or ginger ale
port	Concord grape juice with lime zest or cranberry juice with some lemon juice
orange liqueur	orange juice concentrate, orange zest, orange juice, or marmalade

Swift way to thaw sliced bread. Worried that your sandwich bread will turn stale before you can use it? Keep it in your freezer. It's easy to defrost a few slices at a time as you need them. Just put the bread on a plate in the microwave for about 20 seconds. This method gives you softer bread than if you let it thaw at room temperature. You can also drop frozen bread slices right in the toaster.

Prepare meals to heat and eat. It's hard to beat the convenience of store-bought frozen meals. But why settle for tasteless, overpriced, packaged food when you can enjoy a delicious home-cooked alternative?

Make your own frozen dinners instead. They will be cheaper, tastier, and healthier than anything you can buy in the store. And they're just as easy to reheat in the microwave.

Here are some handy tips for making and reheating your own frozen meals.

- Pop it on a plate. Almost any leftover can be turned into a frozen dinner. Make sure your food has completely cooled, then arrange your protein, veggies, and starch on a plate. Wrap it tightly in plastic wrap first then aluminum foil, and stick it in the freezer.

- Control portions with containers. Foods with a high water content, like soups, stews, sauces, and casseroles, work best. Put individual servings in containers that can safely go in both the freezer and microwave.

- Take notes. Make sure to label and date each container or wrapped plate. Most meals will last two to three months in the freezer.

- Double your pleasure. You don't even have to find extra time to prepare your frozen meals. Next time you cook, simply double your recipe and freeze the extra food. It's like getting two meals for the price of one.

- Reheat wisely. Remove the aluminum foil and thaw your frozen meal in the refrigerator. Or defrost it in the microwave. Then just heat it up and enjoy.

Pop corn for pennies. There's nothing magical about microwave popcorn – unless you count some shady ingredients and an inflated price tag. Make your own microwave popcorn for a fraction of the cost. All you need are some popcorn kernels and a brown paper lunch bag. Pour half a cup of popcorn kernels in the bag, fold it over twice, and stick the bag in the microwave for one and a half to three minutes. Listen for when the popping slows down so you know when it's done. Add salt, butter, garlic powder, cheese, or whatever other toppings you choose.

Cool tips for your freezer. Your freezer can be one of the most useful parts of your kitchen, a perfect place to store and preserve a wide assortment of foods. But too often, it just serves as a chilly holding area for leftovers before they get tossed in the garbage.

Don't let your freezer become a frozen wasteland. Follow these helpful freezing and thawing tips for long-lasting, good-tasting food.

- Shop smart. When buying frozen food, avoid packages with ice crystals or other signs of melting and refreezing. Buy frozen foods last, just before you check out. Go straight home and put them in your freezer.
- Cool down. Let food cool to room temperature before sticking it in your freezer. This helps it freeze more quickly and evenly.
- Choose the right equipment. Put your food in containers, bags, and jars designed to withstand the freezer.
- Downsize. Small containers help food freeze faster and taste better later. They also make storage easier.
- Squeeze all the air out of plastic freezer bags. Double bag for extra protection from freezer burn.
- Leave a little room at the top of containers and jars because liquids will expand in your freezer.
- Label and date everything you put in your freezer.
- Put older foods in front, so you use them first.
- Check the temperature. Make sure your freezer is set to 0 degrees Fahrenheit. To speed the freezing process, you can set it to minus-10 degrees temporarily.
- Avoid overcrowding. Don't stuff too much into your freezer at once. Your food may freeze at a slower rate and lose some of its flavor. Arrange containers in one layer with some space between them so air can circulate.

- Save space. Stack containers once their contents have frozen. Freeze liquids in flat freezer bags, then stack the bags or put them on their side for easy storage. You can also freeze liquids in ice cube trays.

- Thaw safely. Thaw frozen food in a refrigerator set at 40 degrees F or lower. To speed defrosting, you can put frozen food in a plastic bag and dunk it in cold water or use the "defrost" setting on your microwave. Never leave food out on the counter to thaw.

- Cook thawed foods right away – and cook them thoroughly. Freezing doesn't kill bacteria.

- Don't refreeze food that has thawed or partially thawed.

Super storage suggestions

Food should end up in your belly — not your garbage can. Follow these storage suggestions to keep food fresher longer. You'll waste less and eat more.

Food	Storage suggestion	Shelf life
baking powder	keep in cool pantry	18 months
baking soda	keep in cool pantry	2 years
beef, steaks or roasts	refrigerate or freeze	3-5 days in refrigerator; 6-12 months in freezer
berries	don't wash until ready to eat or freeze	1-2 days in refrigerator; 8-12 months in freezer
butter	store in freezer and move individual sticks to refrigerator as needed	3 months in refrigerator; 1 year in freezer
chicken	refrigerate or freeze	1-2 days in refrigerator; 9-12 months in freezer
chocolate	wrap well and keep in cool pantry, not refrigerator or freezer	6 months for milk and white chocolate; 1 year for semisweet, bittersweet, and unsweetened chocolate

Food	Storage suggestion	Shelf life
citrus fruits	wrap cut edges to prevent loss of vitamin C	3 weeks in refrigerator; 4-6 months in freezer
coffee	store in freezer; let it come to room temperature before brewing	2 weeks in refrigerator after opening can; longer in freezer
cornmeal	keep tightly covered; can also freeze	4-6 months in pantry; indefinitely in freezer
cornstarch	keep tightly covered	18 months
eggs	keep eggs in carton, not refrigerator door	2-5 weeks past sell-by date
fish fillets	refrigerate or freeze	3-5 days in refrigerator; 3-6 months in freezer
flour, white	put in airtight container	6-8 months
flour, whole wheat	keep refrigerated in airtight container; can also freeze	6-8 months
fruit juices, canned	store in cool place	9 months
ground beef or pork	refrigerate or freeze	1-2 days in refrigerator; 3-4 months in freezer
herbs, dried	store in airtight containers in dry place away from heat and sunlight	6 months
honey	store in cupboard	1 year
lobster	refrigerate or freeze	3-7 days in refrigerator; 6-12 months in freezer
lunch meat	put in meat drawer of refrigerator	3-5 days past sell-by date
maple syrup	store in cupboard; once opened, put in refrigerator	a few years unopened in cupboard; 1 year in refrigerator
melons	wrap cut surfaces to keep vitamin C in and odors out	1 week in refrigerator; 8-12 months in freezer
milk	place near back of refrigerator, where it's colder	1 week past sell-by date

Food	Storage suggestion	Shelf life
molasses, opened	store in cupboard	6 months
mushrooms	don't wash before storing in refrigerator	1-2 days in refrigerator; 8-12 months in freezer
nuts	store in freezer	6 months
oils	store in a cool, dark place; keep sesame oil in refriger-ator, others in pantry	several months
onions	keep dry and out of the sun	2 weeks
pasta	once box is opened, trans-fer to airtight container	1-2 years
potatoes	store in cool place, below 50 degrees F	2-4 weeks
rice, brown	keep tightly covered	6 months
rice, white	keep tightly covered	1-2 years
shrimp	refrigerate or freeze	3-5 days in refrigerator; 6-12 months in freezer
spices	store in airtight containers in a dry place away from heat and sunlight	1-2 years for whole spices; 6 months for ground spices
sugar, brown	put in airtight container	4 months
sugar, powdered	put in airtight container	18 months
sugar, granulated	put in airtight container	2 years
turkey	refrigerate or freeze	1-2 days in refrigerator; 6-12 months in freezer
vegetables	don't wash produce until ready to eat, cook, or freeze	3 days to 1 week in refrigerator; 8-12 months in freezer
vinegar	keep tightly covered; don't worry about slightly cloudy appearance	2 years unopened; 1 year once opened
yeast	keep in refrigerator or freezer	note expiration date
yogurt	keep in refrigerator; stir if it looks separated	10-14 days past sell-by date

Little-known use for greasy paper towels. You shouldn't dump bacon grease down your drain. But you can save it in a jar and use it for cooking or greasing pans. Even if you cook your bacon in the microwave, you don't have to waste the grease. Microwave your bacon between two sheets of paper towels, then save these oily paper towels in a plastic bag in your freezer. Take them out when you need to grease a skillet or season a cast-iron pan.

Salty solution to moldy cheese. Break out the cheese and crackers without worrying about uninvited guests – like mold. To prevent cheese from turning moldy, wrap it in a cheesecloth or paper towel dampened with salt water and store it in the refrigerator. The salt helps kill bacteria on the cheese before it can form mold, so you can enjoy your cheese longer.

HERBS & SPICES
Good seasonings ahead

5 easy-to-grow herbs. Sure, you can buy herbs in the supermarket. But nothing beats the freshness and convenience of a home herb garden. You don't even need a green thumb to grow your own herbs. Here are five easy-to-grow, hard-to-kill plants that will beautify any home and garden.

- Basil. Sweet basil, the most common variety of basil, grows 1 to 2 feet tall. It can grow indoors or outdoors, in containers or a garden bed. Basil likes fertile soil, with plenty of moisture and full sun. But it does not like the cold, so don't put it out too early. You can start picking the leaves and using them for cooking in six to eight weeks. Don't be bashful. Help yourself to plenty of basil, because frequent pruning makes your plant bushier.

- Parsley. You may think of parsley as a mere garnish, but this herb adds more than just a splash of color to your plate. It also adds taste. For stronger taste, opt for flat leaf parsley rather than Italian, or curly, parsley. Parsley is very easy to grow in any soil. It doesn't need much water but does require a fair amount of sun. Plant it in a mostly sunny location, but not in direct sun. Some shade is good. You may only have to purchase one parsley plant, because it re-seeds itself freely.

- Mint. You won't have any trouble growing mint, which thrives year after year with very little care. Mint grows in nearly all types of soil and in conditions ranging from partial shade to full sun. Just keep your plants well watered. You may have trouble containing mint, which spreads like wildfire. Watch out or it might overtake your garden. Patio containers may be your best bet.

- Thyme. Anytime is a good time to grow thyme. This herb grows well in almost any condition. In fact, it's sometimes used as a ground cover in dry climates. The type of soil doesn't much matter, but thyme prefers full sun. Starting from seed can be difficult, so you may want to start with cuttings or a potted plant from the nursery.

- Dill. You can use dill's seeds, leaves, and stems to season your food. Perfect for a kitchen herb garden, dill should be harvested before it begins to flower.

HANDY HINT

Handy way to transport flavor

Flavor should never take a vacation. But the kitchens of rental properties often come with old, tasteless dried herbs and spices — or none at all. Instead of buying new ones every time you travel, pack some of your favorite herbs and spices in the individual compartments of a pill organizer. It's a cheap and easy way to get your daily dose of flavor.

WARNING

Easy way to keep basil fresh

You can keep leftover basil fresh and tasty for up to a week in your refrigerator. Just wrap the basil in a damp paper towel and place it in an unsealed zip-close bag. Don't rinse it until you're ready to use it. If you rinse basil before you store it in the refrigerator, it will last only half as long.

Pick the perfect time for picking. The early bird may catch the worm, but early morning is also the prime time for something much tastier – herbs. Gather your herbs early in the morning, after the dew dries but before the sun warms them too much. That's when the leaves have the most essential oils – and the most flavor. Here are more handy tips.

- Harvest herbs right before they bloom, when they have the highest concentration of oils.
- Use sharp shears or scissors. You want to cut stems cleanly to avoid damaging the plant.
- Remove insects and any damaged leaves from your harvested herbs.
- Keep the herbs out of strong light. A cool, dark place works best for drying and storage.
- Give herbs time to settle in. Don't harvest perennial herbs too heavily the first year.
- Get in the zone. If you live in a warmer zone, you can harvest up to two-thirds of your herbs' leaves at a time, once in the spring and again in the summer. But if you live in a cold zone, take only one-third each time and stop harvesting five to six weeks before the first fall frost.
- Tie a piece of cheesecloth or a nylon stocking around the seed heads to catch ripe seeds as they fall. Don't use plastic bags, which trap moisture that can lead to mold.

Cool way to store herbs. Pop your parsley in the freezer. You can freeze your extra herbs in ice cube trays, so you'll have plenty of flavor for later. Here are two ways to make herbal ice cubes.

- Puree your herbs in a blender with some water, then freeze the slush in an ice cube tray.
- Use boiling water to blanch the herbs so they keep their flavor and color. Put a few individual leaves or spoonfuls of chopped herbs in an ice cube tray, then fill with water and freeze. Another trick is to fill the ice cube compartments with water halfway at first, then add the leaves. When the cubes are close to frozen, finish filling the tray with water and pop it back in the freezer. That way, the leaves won't float to the top.

Once the cubes are frozen, remove them from the ice cube tray and store them in plastic freezer bags. Make sure to label the bags. Now you have frozen cubes of herbs at your disposal. Toss them into soups, stews, or other dishes. For instance, throw a few basil cubes into a pot of tomato sauce. You could even add some mint cubes to a refreshing glass of iced tea. Other herbs that make good cubes include chervil, chives, cilantro, dill, fennel, parsley, tarragon, and thyme.

HANDY HINT

Get full flavor from half the herbs

Your recipe calls for fresh oregano or thyme, but you only have the dried versions. Because dried herbs are more potent than fresh ones, simply use half the amount called for in the recipe.

Ditch dull dried herbs. Fresh usually works best when it comes to herbs. But some dried herbs will do in a pinch. Feel free to use dried bay leaf, thyme, oregano, rosemary, marjoram, and sage in chili and other slow-cooking dishes. That's because the flavor compounds in these herbs remain relatively stable at high temperatures, so they keep their flavor through the drying process.

On the other hand, some herbs just don't cut it in dried form. If you value taste, avoid dried basil, chives, dill, parsley, cilantro, chervil, and tarragon. Stick to the fresh forms of these herbs, and your taste buds will thank you.

HANDY HINT

Get the most from fresh ginger

Can't quite put your finger on how to store ginger? Here are some helpful suggestions. You can stash leftover ginger in your refrigerator for a few weeks. Wrap it in a paper towel, put it in a paper bag, or simply toss it in the crisper unwrapped.

For long-term storage, pop your ginger in the freezer. Either put the whole root in a plastic freezer bag or cut it into smaller chunks, so you have ready-to-use portions. As a bonus, frozen ginger is easier to grate than fresh ginger.

Bring old herbs back to life. Dried herbs lose their flavor over time. To revive old, tired herbs, push them through a mesh sieve or crush them between your fingers. This will release the herb's flavorful oils.

Quick trick to create dried herbs. Make sure your homegrown herbs don't go to waste. Dry them in your microwave so you can use them later. Just place a small amount of herbs between two paper towels and zap them for about 30 seconds. Crumble the dried herbs, put them in an airtight container, and store it in a cool, dry, dark place. For best results, use your dried herbs within three months.

Don't discard discolored garlic. No need to sing the blues over blue garlic. Although blue garlic may look unappetizing, it should still taste fine – and it's still perfectly safe to eat.

Garlic may turn blue or bluish-green because of a chemical reaction between garlic's sulfur compounds and copper. Small traces of copper can come from either your water supply or cooking utensils, such as copper pots and pans or tools made of cast iron, tin, or aluminum. Butter, lemon juice, and vinegar can also trigger this reaction. Pickling garlic using regular table salt, which contains iodine, rather than kosher or pickling salt can also discolor your garlic.

When exposed to mild acids, enzymes in garlic can produce blue and green pigments. This reaction is more common when garlic has been stored at cool temperatures for several weeks, usually in the winter when your pantry is colder. To help avoid discoloration, use fresh, young garlic when making a recipe that combines garlic with acidic ingredients.

While your garlic may occasionally turn blue, you don't have to. Just close your eyes and enjoy your meal.

Winning ways to ripen tomatoes. What's black and white and red all over? Tomatoes wrapped in newspapers. All joking aside, this trick really works. Find out how your daily paper can make your tomatoes better.

Once you hear the news about a hard freeze coming, reach for your newspaper. Pick your green tomatoes, wrap them individually in newspaper, and store them at room temperature to ripen.

If wrapping them individually seems like too much bother, you can put the unripe tomatoes on a shelf and cover them with sheets of newspaper. The idea is to trap ethylene gas to speed up ripening. Make sure to check your tomatoes often. Remove the ripe ones as well as any that have begun to rot.

Here are some more helpful hints for ripening and storing tomatoes.

- To really ripen a tomato in a hurry, put an unripe tomato in a brown paper bag with an apple or banana. These fruits give off ethylene gas to hasten ripening.
- Tomatoes that have turned pink, but not yet red, can be picked and left in a warm place out of direct sunlight to ripen.
- Once ripe, tomatoes should be stored at room temperature – not in the refrigerator. To make them last even longer, place them stem-end down on your counter. This blocks air from entering and moisture from leaving your tomato.

Secrets to crisp lettuce and celery. Lettuce looking limp? This technique will put the crisp back in the leaves in just a couple of minutes. Simply pop your lettuce in the freezer for two minutes before eating or serving.

You can also revive lifeless lettuce by adding lemon juice to a container of cold water. Place the lettuce in the container and soak for an hour in the refrigerator. Your salad will once again have that appealing crispness.

To do the same for your sagging celery, trim the bottoms of each stalk and place the stalks cut-side down in a tall, narrow container with at least 2 inches of cold water. Then put the container in your refrigerator. Keep your celery standing at attention for six to 12 hours. It should get its crunch back.

Foolproof tips for freezing produce. You can't beat the taste of fresh, seasonal fruits and vegetables. But produce frozen when it's at its peak may be the next best thing. Buying fresh produce in season and freezing it can even save you money – as much as 50 to 80 percent off what you'd pay in a supermarket.

Follow these tips for frost-free frozen fruits and veggies.

- Blanch vegetables first so they don't lose color, texture, flavor, or nutrients. To blanch veggies, place them in a wire basket and lower them into boiling water for a few minutes, then quickly stop the cooking process by submerging the basket in ice water.

- Pack fruits like strawberries in simple syrup – sugar and water – to reducc thc formation of ice crystals.
- Freeze berries on a baking sheet before storing them in a freezer bag. It will keep them from sticking together.
- Cube fruits like melon, peaches, and bananas and freeze them to use in smoothies.
- Put produce in labeled, dated, plastic freezer bags, and squeeze all the air out. For even more protection, put that bag in a second freezer bag before storing.
- Make sure your freezer is set at 0 degrees Fahrenheit or lower.
- Store most fruits and vegetables for up to one year in your freezer.

Keep fruits and vegetables fresher, longer

Store apples in your refrigerator's crisper drawer by themselves instead of in a bowl on the counter. A temperature of 32 degrees is ideal. Apples, like many fruits and vegetables, emit ethylene gas, which can speed ripening of fresh produce and wilt cut flowers.

Give your veggie steamer a boost. Don't get steamed when you encounter obstacles to steaming vegetables. Get creative. If your steamer basket's stubby legs prevent you from adding enough water beneath its base, give it a boost. Crumple three balls of aluminum foil and arrange them evenly in the bottom of your pot. Then place the steamer basket on top of the foil. Now you have room for extra water.

If you don't have a steamer basket, you can use the same trick with a metal colander. Or just use balls of aluminum foil as a platform for your veggies. You'll be enjoying colorful, flavorful, and nutritious steamed vegetables in no time.

Clean your greens with salt. An old salt like Popeye would appreciate this trick. To wash spinach and other greens, soak them in a bowl of cool salted water for about three minutes. A few tablespoons of salt should do the trick. The coarse salt crystals will help remove any dirt and grit from hard-to-reach areas. After a final rinse, you'll be left with tasty, clean, grit-free greens.

Kill bacteria and viruses on fruits and veggies. Your fruits and vegetables may contain more than healthy vitamins and minerals – they could also carry harmful bacteria and other germs. Luckily, an everyday household staple can help kill these intruders. Just clean your produce with vinegar.

Researchers at the University of Florida found that a 10 percent vinegar solution used on contaminated strawberries reduced bacteria by about 90 percent and viruses by about 95 percent. Similarly, a *Cook's Illustrated* test determined that a mixture of one part white vinegar to three parts water killed 98 percent of surface bacteria on smooth fruits, like apples and pears.

For virtually germ-free produce, rinse or spray your fruits and veggies with a mild vinegar solution, then rinse them under tap water for at least 30 seconds.

Wipe off cucumber wax with ease. Supermarket cucumbers often come with a waxy coating to prevent them from drying out during shipping and storage. To remove this wax, simply rub the cucumber with vinegar, then rinse with cold water.

You could also drop the cucumber into a bowl of water mixed with vinegar. Then scrub, rinse, and wipe the cucumber with a towel. Of course, you could also just peel the cucumber – but then you'd miss out on the crisp, nutritious skin.

Chapter 3

LIVING SPACES

"A woman's work is never done, ... and happy she whose strength holds out to the end," wrote Maine midwife Martha Ballard in her journal in 1795. Indeed, housekeeping seems never-ending. Once you arrange your home just as you want it, you begin the job of keeping it that way. That means cleaning, organizing, and maintaining your house and everything in it. The following chapters can help you care for your floors, furniture, fans, fireplace — and so much more.

Shortcuts to a sparkling clean home. Everyone appreciates a clean house, but few people actually enjoy cleaning. Spend less time cleaning and more time living with these helpful tips. Here's how to clean your house in half the time.

- Control the clutter. The first rule of cleaning saves you the most time and work. Stay on top of clutter, and you'll speed up the cleaning process. Designate a place for everything, and put everything in its proper place as soon as you're done with it. Don't let mail, magazines, and other random items build up. It takes some effort and day-to-day discipline, but keeping clutter to a minimum helps you maximize your cleaning time.

- Lend yourself a hand. Use both hands to speed up tasks like dusting or wiping. Alternate hands with each step so you keep the workload evenly distributed.

- Extend your reach. Buy a long extension cord, so you can vacuum your entire house – or at least an entire floor – without unplugging your vacuum cleaner.

- Move from top to bottom. Dust and dirt fall as you clean. Start at the top, so you don't end up cleaning some areas twice.

- Ban backtracking. Enter each room only once, clean it, and leave.

- Minimize movement. When you clean, dust, or polish items in a room, move them away from the wall. When you vacuum, just push them back as you go. Same with dusting a cluttered shelf. Move everything to the center, clean the sides of the shelf, wipe down each item, return it to its place, then spray and wipe the middle.

- Carry your supplies with you. Put your cleaning products, sponges, dusters, cloths, and other cleaning supplies in a tool belt, basket, or bucket so you can carry them from room to room. A tray, cart, or wagon will also do the trick. You'll waste less time running back and forth to retrieve what you need.

- Scale back on scrubbing. Let the cleaning products do the work. Spray tough areas and let them soak while you clean something else. You'll waste less energy. And don't go overboard with cleaning products. It's easier to add more than to wipe up excess cleanser.

- Ditch all distractions. Turn off the TV and radio. Don't open mail or water plants. Don't even answer the phone. Focus on the task at hand.

- Go downhill. Tackle the toughest jobs first. As your energy wanes, the tasks will get easier. Start with the rooms that require the most work, like the kitchen or bathroom. Within those rooms, start with the most time-consuming task.

ALTERNATE USES

Sock it to dust

Give an old athletic sock a workout. It makes a simple, more efficient alternative to a dust cloth. Wear it over your hand and wipe around, behind, and over every nook and cranny.

Chart a course to stress-free cleaning. Keep your cleaning on schedule so your house never looks like a wreck. This handy chart tells you how often to wash windows, change the sheets, and dust your computer screen, along with many other tasks.

The first trick is to set a daily cleaning time – just 10 minutes or less – when you tidy up your main living spaces, including the living room, dining room, bedroom, and office. Kitchens and bathrooms need special care. By staying on top of the basics, you'll avoid allowing the mess to get out of hand. Be sure your daily routine includes these tasks:

- Take items you have used back to the rooms where they belong. This means dishes go back to the kitchen and tools go to the garage.
- Straighten and fluff cushions and pillows on your couch. Fold up throws or quilts.
- Dust table surfaces.
- Toss daily newspapers, and put magazines and books in their homes.
- Straighten up bookshelves.
- Arrange chairs around the dining room table.
- Set out clean place mats or a tablecloth.
- Make your bed.
- Return shoes and clean clothes to closets or drawers.
- Put dirty clothes in the hamper.
- Open and sort bills, and shred junk mail.
- Empty trash cans.
- Wipe down your desk.
- Rinse the sink and wipe stove top.

Now, add in a few weekly, monthly, and "as needed" chores, and you have a smart cleaning plan. Stick with the routine for a few weeks, and you'll notice a difference in how clean and comfortable your house is with little effort.

Weekly chores	*Monthly chores*	*As-needed chores*
dust knickknacks, lampshades, and artwork	clean light fixtures	wash windows
sweep or vacuum floors	turn or rotate upholstered cushions	clean smudges off walls and light switches
clean mirrors	clean heating and air conditioning vents	wash curtains
dust TV screen and computer monitor	wipe baseboards	shampoo carpet
wipe windowsills	check ceiling corners for cobwebs	clean inside china cabinet
dust furniture	clean ceiling fans	wash crystal and china
toss old catalogs and magazines	flip mattress	wash or dry-clean comforter or bedspread
change sheets and bedding	wash mattress pad	wash blankets
pour cleanser into toilet and swish	wash shower curtain	wash or fluff pillows in the dryer
shake out rugs and wash them	clean inside refrigerator, including door seals	unclog shower head, if needed
clean bathroom sink and tub	replace baking soda box in refrigerator	vacuum refrigerator condenser and grille
change towels in kitchen and bathrooms	wipe down kitchen cabinets	clean exhaust fan and oven
clean inside microwave and top of refrigerator	deodorize garbage disposal	wash cutlery tray

Get wise to hidden dangers. Commercial cleaning products can be costly – and toxic. To save money, you can whip up your own homemade cleaning products. But just because you make it yourself doesn't make it safe. Take some precautions to protect yourself and your family.

- Mix at your own risk. Some products that work well by themselves become dangerous when mixed together. For example, never mix chlorine bleach and ammonia. Read labels carefully and make sure it's safe before you mix and match.

- Store it safely. An empty cleaning product bottle may seem like a perfect container for your homemade cleaner. But that might not be the best idea. Your homemade formula could react with residue left in the bottle. What's more, the information on the bottle won't be accurate. This could cause confusion in an emergency. Don't store homemade cleaning products in food containers. Someone may mistake it for food.

- Shop wisely. Before you buy any cleaning product, consider if you really need it. Check if the product requires safety equipment. Examine the list of ingredients for any red flags, and make sure you can safely store it in your home. Always be on the lookout for a gentler, safer alternative.

Dig up cheap disposable gloves. Need to get down and dirty while getting your house clean? Save those plastic produce bags you tear off in the grocery store and turn them into disposable gloves. Slip the bags over your hands and hold them in place with rubber bands. When you're done, just toss them out.

Battle household enemies with the right ammunition. Chemistry plays an important role in cleaning. To remove fatty or oily grime, get down to basics. That means using solutions with a pH greater than 7, the neutral value of water.

Borax, baking soda, ammonia, and bleach fit into the basic, or alkaline, category. Cleaning products like all-purpose cleaners, oven cleaner, and laundry detergent also have a basic pH. These products get rid of most common messes, including dirt, soot, fats, cooking oils, food stains, and baked-on grease.

In your home, acidic cleaners fight rust, mineral deposits, water spots, and soap deposits. Unlike basic solutions, acidic solutions have a pH less than 7. Household examples of acidic solutions include vinegar, which contains acetic acid, and lemon juice, which features citric acid.

Toilet bowl cleaners, tub and tile cleaners, and cleaning products that fight hard water, mineral deposits, and mold are also acidic. As a bonus, acidic cleaners also act as disinfectants. They change the pH of the environment, making it tough for many microorganisms to survive.

WARNING

Safety tip for reusing containers

It's tempting to save empty bottles and jars, reusing them for any variety of purposes. Before you do, check the label.

Containers that held cleaners and other household chemicals may not be safe to use in another way. The label should say something like, "Do not reuse empty container." If you ignore this warning, your family could be in danger.

ODORS
Making sense of scents

Combat pesky household smells naturally. Researchers have found that certain chemicals in air fresheners and household deodorizers may harm your lungs. This is especially serious if you suffer from asthma or other breathing problem. But it's hard to know exactly what chemicals are in your plug-in air freshener or air-freshening spray, since manufacturers don't have to list all the ingredients.

Keep your family safe by using natural products to fight bad odors in your house. Some have been used for generations to freshen the air.

- Coffee grounds. Save up several days' worth of used coffee grounds, spread them on a baking sheet, and dry them in your oven at low heat. Then use the grounds to absorb odors all around your house – in a dish in the fridge, near a smelly ashtray, or in sachets where you store your tennis shoes.

- Baking soda. Just as natural sodium bicarbonate soaks up bad odors in the fridge, it can also tackle aromas around the house. Baking soda works by neutralizing the pH of bad-smelling acid and alkaline substances. Sprinkle it on carpet or upholstery, add it to a load of laundry, or toss a spoonful in your kitchen drain to knock out bad odors.

- Spices. Banish foul cooking scents and make your whole house smell fabulous by setting a pan of water on the stove and dropping in some cloves or cinnamon sticks to simmer.

- Charcoal. This porous form of carbon is a champ at absorbing odor and moisture. Place a small bowl of activated charcoal in your closet or bathroom to eat up those unpleasant odors.

- Lemon. Rub a lemon slice on your cutting board after you slice onions, then toss it down the garbage disposal to add a sweet scent there.
- Vinegar. Set out a dish of this pantry staple to absorb the smell of cigarette smoke after your friends leave, and place one by the stove while you boil cabbage or fry fish. You can also add a cup of vinegar to the rinse cycle to deodorize a load of gym socks.

ALTERNATE USES

Deodorize with a dryer sheet

Let your scented dryer sheets help control odors around your home. Place a new fabric softener sheet in the vacuum cleaner bag to freshen up a room while you clean. Change the sheet every few weeks or when the scent starts to fade.

Put another dryer sheet in your suitcase when you store it to ward off musty odors, and put one in your linen closet to keep sheets smelling fresh.

Banish kitchen odors at the source. Can you find your kitchen sponge just by smell? If the answer is yes, it's no surprise. The kitchen sponge is a major source of hidden bacteria and related bad odors in your kitchen.

Bacteria are happy to hang out and multiply in the tiny crevices of a damp sponge for weeks. You encourage their growth when you use a sponge for weeks at a time, let it stay damp on your dish drainer, and use the same sponge to clean a cutting board after you cut up chicken – then wipe down your kitchen table. That spreads germs.

You may have heard the advice to disinfect your kitchen sponge by putting it in the microwave, but that's a bad idea. True – the microwave can kill germs. But your sponge may catch on fire if it contains certain kinds of impurities, if it's not wet enough, or if your microwave is too powerful.

Instead, follow these four rules to keep your sponge clean and help your kitchen smell fresh.

- Let the sponge or dishrag dry out completely between uses. Bacteria thrive in moisture.
- Run it through your dishwasher on the hottest setting, and you'll kill almost as many bacteria as in the microwave. Place the sponge in the utensil basket to keep it from floating around.
- Wash the sponge or dishrag with bleach in your washing machine, then toss it in your dryer on high heat – at least once a week. You can also clean it thoroughly by boiling it for five minutes.
- Replace your sponge once a month.

4 tricks to end that fishy smell. Get rid of that lingering fish odor on your hands after you're done preparing and eating it. See what's in your cabinet that will work.

- Toothpaste. Use a good squirt of white fluoride toothpaste on your hands as if it were soap, then rinse.
- Lemon juice. Squeeze a lemon so the juice runs onto your hands, then rinse it off with water. Bottled lemon juice also works.
- Mustard. Mix dry mustard with a bit of dishwashing liquid, smear it on your hands, then rinse off.

- Hand sanitizer. Spread a bit onto your hands, then rub them together until they're dry.

Freshen the air with a homemade spritz. Whether you want to save money or simply avoid adding another bottle of chemicals to the growing collection under your kitchen sink, you can simplify life by making your own air freshener spray.

One simple recipe involves plain tap water and a few drops of essential oil. Add water to a 32-ounce spray bottle until it's nearly full, then mix in a dozen drops of your favorite essential oil. Pick a citrus oil like grapefruit to make a bacteria-killing spray, or use lavender oil for a relaxing mist. You can also substitute vinegar for the water, then mix in the essential oil.

If essential oils are not your thing, mix up a spritz with ingredients from your pantry. Dissolve two tablespoons of baking soda in two cups of hot water. Once the baking soda is dissolved, add one-half cup lemon juice and pour it into a spray bottle.

Because the citric acid in lemon juice works as a mild bleach, avoid spraying this mixture near fabrics or carpet.

Give the gift of sweet scents. Gather up some old glass jars or Mason jars and create thoughtful gifts that won't put you over budget. Scent jars let you infuse a room with the fragrance of your choice – then calm it down when you put the lid back on the jar. Select just the right scent for each recipient. Here's how to make them.

First, find a clean, attractive glass jar, preferably one with a lid. If you have saved jars that held candles, spaghetti sauce, or even peanuts, these will work. Decide what mood you want the scent jar to create – like holiday spices, garden blooms, or refreshing citrus.

For a floral scent, place a half-inch layer of rose petals on the bottom of the jar, and add a quarter-inch layer of salt. Continue alternating layers until the jar is about half full. As the salt pulls moisture from the rose petals, scented oils are released into the air. Use orange peels instead of rose petals for a citrus scent.

To create a spicier blend, cover the bottom of the jar with a mixture of cinnamon sticks, cloves, and nutmeg. Add more spices in layers for an attractive look. Sprinkle about a dozen drops of cinnamon bark essential oil onto the spices. Don't forget to give a small bottle of the essential oil along with the scent jar.

Be sure to check with your doctor before using essential oils if you have certain health conditions, like high blood pressure or diabetes.

WARNING

Get help nosing out danger

Your sense of smell naturally weakens over time, and a quarter of people older than age 55 have lost some ability to smell.

Get help if you think your sense of smell is not up to par. Ask a friend to confirm if your milk smells bad, or throw it out if you're not sure. Check the batteries in your home smoke alarms and gas detectors, and consider using multiple alarms. If you can't smell smoke or a gas leak, these alarms may be your only warning.

Create fragrant sachets for your drawers. Give your nose a treat every time you open a drawer or closet by stocking them with homemade sachets.

Make the sachet by gathering up the edges of a cloth handkerchief, then tying it with a ribbon. This trick also works with an unused paper coffee filter or a small mesh drawstring bag.

Fill the sachet with dried eucalyptus leaves, lavender, rosemary, rose petals, or crushed bay leaves. Enjoying the lavender or rosemary sachet may help you feel more calm, while rose petals and lavender can ward off moths. You can also add rock salt and a few drops of your favorite essential oil for a more powerful scent.

Say "so long" to skunk smell. Ah, the distinctive aroma of skunk. You know it when you smell it, whether it's in your car, on your dog, or hanging around your patio. Here's a simple way to make it go away.

Mix a quart of 3-percent hydrogen peroxide with four tablespoons of baking soda and three teaspoons of liquid soap. Use this solution to wipe down your smelly pet or the patio tiles – wherever the odor lingers. Don't forget to wear rubber gloves to protect your hands, and rinse off the solution when you're done.

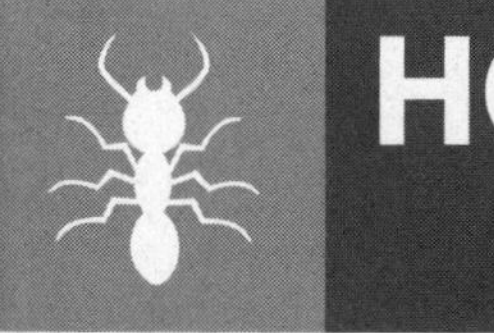

HOUSEHOLD PESTS
Keep creepy crawlies at bay

Amazing tricks to make ants disappear. Ant problems? Learn how to foil, trap, lure, repel, and kill the little pests – keeping them out of your home and yard for good. Dozens of solutions can be found right in your own pantry. Here are a few of them.

- White vinegar. Don't let ant colonies build condos on your lawn. Pour this simple solution on the hills and watch them vacate the premises. Spray full-strength vinegar near doors and windowsills to keep ants out of your home, as well. Repeat if needed.

- Water. Pouring boiling water on anthills also works. Make things even hotter by adding several drops of hot chili oil to the water. Just as with vinegar, you may need to do this more than once, but it will eventually get the job done. Spray soapy water on your countertops and sinks to keep ants away or spray it directly on ants to kill them.

- Coffee grounds. Coffee perks you up – and so will this news. Ants hate coffee grounds. Sprinkle coffee grounds around your plants, yard, garden, and the outside of your house to keep ants away.

- Herbs and spices. If you know where ants are coming into your home, sprinkle cinnamon, black pepper, chili powder, cayenne pepper, bay leaves, or dried mint to block their trail. Ants don't like to cross these substances. Hang sprigs of dried penny royal, rue, or tansy in your kitchen cupboards to keep ants out.

- Salt. Seasoned ant fighters know that ants won't cross salt. Sprinkle it around doorways, windowsills, and anywhere else ants may enter. Ants also won't cross a line of chalk, flour, or baby powder.

- Baking soda. Leave some baking soda in areas where you've seen ants. It should kill them. You can also mix equal parts baking soda and salt, and sprinkle the mixture in problem areas.

- Cream of Wheat. Sprinkle dry Cream of Wheat around the perimeter of your room or pour it on an anthill. When ants eat it, it expands in their stomach and kills them. Minute Rice works the same way.

- Orange peels. Citrus fruits contain natural pesticides. Put orange peels and water in your blender, and blend until smooth. Then dump the mixture on anthills early in the morning, before ants leave their nest.

- Borax. Mix borax with powdered sugar or maple syrup. The mixture will lure and poison ants. Don't use this method if you have kids or pets.

HANDY HINT

Foil fire ants the old-fashioned way

All ants are annoying, but fire ants are also dangerous. These vicious pests boast a painful bite. A swarm of them could even kill a small child. Luckily, you can stop them with an ancient Chinese secret — diatomaceous earth.

The Chinese have been using this nontoxic powder for 2,000 years. Diatomaceous earth, or D.E., is a natural powdery substance that pokes and dehydrates ants as they walk across it. It's perfect for indoor ant trails. You can find D.E. in garden shops and hardware stores.

Diatomaceous earth doesn't work as well when applied directly to an ant mound. But it may help other pesticides work better because it penetrates ants' bodies. In fact, some formulations of insecticides called pyrethrins include D.E. to boost their effectiveness.

"Scents"-ible ways to repel flies. Make your home smell wonderful while making it less welcoming for flying pests. A little peppermint or lavender should do the trick. Tell pesky flies to "buzz off" with these scented oils. They smell lovely to people, but keep flies far, far away. Soak some cotton balls with these oils, and leave them around your house to discourage insect intruders.

You can also shoo away flies with other pleasant scents. Plant mint around the outside of your home or place sachets of crushed mint inside to repel flies. Potted sweet basil plants also keep flies at bay. Cloves work, too. Hang clusters of cloves or small bags of ground cloves in your home. Flies hate the smell of citrus. For a natural repellent, scratch the peel of an orange and place it where flies like to hang out.

Mighty methods to minimize mosquitoes. Itching for an easy way to keep mosquitoes away? Look no further than marigolds. To repel mosquitoes and other flying insects, plant this flower in your garden. It's beautiful and functional. That's because the unpleasant smell of marigold flowers drives away pests. You can also place potted marigolds on your porch or deck to defend against mosquitoes.

Marigolds aren't the only plants that discourage mosquitoes. But for the others to be effective, you need to crush the leaves or stems and rub them on your skin. Catnip, rosemary, and lemon thyme can ward off mosquitoes this way. Test a small patch of your skin first to make sure it's not too sensitive.

Check out these other simple tricks to get rid of annoying mosquitoes.

- Sidestep standing water. Remove any unnecessary puddles in pots, drainage ditches, gutters, and anywhere else water may accumulate in your yard. Change the water in your birdbath, vases, or pool frequently. Standing water serves as a breeding ground for mosquitoes.

- Ban bug zappers. These noisy contraptions do more harm than good. They end up killing more beneficial insects than mosquitoes.

- Defend yourself with dryer sheets. Dryer sheets act as a natural bug repellent. Hang a dryer sheet on your patio or tuck one into your cuff or neckline to drive away mosquitoes.

- Vex mosquitoes with vinegar. Add two teaspoons of apple cider vinegar to a glass of water and set it on your deck or porch. You can also use a cotton ball to rub white vinegar on your skin.

- Slather on a scent. Keep mosquitoes away by making yourself smell horrible to them. Dab some lavender oil on your wrists and elbows. Or rub a slice of onion on your skin. Orange and lemon peels also do the trick. You can also dilute some vanilla extract in water, and wipe the mixture on your skin.

Keen trick to fix a hole in your screen. Are holes in your screen door letting pesky mosquitoes in? You don't need to buy a whole new screen just because of a small hole in your screen door or window.

Push the mesh back in place. Then take some clear nail polish and dab over the hole. Apply three or four coats, letting it dry between applications. The nail polish will seal the hole and prevent it from getting bigger. Rubber cement or model glue should also do the trick.

Encourage mice to run for the hills. Your pantry holds a wide range of kitchen staples, making it a potential smorgasbord for hungry mice. Protect your pantry – and the rest of your home – with peppermint. Make pantry pests scurry away with a cotton ball soaked in this sweet scent.

Look for peppermint oil in the essential oils section of health and vitamin stores. You can also find it online. Soak cotton balls in the peppermint oil, and leave them where you suspect mice are lurking. Look for telltale signs of mouse droppings. Prime spots include cabinets, storage areas, or behind your refrigerator. Mice can't handle the strong scent of peppermint, and they'll run from it.

You can use mint leaves instead of the scented cotton balls to scare mice away. Or plant mint around your doors to discourage mice from entering in the first place.

Baking soda and used kitty litter can also repel mice – but they don't smell as good as mint.

HANDY HINT

Cool tip to protect your pantry

Reading a package's nutrition label helps you know more about what's in your food. But the label won't tell you if there's something living in there. Indian meal moths, beetles, and other bugs may make their home in packaged grains like flour, cornmeal, pasta, rice, or cereal.

Keep the bugs away from your flour and pasta with this simple trick. Pop these susceptible items in the freezer for a few days when you bring them home from the store. The cold temperature should kill any pests. You can even store these items in your freezer or refrigerator to prevent infestation. Make sure to use airtight containers. Pests can worm their way through cardboard, plastic, or paper.

Other ways to guard your grains include inspecting packages for signs of damage, buying smaller amounts of food, and using older and opened products before new, unopened ones. It's also important to keep food storage areas clean and free of crumbs.

Fantastic tips to get rid of fleas. When you have pets, you may also have fleas. These pests can multiply rapidly, bite, and spread disease. Try these tactics to make fleas flee your home.

- Attack them with acid. Spray a mixture of boric acid and salt on carpets, bedding, and any other areas where your pets hang out. It will kill fleas, but won't harm you or your pets.

- Stymie them with soap. Place a bowl of soapy water below a table lamp. Fleas will jump toward the light at night, fall in the water, and drown. Wash pet bedding once a week in hot soapy water to kill any eggs. Liquid dishwashing detergent works well.

- Vanquish them with a vacuum cleaner. After vacuuming carpets and bedding, empty the contents in a plastic bag and dispose of the bag away from your house. Make sure to seal the bag tightly.

- Nix them with natural products. Some oils and extracts serve as natural insecticides. You can use citronella oil, eucalyptus oil, lavender oil, tea tree oil, balsam, and citrus peel extract to kill fleas.

Squelch spiders with ease. Tired of finding creepy cobwebs in the corners of your home? Here's a nifty trick to keep spiders away from your walls. Add a teaspoon of coconut oil to some white distilled vinegar, and spray the mixture around your house. Your house may smell like vinegar for a while, but it should also stay spider-free.

Another homemade spider repellent involves mixing one cup of vegetable oil, one-quarter cup of liquid dish soap, and one teaspoon of vanilla extract. Dilute it with water – one cup of water for each tablespoon of the mixture – and spray away your spiders.

But you don't even need fancy concoctions to solve your spider problem. Virtually eliminate spiders from your basement in a matter of weeks with two easy steps.

First, vacuum and dust regularly to remove webs and egg sacs. Then make sure spiders have nothing to feed on by keeping other insects out. Seal any cracks, screen vents, and maintain seals on window screens and doors.

Critter-proof your house. As Dorothy from "The Wizard of Oz" discovered, there's no place like home. Unfortunately, furry creatures sometimes make that same discovery. Raccoons and squirrels and rats, oh my! Keep the critters away from your house with these four tips.

- Limit food sources. Don't leave pet food bowls or bags of pet food outdoors. Hang bird feeders in hard-to-reach areas – like on a wire between two high tree branches – or bring them in at night.
- Guard your garbage. Keep garbage securely covered in sturdy cans. Tie down the lids with ropes or bungee cords, if necessary. Keep the garbage can in your garage or shed if all else fails.
- Trim your trees. Remove any tree branches within reach of your roof. Watch out for trellises, too.
- Repair your roof. Fix any holes in your roof and cover any possible entrances. Screen attic vents. Cover your chimney with a chimney cap or netting.

Be just as vigilant inside your house, keeping an eye open for cracks leading to the outside. Plug a mouse hole with a mixture that scares off the toughest mice. Stuff steel wool into any hole bigger around than a pencil, seal it with caulk, and smooth.

Repel flying insects with a pleasant-smelling potpourri. Mothballs may protect your clothes from destructive moths, but what will protect your clothes – and you – from the unpleasant smell of mothballs? Try this spicy sweet alternative – whole cloves. Bugs hate them just as much as mothballs.

Simply put some cloves in cheesecloth or a small muslin drawstring bag. It's an ingenious way to repel bugs and freshen clothing. Just tuck your clove sachet into a drawer or closet. No more mothball odor. You can also just put a few individual cloves in the pockets of your wool coats and jackets.

Lavender sachets also do the trick. Tie a handful of dried lavender into a muslin square. Put this in your drawers or closets to repel insects and make your clothes smell springtime fresh.

Moths also dislike the smell of citrus fruits. Scatter dried citrus peels in your dresser drawers to keep moths out. Another trick to keep insects away and freshen the air is to put bars of soap in drawers, closets, and suitcases.

Beware of liner paper in dresser drawers

Don't line your dresser drawers with ready-pasted wallpaper or adhesive liner paper. The glue will attract moths and other pests.

6 ways to dodge bedbugs. You may not be the only guest in your hotel room. You could be sharing your quarters with bedbugs. And, if you're not careful, you could end up bringing these unwanted souvenirs home with you. Here's how to keep bedbugs at bay when you're on the road.

- Watch where you put your bags. Don't put your luggage on the bed, carpet, or upholstered furniture. That's where bedbugs make themselves at home. Use the coffee table, desk, or metal luggage rack instead. Just make sure these items aren't too close to the bed.

- Check out your room. Examine the bed and surrounding furniture for bedbugs. These tiny reddish-brown bugs could be hiding in the seams of the mattress, the box spring, headboard, or night stand. If you spot any bedbugs, ask to change rooms. Then carry out a similar inspection of your new room.

- Guard your garments. Don't unpack your suitcase and put your clothes in the hotel's dresser drawers. Hang all your clothing or leave it in the suitcase, far from the bed.

- Leave personal comforts at home. Resist the temptation to bring your own pillow or sheets on the road with you. They could harbor bedbugs from the hotel mattress.

- Turn up the heat. When you get home, empty your suitcase and throw all your clothes – whether you wore them or not – in the dryer for 15 minutes on high as an extra precaution. Extreme heat can kill bedbugs.

- Clean your suitcase. Vacuum out your suitcase when you get home. You can also leave your empty bags in the car on a very hot or very cold day to kill any critters that may have hitched a ride home with you.

Detect bedbugs with dry ice. Find out if you have bedbugs with a handy homemade bedbug detector. Developed by a Rutgers University professor, this economical contraption works as well as any equipment used by professional exterminators. Here's how to set it up.

- Scuff the outer surface of a plastic pet food dish with sandpaper.
- Turn the dish upside down and dust the inside lip of the overturned dish with talcum powder.
- Buy an insulated jug – one-third of a gallon – at a sports or camping store and fill it with 2 1/2 pounds of dry ice. Always wear gloves when handling dry ice.
- Set the jug on top of the overturned dish. Open the pour hole slightly.

As the dry ice evaporates, the jug leaks carbon dioxide. Because humans exhale carbon dioxide, this makes bedbugs think there's a living, human target nearby. The bedbugs easily climb the overturned pet food dish, since the scuffed surface provides traction. But once they reach the top, they slide down the other side – thanks to the slippery powder.

With this gizmo, you'll be able to discover bedbugs before they become a big problem. If you do detect any bedbugs, call an exterminator right away.

Repel roaches with simple remedy. Here's a sweet way to get rid of cockroaches. Mix equal parts of baking soda and powdered sugar, and sprinkle the mixture in problem areas. You can also leave some in strategically placed shallow dishes. It will attract the roaches and kill them. Keep this remedy out of the reach of children and pets.

Vinegar trap foils fruit flies. Fruit flies swarm your kitchen seeking fermenting fruits and vegetables. Give them what they want – plus an added surprise. Pour some apple cider vinegar in a bowl or small container, and add a few drops of dish soap. Place this cheap, simple trap in an area where you've seen fruit flies. The smell of the vinegar will lure the flies, while the soap breaks the surface tension of the water. They can't escape and drown in the trap.

Sticky solution for summer pests. Stick it to bothersome flies with some homemade flypaper. In a shallow pan, mix one-quarter cup of maple syrup with one tablespoon each of brown sugar and white granulated sugar. Cut or tear a brown paper bag into several long strips, and soak the strips in the sticky mixture overnight. Punch a hole in one end of each strip and insert a string. Hang your homemade flypaper near open doors and windows to catch those annoying summer pests.

Frighten flies away for pennies. Sometimes folk wisdom is the best wisdom. Try this homespun trick to keep flies away. Fill a plastic sandwich bag halfway with water, and drop in a few pennies. Zip the bag shut and hang it over a doorway or window. Flies should steer clear of the area.

Nobody knows why this homemade fly repellent works. Some say the reflection scares flies away. Others say flies mistake the hanging bag for the nest of a predator. Others dismiss the whole thing as poppycock.

Even if there's no clear explanation for its success, it's worth a try. After all, it only costs a few pennies. But the payoff – a fly-free home – could be priceless.

Build your own mousetrap. You don't need poison or deadly snap-traps to get rid of that pesky mouse in your house. A makeshift mousetrap using everyday household items will do the trick. It's a cheaper, safer, and more humane alternative to other traps.

All you need is an empty toilet paper tube, a tall garbage can or bucket, some newspapers, and some bait. Here's how to set it up.

- Flatten one side of the empty toilet paper tube so it can rest on a flat surface without rolling.
- Put some kind of treat, like bread crumbs or a dab of peanut butter, at one end of the tube.
- Balance the tube so the end with the treat hangs well over the edge of a table or counter.
- Position the garbage can or bucket directly under the dangling end of the tube.
- Stuff some crumpled newspapers at the bottom of the garbage can or bucket. You can also put more treats in there.

The mouse will crawl into the toilet paper tube toward the treat. As it moves further along the tunnel, its weight will cause the tube – and the mouse – to fall into the garbage can or bucket. The newspaper will cushion its fall, and the treats will keep the mouse from trying to escape.

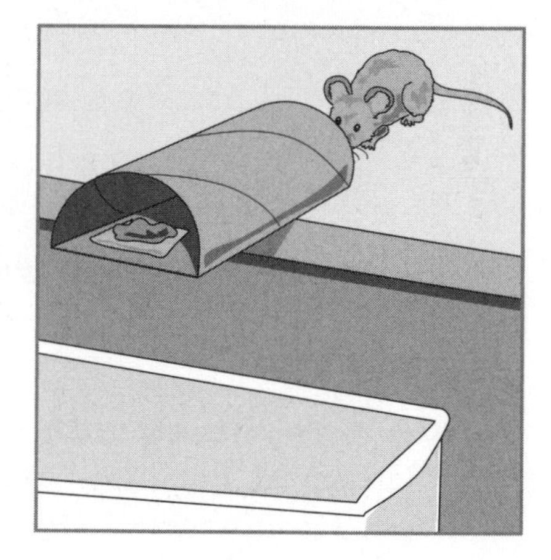

Once you trap the mouse, release it far from your house. Either dump the mouse by turning the trash can or bucket upside down or set it on its side so the mouse can run out.

Relieve bug bites with everyday items. In spite of your best efforts, you got a nasty bite. Fortunately, you can soothe insect bites and stings with everyday household items. Try these handy remedies.

Remedy	How to apply
Alka-Seltzer	Dissolve two tablets in water, soak a cotton ball in the solution, and place on bite for 30 minutes.
antiperspirant	Dab some roll-on antiperspirant directly on the bite.
aspirin	Wet your skin and rub aspirin over the bite or sting. Or crush a tablet, mix with water to form a paste, and spread it on your sting.
baking soda	Spread a paste of baking soda and water on bee stings and other bites.
basil	Crush fresh basil leaves and rub them on your bug bite.
hot peppers	Crush them and spread over your skin. The heat will take your mind off the pain. Hot sauce also works.
meat tenderizer	Make sure it contains papain but no added seasonings. Add water to form a paste. Spread it over the bite.
milk	Make a paste of one part powdered milk, two parts water, and a pinch of salt. Dab on the bite.
onion	Apply half an onion to a bee sting.
peppermint oil	Apply a drop or two to the itchy area. Toothpaste that contains peppermint oil also works.
salt	Soak a mosquito bite in salt water, then coat the area with vegetable oil.
vinegar	Rub some apple cider vinegar on insect bites.

Battle mosquitoes with bats. In the comic books, Gotham City flashed the Bat Signal to summon Batman to the rescue. You don't need a superhero to fight mosquitoes, but you can still summon some winged help. Just build or buy a bat house to lure bats to your property.

Why do you want to lure bats? Because bats gobble up mosquitoes and other pesky insects. In fact, a bat can eat up to 1,000 mosquitoes an hour.

For cheap, nontoxic mosquito control, install a bat house. Also known as a bat box, a bat house is open at the bottom with a roof on top. It's very narrow, unlike a bird house, because bats like tight spaces. They also like it warm, so you should paint the box a dark color to absorb the sun's rays. However, if summer temperatures regularly exceed 95 degrees where you live, a lighter color will do. The inside of the box should be rough to simulate the bark of a tree and to give bats something to cling to.

Hang your bat house on a tree, a pole, or a building. Place it in a sunny spot about 15 feet high. Your mosquito problem should be solved. As a bonus, providing bats with an alternative roost will keep them out of your house.

ORGANIZING
Space-savvy storage

Top tip for easier organizing. Are you a hunter in your own home? End the frustration of having to search for important items.

Make your stuff easier to find, while you save time and space, with one simple technique – make a home for everything, and put everything in its home.

It's just that simple. Designating a certain location for each item means you always know where to find it, whether you're looking for a flathead screwdriver or your favorite silk blouse. Here's how to start the process.

- Organize based on how often items are used. For something you use every day, like your favorite hairbrush, designate a location where it's easy to reach. But a gadget that gets used only rarely, such as a fondue pot, can have a home that's tucked away.

- Place similar items together. Create a space for all cleaning supplies, and another for your tennis gear. Then there's no confusion about where to put your tennis racket when you come home. In fact, as you sort similar items, you may find you have more of one thing than you need, so you can cull extras and donate them.

- Keep it simple. Don't clutter up your home with a complicated system of boxes, bins, or shelves that makes putting things away difficult. A complex plan pretty much guarantees you won't follow it.

- Don't wait. When you bring in the mail, sort it immediately and deal with each bill and catalog once. Toss the trash right away – don't set it down to look at later. This habit leads to piles of clutter you'll have to sort through.

Take control of clutter in just 15 minutes. Still waiting for that free weekend so you can get organized? Be realistic – it'll never arrive. Instead, block out 15 minutes each day to tackle one small clutter problem.

Be specific about what you'll do, like cleaning out files on Monday, sorting items in the junk drawer on Tuesday, and seeking out old clothes or shoes to donate on Wednesday. Write down your plan, then follow through. By the end of the first week, you'll feel more in control of your belongings and ready to continue the project.

You can do anything for 15 minutes, so you won't feel overwhelmed by the job. Just keep telling yourself that getting a handle on your home is a marathon – not a sprint. Do a little work at a time, and soon you'll see real progress.

HANDY HINT

Find your keys in a flash

Create a drop zone for the most commonly misplaced items in your life. For many people, key rings, cellphones, and sunglasses seem to disappear just when you need them most.

Your drop zone should be a place set aside for just that purpose, with some kind of holders to contain your must-haves. Consider hanging a small shelf with hooks in your front hallway or near the door to your garage. You can even buy a wall organizer with these features, plus a wipe-off message board or chalkboard to write notes or reminders. Place a basket beneath the shelf to hold your purse, and you're set.

Get in the habit of putting your keys on the hooks and setting your sunglasses and cellphone on the shelf every time you come home. With the drop zone located on your way into the house, good habits will come easily.

Get a ship-shape kitchen without spending a dime. Keep your kitchen clean and organized by reusing items you already have.

- Make a countertop spice tray from a round cake pan. Clean it, sand any rust, spray with a paint made for metal, and set it on your counter. Then pull out the spices you use every day – maybe salt, pepper, garlic powder, and cinnamon – and arrange in the pan. Now, you can stop searching through a dark cabinet.

- Save that clever little canister stacked chips come in to store your spaghetti once the box is opened. You won't have to deal with spilled pasta again. Just be sure to clean out the can first.

- When you buy ice cream in a large plastic tub, you're also buying a great sealable container. Save up several, and use them to keep baking supplies like flour, sugar, and cornmeal away from pantry pests.

- Use an old shoe box or rectangular tissue box to sort gravy, sauce, and spice packets. You can also put an old loaf pan to use for this job.

- Upgrade your silverware drawer with a new cutlery tray, then reuse the old one. Place it in a deep utensil draw, and sort items into the sections. If you have several trays, you can stack them in the drawer with items you use often, like a spatula or can opener, on the top level. Hide away items you rarely use, such as a garlic press, underneath.

- Use plastic berry baskets to corral small jar lids in the dishwasher to keep them from getting lost in the bottom drain. Put your items in one basket and put another on top. Secure them together with a rubber band.

- Create cubbyholes on your pantry shelves, and you'll be able to see items and organize them. Use plastic crates, wire baskets, or transparent storage boxes.

- Install long metal kitchen cabinet handles horizontally inside a cabinet door and hang small hooks from them. You now have a hidden storage space for soup ladles and slotted spoons.

Clever hidden storage for plastic grocery bags. Keep those supermarket plastic bags clean and ready to be reused. Create a makeshift storage place by tacking an empty tissue box to the inside of your pantry door at a convenient level. You'll never have trouble finding a bag when you need to line a wastebasket or gather up snacks for the road.

Divide and conquer your junk drawer. Get a handle on that drawer where you stash paperclips, batteries, pens, and grocery coupons. A homemade set of dividers lets you organize all the items in your junk drawer.

First, empty the drawer completely, and toss out any trash or items you don't need. Measure the drawer, and cut partitions from cardboard to create a grid. You can use larger pieces of cardboard from corrugated boxes, or cut apart shoe boxes or tissue boxes for smaller pieces.

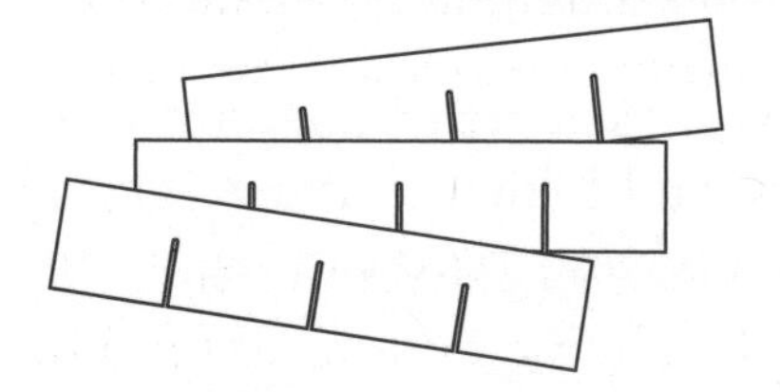

You'll need a sharp utility knife, so be careful. Create large and small divisions to fit the items you'll be storing. Cut notches halfway through each cardboard piece.

Fit together the pieces into a grid, and set it into the empty drawer. Since you weeded through the junk, what's left should be useful stuff you can easily sort into the sections. Get into the habit of keeping your drawer neat.

More closet space without renovations. No matter how large your closets are, they're never big enough. Make your closets hold more stuff neatly. Just follow these simple steps for closets you can be proud of.

First, take a look at the items you want to store. Do you have mostly hanging clothes? lots of shoes? loads of accessories? Or do you really need more space for folded items? Once you determine what kind of space you need, you can start designing a system to hold it all.

Second, make more space. Browse through magazines or brochures of custom closets, and you'll see that the best spaces feature more than a single hanging rod. They usually have multiple rods, shelves at various heights, baskets, hooks – many ways to store and organize your clothing. Consider these additions.

- Hang shower curtain hooks onto your clothes rod, and use them for belts and ties.

- Install a towel rod on the back of your closet door. It's a great space to hang scarves so they won't get wrinkled.

- Put hooks at various levels on the wall inside your closet. They'll work great to hang out-of-season purses and belts.

- Measure the floor area in your closet, then create a cubby system to define space for shoes, bags, and folded clothing. The beauty of using cubbies rather than boxes is you can see what you have at a glance.

- Put up a second rod. Designate a section of your closet where you'll hang slacks and other short items. Then install a rod below the top one. You can find one that hangs suspended from the top rod, so you don't need to drill holes in the wall.

Finally, get sorting. Be honest – you probably have clothes you never wear. Cull the extras, and pass them on to someone who can use them.

ALTERNATE USES

Save space with three-ring binders

When file cabinet space is lacking but shelf space is plentiful, use three-ring binders as your filing system. Just add plastic sheet protectors or file pockets, and you can use binders to keep various kinds of documents organized and easy to find.

- Paperwork for appliances. Gather warranties, owner manuals, dates of purchase — even the phone number of your favorite repair service — in a single place.
- Medical information. Designate a separate binder for each family member, and keep bills, test results, and prescription information together. Having this information handy when you need it can be a real lifesaver.
- Recipes. Organize recipes and menu ideas you clip from newspapers or print from your computer in a binder rather than copying them onto index cards. You'll save time and have your favorite recipes in one place.

8 unusual uses for accordion files. These handy, expandable file folders are tops when it comes to sorting important documents. Did you ever think about using them to file more than just papers? Grab a bundle of accordion files when you see them on sale, and try these super organizing ideas.

- Sort manuals and warranties for all your appliances and gadgets.
- Get a handle on patterns, templates, and swatches for sewing and knitting projects.
- Keep samples and swatches from a home-decorating project. You'll know just what paint or wallpaper to buy when the room needs a touch-up.

- Plan ahead and keep greeting cards handy for birthdays, anniversaries, and holidays. You can even get a 12-section file, designate one pocket for each month, and prepare cards for the entire year.
- Organize medical records by person, procedure, or doctor.
- Sort sandpaper according to grain and material to keep sheets flat and clean.
- Corral coupons into categories like hair products, dairy items, and cleaning supplies.
- Track taxes all year. Designate a section for charity receipts, another for bank statements, and a third to hold W-2 forms.

Attract neatness with a magnetic strip. A wall-mounted magnetic strip can help clear clutter from your bathroom drawers. Install a strip horizontally inside your medicine cabinet, and use it to hang tweezers, scissors, metal combs – anything that will stick.

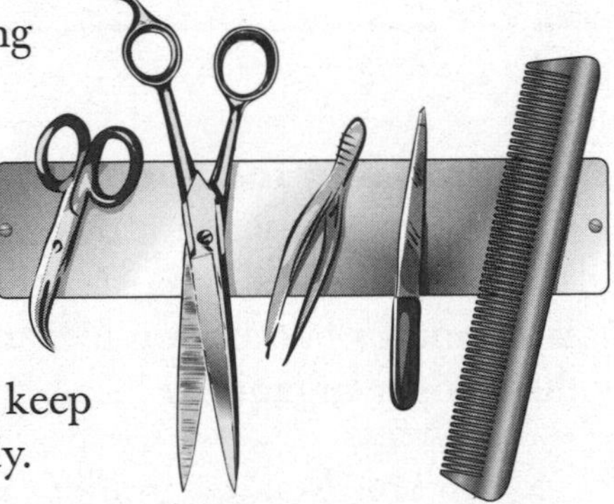

You can also put a magnetic strip in your kitchen to hang knives. Or install one in your garage or workshop, and use it to keep paintbrushes and other tools handy.

Handy hang-up for paper bags. Save old skirt hangers with metal or plastic clips, and use them to store oversize paper shopping and gift bags. You can fill part of a coat closet with neatly folded bags ready to be used to deliver old magazines or wrap a birthday gift.

HANDY HINT

Stop junk mail cold

Keep junk mail from cluttering up your home by stopping it with the help of a service called Precycle.

For a one-time fee of $10, the service will remove your name and address from many marketing lists, cutting down on the junk mail you receive. Sign up online at *http://precycle.tonic.com*.

To stop most junk mail for free, contact the Direct Marketing Association's Mail Preference Service at P.O. Box 643, Carmel, NY, 10512. Or navigate to the group's website, *www.dmachoice.org*, and click on the link "Give your mailbox a makeover." You'll have the options to limit or stop various types of unsolicited mail, catalogs, and magazine offers. You should get less junk mail for the next five years.

Shoe bag helps kick clutter. You may have too many shoes for your over-the-door shoe organizer, but it can provide great storage options throughout the house.

- In the closet. Sort your socks by color, or fold up scarves and place one in each pocket with a corner sticking out so you'll find it easily. If chunky bracelets or strings of beads overtake your dresser, keep them out of the way in the pockets of a clear vinyl shoe hanger.
- In the laundry room. You can never have enough storage space here. Corral cleaning supplies, rags, and extra light bulbs in the pockets.
- In the bathroom. Clear off your counter and keep bottles of shampoo, conditioner, and lotion in the pockets. You can even designate pockets for nail polish and manicure tools.

- In the pantry. Sort spice mixes, gravy packets, and small bottles into the handy pockets. If that box of cornstarch won't fit, repackage it in a resealable baggy and label it. Remember to attach the bottom corners of the shoe organizer to your pantry door so it stays still when the door opens.

HOME DECOR
How to show it off

Group your pictures like a pro. A well-planned picture grouping on a wall can make any room look more polished. Don't be intimidated by the job of getting each picture hung in the right place. Put a large piece of craft paper to work as a template, and the group will come out looking perfect.

- Begin by laying the piece of craft paper on the floor and arranging your pictures as you would like them on the wall. This is your opportunity to try out various layouts, since you're not making holes in the wall yet.

- Once you're happy with the plan, trace around each picture frame on the paper.

- Number each picture, marking it with a piece of tape and writing that number on the craft paper. You can even create a small sketch of the layout, including numbers, so you don't get confused.

- Measure each picture frame to find the distance from the top of the frame to the hanger. Draw in the hanger's location on the template for each picture.

- Using painter's tape, attach the template to the wall. Stand back and examine it to be sure the pictures will be just where you want them. Take your time with this step, perhaps waiting to view the arrangement in different light.

- Mark each nail hole through the paper. You can even go ahead and install the nails or hanging bolts with the paper still on the wall.

- Take down the paper, put up the pictures, and enjoy your perfect grouping.

Hang pictures straight the first time. Stop the annoyance of pictures that hang at a slant – even after you've straightened them for the umpteenth time. Use these decorators' secrets to get your pictures positioned perfectly and hanging straight in a jiffy.

First, get the nail exactly where you want it. Whether your picture will hang from a wire stretched across the back of the frame or from a mounting bracket, you need to figure out where the nail should be. You can measure the distance from the top of the frame to the bracket or wire, or you can take this measure-free shortcut.

Attach double-sided tape to the head of a thumbtack, and attach it to the back of the picture just below the mounting bracket or wire. Be sure the thumbtack is centered from side to side on the picture. Hold the picture up to the wall where you want to hang it, and press it against the wall, letting the tack make a small mark. Use that mark as a guide to install your nail or hanging screw.

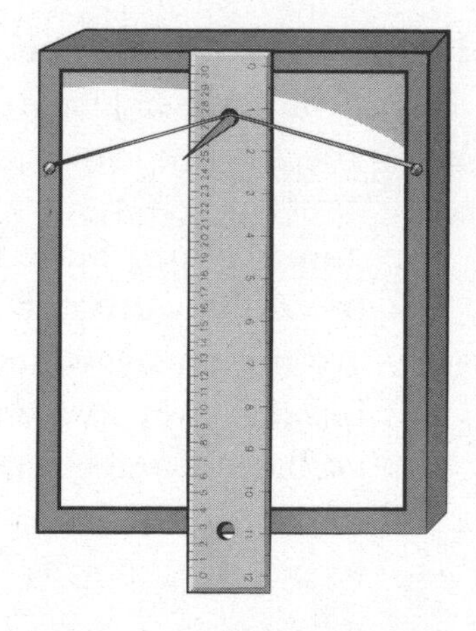

You can also use a ruler with holes down the center, placing a tack or small nail in one of the holes. Allow the picture's wire to hang on the nail while you hold it up with the ruler, then press the whole thing against the wall where you want to hang the picture. The nail will leave a small mark to use as your guide.

Second, keep your pictures from sliding to the side and hanging askew. Even if the picture hangs on a single nail, a small amount of something sticky will keep it in place. Place a tiny bit of window caulking or even Silly Putty along the frame in one corner. You need a substance that won't dry out quickly, yet won't damage the wall. Or you can wrap a bit of tape, sticky side out, around toothpicks and wedge them between the wall and the back of the frame.

HANDY HINT

Hang a picture with floss

Skip a trip to the store for hanging wire, and use that extra spool of dental floss.

Dental floss is super strong, and you can thread two or three strands across the holders on the back of the picture for extra support. Try it for small framed photos or art, holiday ornaments, sun catchers, or wind chimes.

Keep your florals from fading. Enjoying cut flowers for the longest time possible starts at the store and continues once you bring them home. Success is in the details.

- You may pay more for flowers at a specialty florist, but it's probably worth it. Flower bouquets on display at a supermarket are not always cared for properly. Florists take more care because they lose money when they have to toss flowers that go bad. When selecting cut flowers, look for buds just starting to open, firm flowers, and undamaged stems. Sniff the water to be sure it smells fresh.

- Prepare the flowers before you place them in a vase. Cut the stems at an angle to give them more surface area to take up water. It's best to do this job with a sharp knife, preferably while holding the stems under running water. And be sure everything that comes into contact with your flowers – knife, vase, even your hands – is clean. Bacteria on the flowers will make them wilt.

- Maintain a flower-friendly environment. That means keeping the flowers out of direct sunlight, a drafty room, or high temperatures. And don't place a bowl of fruit near the flowers, since ethylene gas from ripening fruit will hasten the demise of your buds.

Bubble away grime inside a flower vase. Here's a clever way to clean the inside of a narrow vase that's too small for your hand. Put the fizz of Alka-Seltzer to work. Just fill the vase with water and drop in two Alka-Seltzer tablets. The bubbling action from carbon dioxide release will gently scrub the vase.

Keep pollen from staining your decor. Avoid the mess and damage of pollen shedding from your cut flowers. When you include flowers like lilies in an arrangement, be sure to cut off the pollen-bearing anthers from the stamens and throw them out. Turn the flower upside down and use sharp scissors to snip them.

Extend the life of cut flowers. That little packet of powder you get from the florist to feed your cut flowers really works to help them last longer. In fact, you might want to ask for an extra packet or two when you buy a bouquet.

Flower-saving packets contain three types of ingredients – a chemical biocide to kill the bacteria and fungi that feed on plants as they wilt, an acidifier like citric acid to help flower stems take up water, and sugar that the plant uses as nutrition.

Recipes for homemade cut-flower solutions contain some or all of these components. Try these when you run out of packets.

- Lemon-lime soda. Adding a bit of this to the water gives your flowers sugar and some acidity.
- Crushed aspirin. This remedy provides acid, similar to lemon-lime soda.
- Vinegar and sugar. Several tablespoons of white distilled vinegar and a spoonful of sugar provide nourishment and acidity.
- Bleach. Just a few drops of this disinfectant will kill the bacteria that speed up the demise of your lovely flowers.
- An old penny. Drop a copper-containing penny – one minted before 1982 – into the vase of water. The copper works to kill fungi and extend the life of your blooms.

Whichever flower-extending recipe you choose, be sure to change the water in the vase every few days to keep it fresh.

2 tricks for shinier brass. Brasso – it's a great product when you want to remove tarnish and grime from brass pots, buckles, and hinges. But when you run out of Brasso and need a substitute, look no further than your produce drawer.

- Lemons. A lemon half sprinkled with salt makes a great brass polisher. Just rub the brass until it's clean, then rinse. You can also polish brass with plain lemon juice. Use lemons or juice only if your brass is solid – not brass plated. Otherwise you'll end up with scratches on the surface, or you may even rub the brass plating right off.
- Onions. Bring a pot of chopped onions to a boil and let it simmer for two hours. Strain out the onion bits, then use the onion juice to polish your brass. Be sure to rinse off the brass when you're done.

WARNING

Mold-free way to clean blinds

Don't clean your window blinds by dunking them in your bathtub. Doing so may get the blinds clean, but it will also soak the strings that hold up the blinds. This can lead to mildew or mold growing and damaging your blinds.

Instead, wipe down the blinds with a damp cloth or sponge, or simply wipe off the dust using an old dryer sheet to cut down on static, which attracts dust.

5 ways to decorate with a wooden ladder. Give your home decor some panache by recycling an old wooden ladder. This sturdy yet rustic-looking item can serve several purposes with just a little work and creativity.

- Drape quilts. Cut a ladder to size, sand the rungs, then trim the top rails at an angle so the ladder leans flush against a wall. You can even glue on felt pads to avoid scratching the wall. Fold and drape a quilt over each rung to add color to a room or hallway.
- Display art. A ladder with flat rungs gives you a great vertical art gallery for paintings or framed photos. If the rungs are wide enough, use stand-up picture easels. Otherwise, you can install a hanging nail at the center of each rung.
- Hang pots and pans. A short ladder section makes a great overhead rack in the kitchen when it's hung horizontally. Be sure to attach it securely to the ceiling with metal chains and hooks secured to the ceiling joists, then hang your prettiest copper pots using S-hooks.
- Collect houseplants. Clean up a small stepladder, and put it to use as a plant stand. You'll be able to water all your

houseplants at once when they live together on a single stand. If a step on the ladder is not wide enough for a large pot, attach a piece of plywood to extend it.

- Store books. Cut a ladder into two equal lengths, making sure the rungs are at the same height on each section. These can stand as side supports for a bookshelf, with lengths of wood held up between the rungs as shelves. Bolt the whole thing to the wall to keep it stable.

MYTHBUSTER

Common-sense candle care

You may have heard the advice to store candles in your refrigerator so they will burn longer. Don't waste the space in your fridge.

The National Candle Association says that, although a candle will be colder straight out of the fridge, it won't make much difference in burning time. Within a few minutes of lighting, the candle will be back at room temperature — just as if it had never spent time in your fridge. Store candles in a cool, dry, dark location.

HOUSEPLANTS

Pots with pizzazz

Know when to water. Yellow leaves on a houseplant can mean too much water – or not enough. But doing the wrong thing can kill your plant. Discover two simple signs that tell you whether to water, or wait.

- Sign #1. Houseplant roots often live in the bottom two-thirds of the pot. You don't want to water until the lower portion of the pot is almost completely dry. To test this in a 6-inch pot, push your finger down 2 inches deep into the soil near the pot's edge. For most people, that means the top of the soil is about even with the second joint of your finger. If the soil feels damp at your fingertip, don't water yet. Just repeat this finger test every day. When the soil at your fingertip is dry, water thoroughly.
- Sign #2. Push a pencil down in the dirt and then remove it. Don't water the plant if you find dirt or moisture on the pencil. You'll know it's time to water if the pencil comes out dry and dirt-free.

Stop houseplants from leaking

Before potting your plant, lay down a drainage layer of gravel or packing peanuts, then throw in a handful of tea bags before adding the soil. Most plants will love you for this and here's why. When you water, the layer of tea bags will absorb excess water. Not only does this prevent leakage, it also holds in moisture so roots will thrive. Nutrients from the tea bag may even help nourish your houseplants.

Find the perfect spot for your new plant. All houseplants love light, but some need more than others. To make sure your plant gets the right amount of light, do a shadow test in the spot where your plant will live.

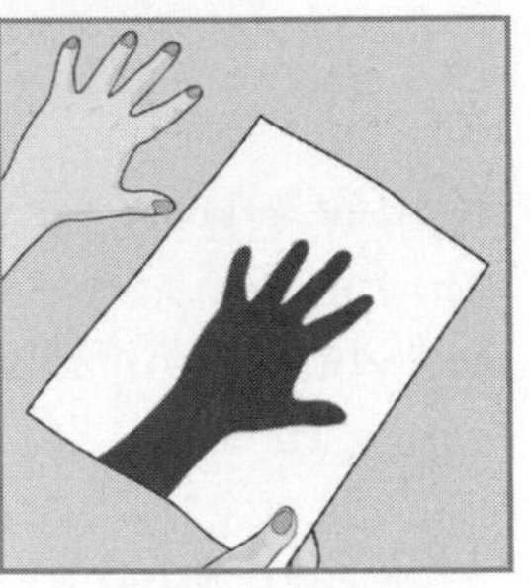

First, check the plant label to see whether it recommends low, medium, or high light. If the label doesn't have that information, search for it on the Internet or at your local library.

Grab a sheet of white paper and go to the spot where your plant will dwell. Do this on a sunny day when the light in the room is at its brightest. Hold the paper where the plant will be and angle it so it faces the nearest source of natural light. Now place your other hand between the paper and the light source, keeping your hand roughly a foot away from the paper.

If your hand's shadow is sharply defined on the paper, the plant can expect a high amount of light. If the shadow is dimmer and fuzzy around the edges, the light is medium. A faint shadow means this is a low light location.

Keep in mind that different seasons bring different levels of brightness. Test the spot again in early winter and in early summer to make sure your plant still gets the right amount of light.

If the light isn't right, notice which way the windows in the room are facing. You can raise or lower the light available to a plant by moving it to a window that faces in a different direction. If not shaded, south-facing windows provide the most light, while north-facing windows offer the least. Unshaded windows that face east and west fall somewhere in between, but plants get hotter near a west-facing window. You can also try moving the plant closer to the window for more light or farther away for less light.

14 houseplants that love low light. If you have a room that just cries out for beautiful plants, but gets little sunlight, check out this list of 14 attractive houseplants you can grow in rooms that sometimes seem almost as dark as a cave.

- Chinese evergreen *(Aglaonema)*
- cast-iron plant *(Aspidistra elatior)*
- pothos *(Epipremnum aureum)*
- heart-leaf philodendron *(Philodendron scandens)*
- snake plant, mother-in-law's tongue, or sword plant *(Sansevieria)*
- zz plant *(Zamioculcas zamiafolia)*
- parlor palm *(Chamaedorea elegans)*
- dumb cane *(Dieffenbachia amoena)*
- Swedish ivy *(Plectranthus nummularius)*
- corn or cornstalk plant *(Dracaena fragrans* – Massangeana)
- arrowhead vine *(Syngonium)*
- spider plant *(Chlorophytum comosum)*
- German ivy *(Senecio mikanioides)*
- grape ivy *(Cissus rhombifolia)*

Keep in mind that no plant can grow in complete darkness. To test whether your low-light plants get enough light, sit next to them and try to read during daylight. If the light is too dim to read by, consider placing the plants near fluorescent lights for 12 to 16 hours a day.

WARNING

Watch out for symptoms of light deficiency or overload

Feeding your plant or giving it more water won't help if your plant is ill from a lack of light. Learn to recognize the signs of too much or too little light, so you'll know when to move your plant to more appropriate lighting.

Your plant may not be getting enough light if:

- new leaves are smaller than older ones.
- leaves drop off.
- the plant stops growing or grows very slowly.
- a flowering plant stops producing flowers or produces far fewer flowers than usual.
- the plant leans toward the light.
- growth is spindly and elongated.

Your plant may be getting too much light if:

- the leaves become faded, develop brown burn spots, or dry out and drop off.
- growth is stunted.
- new growth turns yellow.
- the plant wilts during the hottest part of the day.

Wonderful way to clear the air. The air in your home may look clean, but it's probably dirty enough to break U.S. laws and threaten your health. Studies suggest indoor air contains more pollutants than federal regulations normally allow in outdoor air.

The scariest pollutants may be volatile organic compounds (VOCs.) These may be emitted by air fresheners, aerosol sprays, cleansers, and many household products. VOCs and other indoor air pollutants may lead to health problems like headaches, respiratory problems, nervous system disorders, and even cancer.

A 1989 study by NASA suggested houseplants might have the power to remove these harmful pollutants from indoor air, but the Environmental Protection Agency and other scientific authorities did not find enough evidence to take the study seriously. Yet, new studies like these hint that NASA may have been right all along.

- A University of Georgia study found that five "super-ornamentals" can significantly improve the quality of indoor air by removing several kinds of dangerous VOCs. These include asparagus fern *(Asparagus densiflorus)*, the purple waffle plant *(Hemigraphis alternata)*, English ivy *(Hedera helix)*, variegated wax plant *(Hoya carnosa)*, and the Purple heart plant *(Tradescantia pallida)*. Several other plants were good at removing one or more kinds of VOCs including nerve plant *(Fittonia argyroneura)*, weeping fig *(Ficus benjamina)*, and Ming aralia *(Polyscias fruticosa)*.

- A related study discovered that Japanese fatsia *(Fatsia japonica)* and weeping fig *(Ficus benjamina)* help remove the formaldehyde gas emitted by carpets, curtains, furniture, and cabinets.

- Australian researchers discovered that three corn plants – Janet Craig *(Dracaena deremensis)* – or one corn plant and five peace lilies – Sweet Chico *(Spathiphyllum)* – could reduce VOCs up to 75 percent in offices measuring between 32 and 39 square feet.

The studies suggest that soil microbes and pores in the plant leaves may help clean the air. But more research is needed to know whether houseplants consistently clean the air well, so stay tuned.

6 surprising ways to water your plants for "free." Most people give their houseplants a drink with water straight from the tap. But sometimes water from a more unusual source may be healthier for your plants. Give these options a try.

- Water from cooking or steaming vegetables. As long as you didn't add salt to this water, you can use it. Just let it cool to room temperature before pouring it on your plants.
- Club soda. Occasionally, save your leftover club soda, let it go flat, and water your potted plants with it. This gives them a mineral boost.
- Coffee. Top off your watering can with leftover coffee. Make sure your coffee-laced water is cool before giving it to your houseplants.
- Freshwater aquarium. Reuse the water from cleaning out your freshwater – not saltwater – aquarium. Once you have removed the fish, siphon your used aquarium water into a bucket. This water is rich in nitrogen and phosphorous that can benefit your plants.
- Water from boiling eggs. Let this cool before using.
- Water from your dehumidifier. Only use this water if you clean or disinfect the dehumidifier regularly to prevent mold and mildew.

7 ways to reuse plastic nursery pots. You hate to throw out those plastic nursery pots, but they're beginning to pile up. Put them back to work with these tips.

- Use plastic cell packs to organize small garden items, or use them to start plants from seed next spring.

- Turn a pot upside down and use it to protect a small plant from early autumn or late spring frosts.
- Donate nursery pots to a plant sale, a school garden, or another charity; offer them to a plant nursery; give them to a grower at your local farmer's market; or offer them on Freecycle.
- Line one with a plastic grocery bag and use as a temporary garden wastebasket for wrappers, paper towels, and other disposable items you'll later throw in the trash.
- Store small garden tools in them.
- Paint the outsides of the pots with paint made for plastic. Some paints can make your plastic pot look like it is made of stone or copper.
- Use 14-inch or larger plastic nursery pots as molds for hypertufa planters – pots that look like concrete or old stone but weigh much less. To make the hypertufa mixture, you'll need perlite, peat moss, and Portland cement from your local home improvement store. Spread a drop cloth or plastic sheeting over a shady work area and put on gloves and a dust mask. Mix three parts perlite, three parts peat moss, and two parts Portland cement in a wheelbarrow or plastic tub. Add enough water to give your mixture the consistency of cottage cheese. Spray your plastic nursery pot with non-stick cooking spray. Let dry a little and line the inside of

your pot with handfuls of the mixture. Aim for smooth walls at least three-quarters inch thick on the sides and about 1 1/2 inches thick at the bottom. Create a drainage hole by pressing a wooden dowel through the drainage hole at the bottom of the pot. Cover with plastic and let cure for several days – then separate the mold from the pot. Put the pot back under plastic for 10 days, remove the plastic, and let dry for two more weeks. Your pot is now ready for planting.

3 little-known African violet secrets. These beautiful plants can sometimes be tricky. If you have struggled with African violets in the past, don't give up. Just remember these tips to help your plants thrive.

- Don't touch. Researchers from Oklahoma State University discovered that touching African violet plants, even briefly, causes damage and stunted growth. The problems become even worse if you use lotion on your hands.
- Plant your African violets in a mix of pine bark and sand. These ingredients give you a slightly acid soil that has excellent drainage – qualities that make African violets thrive.
- Learn how to water. Watering the wrong way can cause white spots on your African violet leaves. If you water from above the plant, pour the water directly on the dirt, not the leaves, and always use room temperature water. Remove any extra water that drains through to the bottom of the pot. To water from below, put the pot in a dish containing about an inch of water. When the top of the soil becomes damp, remove the pot from the water and let it drain.

Treat yourself to dinner and free stakes. The next time you eat out at an Asian restaurant, save your chopsticks. They make excellent stakes for floppy houseplants.

Simple way to get rid of fungus gnats. Those little black bugs that love to fly around your houseplants and constantly hover around your face may be fungus gnats. They love wet soil, so try waiting until the surface dirt dries to water your plants. If you can allow the first inch or two of dirt to dry out, that's even better. To check, poke your finger in the soil near the edge of the pot.

Or spread cedar chips over your houseplant soil. Most insects don't like the smell. Then coat the surface of a yellow sticky note or small squares cut from yellow poster board with petroleum jelly. Hang these near your plants to catch the gnats.

Squelch houseplant mold. The Mount Sinai School of Medicine in New York suggests this attractive way to prevent mold on your houseplant soil – cover the soil with shells or aquarium gravel. Your plant will look lovely and its soil will stay mold-free.

CARPET
Flooring fix-ups

4 surefire solutions for stains. Baby wipes offer a cheap, quick, and easy way to wipe away fresh carpet stains. Try them on especially tough stains, such as blood and motor oil. Scrub them while fresh, before they set in.

Some brands of baby wipes may work better than others. You may need to test a few until you find one that can tackle your tough messes. Try these other tried-and-true methods for cleaning carpet stains.

- A solution of one part liquid dish soap to one part hydrogen peroxide will make short work of many stains and smells. Just test it on an inconspicuous part of the carpet to be sure it won't harm the color. Blot with a sponge, then rinse with warm water.

- White shaving cream works wonders, particularly on dark stains. Spray a dot on the spot, then blot. For dried, crusted dirt, spray the base of the carpet fibers, then scrape off the stain with a credit card. Clean up with cool water.
- Club soda will wash out freshly spilled food and liquids. Pour on club soda, blot, and repeat until the stain lifts away.

Keep carpet looking new longer. Want your carpet to last a long, long time? Then follow these four steps.

- Buy carpet with a high pile density and tight twist, both of which make it more durable.
- Opt for the best carpet pad you can afford. The cushion matters more than the carpet itself.
- Vacuum regularly. Dirt has tiny but sharp edges, which saw away at carpet fibers.
- Avoid wearing shoes in the house. Keep a pair of house slippers by the door to put on when you walk in.

Banish bad odors naturally. There's a smart way to refresh your carpets, hidden in your bathroom cabinet. Baby powder made with cornstarch makes an easy, affordable carpet deodorizer. Mix one-quarter cup of cornstarch baby powder with three-quarters cup of baking soda. Sprinkle on the carpet, let sit for 15 minutes, and vacuum thoroughly to banish bad odors.

Love having your pet inside but hate the smell? Tweak this recipe to make a lemony fresh carpet deodorizer. Just add a few drops of lemon essential oil to your baby powder deodorizer for a light, upifting scent.

Freshen the air while you clean

Squeeze 15 drops of your favorite essential oil on a cotton ball and drop it in the vacuum bag before you clean. Your whole house will smell fresh naturally.

Make minor damage good as new. A little damage doesn't have to mean a big repair job. Cigarette burns and other small stains are easy to fix.

If only the tips of the carpet pile are damaged, try trimming off the bad part. Use a sharp pair of manicure scissors, or even nail clippers, to carefully clip off the ends of the pile.

If the damage goes deeper, you'll need to cut the pile at the base, where it meets the carpet backing. Snip away only the damaged fibers. Now borrow some fibers from an out-of-the-way place. Head to the most hidden corner of your closet, and snip a few pieces of healthy pile.

Take a toothpick and apply a drop of clear, waterproof glue to the bottom of each piece of pile, then place the fibers against the bare carpet backing. Tweezers can help do this delicate work. Let the glue dry, and lightly trim the top of the transplanted pile level with the old.

Easy repairs for unraveled carpet. Repairing a snag in berber carpet is as simple as fixing a snag in a sweater. You can even use the same tools. A crochet hook or knitting needle can pull a line of berber back into place in no time.

Berber carpets are made of loops woven in and out of the backing. Start by finding the first good loop in the snag. Slide a small screwdriver or knitting needle through the loop, so you don't accidentally pull it through the carpet backing.

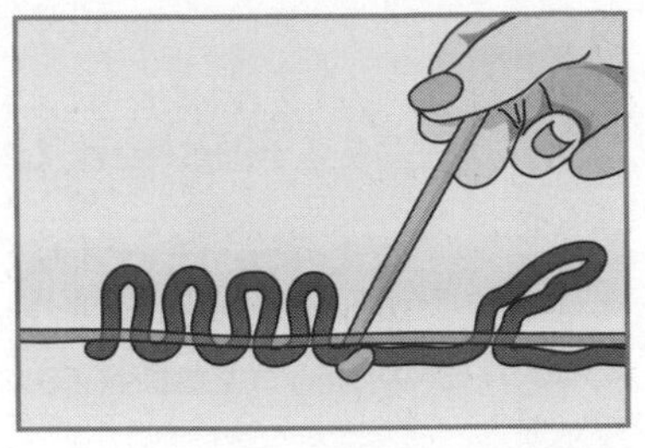

Next, slide a crochet hook or knitting needle through the backing next to the good loop. A magnifier can help you see. Dig your hook around until you catch the pulled strand of carpet. Tug it up through the backing until you have a loop slightly smaller than the others. Repeat the process until the snag disappears back into the carpet.

Runs require a different approach. With a little glue and a knitting needle or screwdriver, you can glue the strand back into place. Find the first good loop at the end of the run. Now form a small loop in the loose strand. Press the screwdriver or knitting needle at the base of this loop, so it touches the carpet backing. Add a drop of glue to that spot, and continue pressing the loop in place until the glue holds.

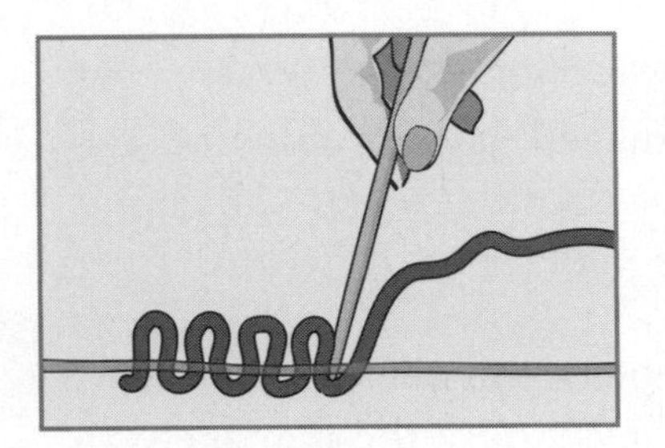

Repeat along the length of the strand, until all the loops are back in place. Use the weight of a book to hold them in place while they dry.

Stop creeping rugs in their tracks. Velcro and double-sided tape can keep rugs from creeping or suddenly sliding out from under you.

- For rugs on hard floors, attach a piece of heavy-duty, double-sided tape to the bottom of each corner. Or cut strips of Velcro. Stick the stiff side on the hard floor and the soft side on the underside of the rug. Press down firmly.

- For rugs on carpet, try the Velcro trick. This time, attach the stiff strip of Velcro to the underside of the rug and press it into the carpet beneath.

Get gum out of carpets for good. Don't rush out and replace your carpet just because you tracked in chewing gum. Fill a plastic bag with ice cubes and set it on the gum for several minutes. This will harden the goo, making it easy to shatter and scrape off with a butter knife.

Sometimes the ice cube trick doesn't get all the gum off. Sugarless gum can pose a special problem, since it doesn't really freeze. Turn to heat, instead. Melt the gum with a hair dryer. Hold the dryer far enough away so it doesn't melt the carpet fibers. Then pull off as much goo as you can with a plastic bag.

Either method may still leave a little hard-to-clean gunk stuck to the fibers. These two common products can lift out the last of it.

- Spray some WD-40 on the remaining stain. Scrape off what's left with a dull knife or rub gently with a soft cloth.
- Work in a topical pain reliever made with methyl salicylate, such as BENGAY, and use a rag or plastic bag to remove the rest of the gum.

Wash away the last of the stain with water and liquid dish soap, to dissolve the WD-40 or pain rub, and rinse.

Best way to take out soot. Resist the urge to brush away soot that's sifted onto your carpet. Doing so will only work it deeper into the fibers. Try this advice, instead, from the American Cleaning Institute.

- Vacuum up soot with a canister or handheld vacuum. Avoid the upright kind, since the spinning brush can actually spread the soot.

- Suck up the grime, starting around the edges and working your way toward the center.
- Pour a little rubbing alcohol onto a clean cloth and blot what's left of the stain until it disappears. Don't saturate the carpet with alcohol because it can damage the backing.
- Finish up by blotting the spot with liquid dish soap and water.

ALTERNATE USES

Find dropped items with ease

Stick a sock in it — or a nylon stocking. The next time you lose an earring or something else under your dresser, don't bother getting on your hands and knees. Reach for your vacuum.

Slide one leg of knee-high nylon over the hose of your vacuum cleaner. Secure the leg over the mouth of the hose with a rubber band. Flip the switch and suck it up. When you turn off the vacuum, simply fish the item out of the stocking.

5 ways to protect yourself from carpet chemicals. New carpet can release lots of chemicals into the air of your home, as can the padding that goes under it and the adhesive used to glue everything together.

These chemicals, called volatile organic compounds (VOCs), can trigger headaches, shortness of breath, coughing, and irritation of your eyes, nose, and throat. That's why the American Lung Association offers these tips for dealing with new carpet.

- Ask the retailer to unroll the carpet in a clean, well-ventilated area to air it out before installation.
- Plan to be away from home while the new carpet is being installed.
- Have the installers use adhesives low in VOCs and free of formaldehyde.
- Leave doors and windows open during and after the installation to draw in fresh air and cut down on your chemical exposure.
- Run window fans and room air conditioners for two to three days to vent fumes to the outside.

The Carpet and Rug Institute now tests carpets and adhesives for chemical emissions. Those that give off very low levels of VOCs, compared to regular carpets, get certified with the CRI Green Label Plus seal. Shop with this seal in mind if you're concerned about carpet chemicals.

No-mess secret to cleaning blades. Make short work of even the grimiest ceiling fans. Grab an old pillowcase and spritz the inside with a mixture of white vinegar and water.

Slip the pillowcase over each blade. Gently pull down and back to collect and trap built-up dust. You may need more than one pillowcase, depending on how dirty the blades are. Wipe the blades with a slightly damp cotton cloth to banish any remaining dirt.

Simple steps to stop the wobble. Wiggling, wobbling fans are a disaster waiting to happen. Luckily, a couple of quick fixes should have them humming along in no time.

- Clean the fan blades and motor housing. It sounds simple, but this may calm the wobble. Even a little dirt buildup can throw a fan off balance.
- Tighten the blades. Take a screwdriver and tighten the screws that attach each blade to the arms of the fan and each arm to the body.
- Secure the body. Stand on a step ladder, put your hands around the body of the fan, and give it a wiggle. If the whole thing moves easily, the fan itself is loose. Have a helper hold the fan as you unscrew the canopy, then tighten the screws holding the fan to the junction box.

Still can't find the culprit? Unbalanced blades may be to blame. Clip a clothespin halfway down one blade, then turn the fan on low and see if it still wobbles. Try the clothespin on each blade until the wobble disappears.

Once you find the problem blade, bring it back into balance with a little pocket change. Move the clothespin up and down the blade until you find the spot that seems to steady the fan.

Tape a coin to the top of the blade in that spot and see if the wobble goes away. Keep adding coins until it does. Once you find the magic number, glue them in place with some strong epoxy.

Update an outdated fan. Don't replace an outdated ceiling fan. Give it a face lift. For a few dollars at the hardware store, you can swap out the blades and blade arms, and even the light globe, for a fresh look.

When changes like these are out of your price range, try paint. Remove the blades and the metal arms. Clean the blades well, then spray them with a clear primer. Let that dry, then spray or brush on the color of your choice.

Find the perfect size

Don't buy more fan than you need. Measure the longest wall in the room. If it's less than 12 feet long, you need a ceiling fan that's 36 inches in diameter. A 12- to 15-foot wall requires a 42-inch fan, while a wall longer than 15 feet will take a 52-inch fan.

Reverse blades for warmth in winter. Ceiling fans can keep you cool in summer and warmer in winter. Just change the direction the blades turn.

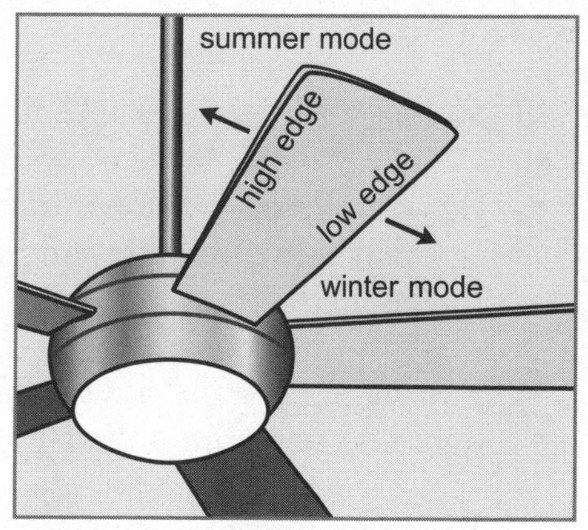

Most fans are reversible with the flick of a switch, generally on the outside of the fan body. You can tell if it's in warm mode or cool by which direction the blades are rotating.

Fan blades swoop at an angle, with one side higher than the other. Watch the blade as it spins. If the high side leads, then the fan is in cooling mode. If the low side leads, the fan is in warming, or winter, mode. In summer, the low side of the blade pushes air downward to create a cooling breeze. In winter, it scoops air up toward the ceiling. This updraft pushes the warm air near the ceiling down into the room.

Prevent a little-known cause of house fires. Nearly one-quarter of home heating fires are caused by a buildup of creosote. This grayish-black residue collects on your chimney walls from burning wood or coal. To prevent a dangerous fire, keep creosote under control.

The speed of creosote buildup depends on factors like how often you use your fireplace, whether the wood burns quickly or smolders, and draft of the chimney. That's why it's hard to know how often to get the chimney cleaned. You may notice a bad smell coming from your fireplace, especially when the air conditioner is on. That smell is creosote.

You can check creosote buildup yourself.

- Be sure there's no downdraft from your chimney. If there is, open some windows and wait until the air is flowing up the chimney.

- Put on goggles and a disposable dust mask, and gather a flash-light and your fire poker.

- Reach up into the fireplace with the poker, and scratch the black surface of the wall above the damper. Check the depth of the groove formed.

Experts say a masonry fireplace with a creosote layer of one-eighth inch should be cleaned soon. If the layer is one-quarter inch, don't use the fireplace again until it's cleaned. If you have a factory-built fireplace, get it cleaned once there's any noticeable buildup.

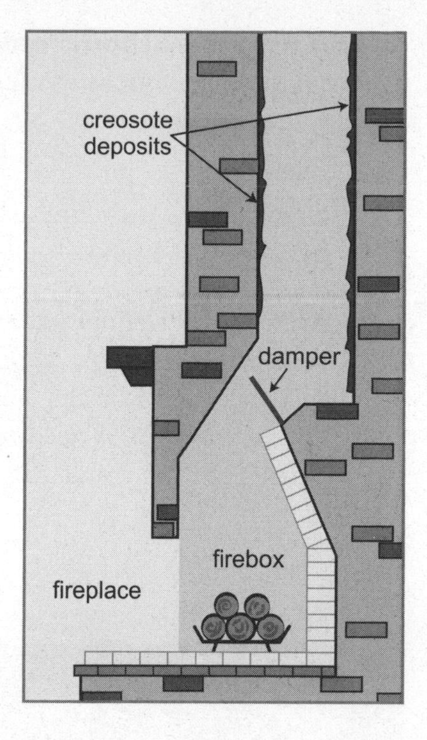

The best idea may be to ask an expert to inspect your chimney. Contact a chimney sweep certified by the Chimney Safety Institute of America, and ask for a Level 1 chimney inspection and sweeping. If the sweep doesn't know what that means, find one who does.

Cut the dust with coffee. Avoid choking in a cloud of ashes when you clean out your fireplace. Sprinkle some wet used coffee grounds on the ashes, then scoop up the whole mess. No more ashes in your face.

You'll get bonus benefits in the garden by spreading the ashes and grounds around your plants. Ashes provide calcium, while coffee grounds give your plants nitrogen and other nutrients.

Sprinkle away sooty buildup

Don't flirt with fire hazard. Every so often, sprinkle a handful of salt on the flames in your fireplace. According to the Salt Institute, salt works to loosen soot and keep your chimney burning clean. You'll even enjoy the bright yellow-orange flame while the salt burns.

Clean bricks without making a mess. Follow these steps to get your fireplace bricks as clean as new.

- Protect the surrounding floor with a drop cloth.
- Sweep or vacuum out ashes, debris, and loose mortar from between the bricks.
- Mix together equal parts liquid dishwashing soap and table salt. Stir in enough water to make a thick paste. Spread this mixture on the bricks, and wait for a few minutes to let it dry completely. You'll need to scrub away the crud with a stiff brush, but the result will be worth the effort.

LINENS
Sheet smarts

Tricks to make linens last longer. You paid good money for top-quality sheets. Protect your investment by treating them right.

- Don't wash them too often. The laundry room can be harder on your linens than the bedroom, so don't overdo the washing schedule. Every week or 10 days is fine.
- Keep them out of hot water. People with allergies tend to use hot water to kill dust mites and other critters. If you don't have those problems, washing linens in cold water is gentler on them.
- Watch your detergent. Experts say using too much detergent to launder sheets and not rinsing it out completely are two

common errors. Use half the amount specified on the detergent container, and rinse the load twice to remove residue.

- Skip the bleach. Some people buy white sheets so they can bleach them regularly. It's true that bleach is a good disinfectant, but it ages your sheets prematurely. If you must use bleach, use it sparingly and not too often. And add it to your washing machine after it's filled with water.
- Avoid the dryer. Why put your sheets through the wringer when you can dry them gently the old-fashioned way? Hang them on the line to dry, and they'll bring the fresh scents of outdoors into your bedroom.

MYTHBUSTER

Don't overpay for high thread count

You can pay hundreds for a set of sheets with a high thread count, which is the number of threads in 1 square inch of fabric. Rough muslin has a thread count of about 140 to 180, while a tightly woven luxury sheet is more like 300 or higher.

Some people say the higher the thread count the better, and it's true that sheets with a high thread count get softer with each washing.

In reality, you probably don't need to pay extra for a thread count higher than 600. Beyond that, you may be paying more to get a sheet that's thicker — not better. Also, look for 100-percent cotton on the label.

Hold the fabric softener for better absorbency. For towels that stay fluffy and absorbent, don't use fabric softener. It can build up on towels and even make them less absorbent. Instead, add one-quarter cup of white vinegar in the final rinse.

You can make those towels even softer by fluffing up each one as you move it from the washing machine to the dryer, then again when you take them out to fold. And don't even think about drying them on a clothesline if you want them to be soft. The dryer is your best bet.

20 uses for an old pillowcase. Don't toss those old pillowcases when you update your bed linens. Put them to use elsewhere in your house. Some of these ideas require a bit of sewing skill – but not much.

- Add a drawstring to several pillowcases, and use the bags to sort your dirty laundry.
- Use a pillowcase to wash delicates, and you can skip buying a mesh laundry bag.
- Cut off the hem to make handles, then reattach and use as a tote bag or reusable grocery bag.
- Make washable seat cushions for your patio chairs or benches.
- Stuff with plastic grocery bags and use as a doggy bed.
- Slip a pillowcase over the end of a broom, tie it around the handle, and attack cobwebs on your ceiling fan or in the corners.
- Store sweaters and other seasonal clothing to keep items clean and dry.
- Find a coordinating ribbon, and use to gift-wrap odd-shaped presents.
- Make a travel pillow that's just the right size.
- Pack hiking boots or other camping supplies in pillowcases to keep dirt from spreading through your duffel bag.

- Keep fragile items clean and safe in storage by packing them in pillowcases.
- Make an apron you won't be afraid to get dirty.
- Tear into strips and use as plant ties in your garden.
- Make a set of matching place mats.
- Create a protective pillow cover by whipstitching the case onto a pillow. Then use your new pillowcase right over the top.
- Put a hand-embroidered pillowcase to use as a dresser scarf, so you can continue to enjoy the beautiful stitching.
- Protect your grandson's teddy bear in the washing machine by using a pillowcase as a laundry bag.
- Get out some wide ribbon, and sew a simple shift dress for your granddaughter.
- Fill with shredded paper and surround a casserole dish to keep it hot when you take it to a potluck dinner.
- Take on your next airplane trip, and use it to cover the head-rest. Your seatmates will wish they had planned ahead, too.

Avoid fold damage to heirloom quilts

Slow down aging of your heirloom quilts with this simple habit. Each time you get out a vintage quilt to air it or show it off, fold it differently from the last time. If the first crease was in the middle, this time fold it into thirds. Over time, creasing the fabric in the same place causes damage to fragile textiles.

Keep your down comforter at its cozy best. A down comforter is tops for keeping you warm on cold winter nights. Keep yours fresh without damaging it.

First, don't wash your comforter any more often than you have to. Goose down tends to lose fluffiness with every washing or dry cleaning. You can protect it from stains by using a duvet cover and spot-cleaning when possible.

But eventually it will be time to clean your comforter. Some people say to do it every few months, or more often if you have asthma or allergies to dust mites. It's always a good idea to clean it when you take it from storage in the fall.

When it's time, use a gentle detergent and low heat. Be sure to dry your comforter thoroughly to prevent mildew or disintegration of the fill. Save your dryer's motor, and don't overload it with multiple heavy comforters at one time.

To get rid of dust while you freshen your comforter, try this trick. Put it in the dryer with two clean tennis balls, and run it for 20 minutes on the fluff cycle. Agitation from the tennis balls will redistribute the feathers and fluff up the comforter. You can also add a fabric softener sheet to make the comforter smell fresh and clean.

3 ways to fluff up pillows. Bring tired pillows back to life – whether they're filled with down or fiberfill. Pick your favorite trick.

- Get smacking. Sometimes a little elbow grease is all it takes to redistribute feathers and add some fluff to down pillows. Shake them around, whack them on the mattress or the floor, and watch your pillows come back to life.

- Make friends with your dryer. If your pillow is small enough, put it in your dryer, pop in a couple of clean tennis balls, and run it on the fluff cycle for 20 minutes. Your pillow will come out fluffier and fresher – just like your comforter.

- Take your pillows outdoors on a nice day, hang them over your clothesline, and let nature do the rest. Several hours in the fresh air and sunshine will remove bad odors and liven up your pillows.

Extend the life of kitchen towels. Drying your hands and your dishes with cloth towels can save you from buying lots of paper towels. When your dish towels start to look ragged, try these tricks to give them new life.

- Sew two towels together along the outside edges, placing them so a worn spot on one towel covers up a worn spot on the other.

- Make a towel into a dusting mitt to easily clean shelves or blinds. First, make a pattern by placing your hand on a piece of paper, fingers closed but thumb spread out. Trace a line an inch or so outside of your hand, like a big mitten. Fold the dish towel in half, right sides together, and use the pattern to cut out two layers of the towel. Sew them together, leaving an opening for your hand.

- Turn your dusting mitt into a bath mitt by adding a pocket in the palm of the mitt described above. Slide soap slivers into the pocket.

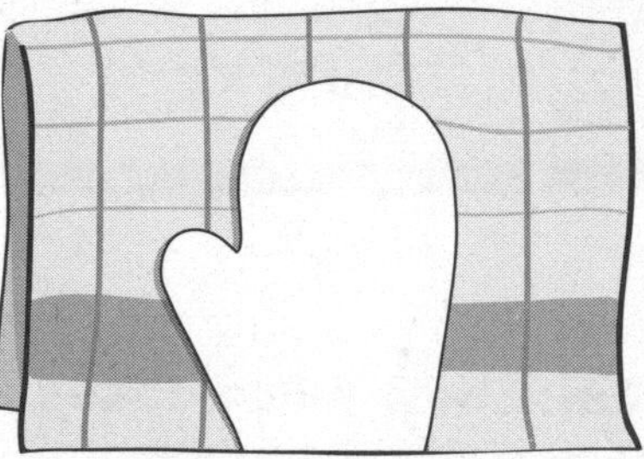

Fold a fitted sheet in seconds flat. Fitted sheets take up less space in your linen closet when you fold them neatly. The trick is not to fight the corners.

Stand up and hold the fitted sheet in front of you, placing your hands into two of the corner pockets. Bring your hands together, placing one pocket over the other so you hold both corners in one hand. Smooth those two pockets together.

With your free hand, gather up the other two corner pockets, placing one inside the other and holding them smooth. Now each hand holds two corner pockets folded together. Hold your hands in front of you and bring them together, transferring all four corner pockets of the sheet to one hand. Smooth them all together.

Now lay the sheet flat on a table, with all four pockets folded together. Smooth out the sheet and fold it in thirds toward the center. Then fold it in thirds the other way, and it's flat and ready to put away.

HANDY HINT

Clever way to store your sheets

Rather than separating matching sheets and pillowcases in your linen closet, then having to find each piece when it's time to make the bed, store them all together. Fold matching fitted and flat sheets and one pillowcase and slip them inside the other pillowcase. Fold over the end and stack in the closet. Next time your bed needs a change, just grab and go.

Make new pillowcases from old sheets. Use the unworn portion of your favorite flat or fitted sheets to make pillowcases with this simple beginner sewing project.

First, find a pillowcase that's the size you want to make to use as a pattern. Lay out the old sheet, folding it in half with a section of unworn fabric at the fold. Lay the pillowcase with its long edge along the fold.

Measure about one-half inch away from the pillowcase, and mark lines all around on the sheet. Add an extra 4 inches at the end where the opening will be. Cut the sheet along these lines.

With right sides together and your sheet fabric still folded, sew along one short and one long side of the fabric. Press the seam open, then turn the pillowcase right side out. Fold over the edge of the opening about 4 1/2 inches. Finish the edge by folding it under another one-half inch and sewing about one-quarter inch from the fold line. Your pillowcase is done.

MATTRESSES
Snooze control

Make your mattress last longer. A new mattress set will run you hundreds or even thousands of dollars. Ensure a long life for your mattress by taking good care of it.

The main thing you can do to preserve your mattress is to flip it every few months or as recommended by the manufacturer. Turn it side to side one time you do the job, then end to end the next. Doing this simple task will help your mattress wear more evenly. If you have a pillow-top mattress that can't be turned over, at least rotate it so the head of the bed is now at the foot.

Also, take care of your mattress by airing it out every so often and vacuuming it to get rid of dust and dead skin cells. You should also use a mattress cover to protect it. And don't opt for a cheap box foundation – like box springs but without the springs. These contraptions can allow your mattress to age more quickly than it should.

No matter how much TLC you give your mattress, eventually it will wear out. How long it lasts depends on things like how it's made and how it's used, but you should think about replacement after about five to seven years.

Here are some signals it may be time to shop for a new mattress.

- Your mattress shows its age in lumps, sagging, or other signs of wear.
- You often wake up feeling stiff or achy.
- A night spent away from home – visiting a relative or sleeping in a hotel – leaves you feeling more rested and refreshed than a night in your own bed.

HANDY HINT

Dispose of an old mattress for free

When the time comes to replace your old mattress and box springs with a new set, don't burden your children with the old ones. A used mattress is not much of a gift.

The Better Sleep Council suggests these methods for disposing of old mattress sets.

- When you buy your new mattress, ask the salesman to have the delivery driver haul off the old set. They may offer this service for free.
- Contact your garbage collector or local municipality to arrange a pickup. Advance notice is often required for larger items.

Freshen up an old mattress. Get out your vacuum if a musty smell in your mattress is keeping you up at night. In the morning, remove the sheets and sprinkle some baking soda directly on your mattress. Leave it on all day to absorb odors, then vacuum the baking soda at night before you go to bed.

UPHOLSTERY

Make yourself comfortable

Whip up your own upholstery cleaner. You can always pay to have your sofa and chairs professionally cleaned, but you don't have to. Save a bundle by cleaning upholstered furniture yourself. It's a breeze.

For spills, use a combination of cornstarch and club soda. First, apply some cornstarch to absorb the mess. Then pour a little club soda to lift the stain.

You can also whip up a homemade upholstery cleaner. Mix one-quarter cup hand dishwashing liquid in a cup of warm water. Use a wire whisk or hand mixer to whip up lots of suds. Or put a lid on the container and shake it up until foam forms.

With a sponge, cloth, or soft brush, apply the froth – but not the liquid underneath – to your upholstery. Rub gently over the entire surface, one small area at a time. Start with a hidden area to make sure the treatment doesn't cause the colors to run. Remove the foam with a damp cloth or sponge. Let your furniture dry completely before sitting on it.

Give pet hair the brushoff. Pet hair on clothing, furniture, and carpet driving you nuts? This handy solution will save your sanity. Simply rub a dryer sheet over your sofa, rug, and other surfaces to remove unwanted pet hair. It's quick, easy, and your furniture will smell great.

Here's another "handy" solution. Put on a rubber glove and rub your hand over the upholstery. You'll find the pet hair rolled up into an easily removable ball.

You can also make an impromptu lint brush using tape. Wrap some wide tape, like duct tape, around a paint roller, sticky side out. Then roll it over furniture or carpets – or even your clothing – to remove stubborn pet hair. You don't even need the paint roller. Wrapping the tape around your hand should also do the trick.

"Foil" overly frisky pets. Your cat has a perfectly fine scratching post, but prefers to sink its claws into your sofa. Instead of constantly yelling at your pet or shooing it off your upholstery, look to your kitchen for a simple solution – aluminum foil.

Here's how it can protect your furniture. Tear a long piece of foil and lay it on your couch cushions. Most cats hate the feel and sound of the foil and will jump off the couch right away. This simple training technique should help your cat learn to stay off your furniture.

You can also use two-sided sticky tape to discourage cats from climbing on your couch. Or drape some netting over your furniture. Cats don't like to snag their claws when scratching. Once your cat realizes it's no fun to sit on or scratch your furniture, it will change its behavior – and spare your sofa.

HANDY HINT

Keep pets away from furniture with vinegar

Try vinegar in a spray bottle to keep pets off your furniture. Both cats and dogs hate the smell of vinegar, so it serves as an effective pet repellent. Spray a mixture of vinegar and water on your upholstery to protect it from your pets. They won't want to walk, sleep, or scratch on anything that smells like vinegar.

Freshen fabrics for pennies. Eliminate furniture odors while also eliminating expensive scented products. Make your own fabric freshener for a fraction of the cost of Febreze.

Just mix one cup of baking soda and one cup of your favorite liquid fabric softener with two cups of warm water. Put the mixture in a spray bottle, and shake well. Spray it on your furniture, carpets, and curtains to give your home a pleasant, fresh scent.

Variations on this recipe include leaving out the baking soda or swapping vinegar or rubbing alcohol for the baking soda. As long as you use a blend of fabric softener and water, you should be OK. To jazz up your homemade solution, you can use unscented fabric softener and add a few drops of essential oil to create just the right scent.

Overpower stains with baby powder. Get to work on that fresh grease stain on your sofa right away. Sprinkle a generous amount of talcum powder on the spot. Let it sit for a while, then brush it off. The powder should absorb the grease. You may need to repeat the treatment if the grease mark doesn't disappear entirely. Salt or cornstarch should also work.

Similarly, you can make a paste of talcum powder and water. Apply it to the greasy stain, let it dry, and vacuum it off.

Easy way to remove wax. Candlelight helps create atmosphere, but candle wax can spoil the mood – and your furniture – in a hurry. Do not despair if you accidentally drip candle wax on your upholstered sofa or chair. Simply lay a brown paper bag over the hardened wax and slide a hot iron over the bag. The wax will soften and transfer itself to the bag.

Save your sofa with socks. You love your grandchildren – but they love to jump on your furniture. If you have little ones visiting that will be climbing on your couch, don't worry about dirty shoes.

Slip an old pair of socks over their feet, shoes and all, and let them play. That way, you eliminate the hassle of taking shoes off and putting them back on again.

Give your living room a cheap makeover. Invest in slipcovers and you'll get a whole new look without spending big bucks on new furniture. Slipcovers come in a variety of attractive fabrics – or you could even sew your own.

Just make sure you take good care of them. To prevent shrinking, remove slipcovers from the dryer while still damp. If you put them back on your couch or chairs immediately, they'll dry smoothly and won't need ironing.

WINDOWS & GLASS

Let the sun shine in

Thrifty way to make glass sparkle. A 32-ounce bottle of distilled white vinegar costs about $2.40. Compare that to $4.50 for a smaller bottle of Windex. Considering that you'll water down the vinegar to use as a window cleaner, it's a huge savings over buying specialty window cleaner. The question is – does vinegar work well to clean glass?

The answer is yes. First, vinegar behaves like a gentle solvent, so it removes sticky substances from glass. That makes it a great choice to take off the price tag from the glass on your new picture frame or a holiday sticker from your window.

Second, vinegar is a mild acid, erasing those hard water deposits from your glassware or glass shower doors. Finally, vinegar cuts through grease and oil, so it quickly removes all kinds of gunk from your picture window or your bathroom mirror.

You'll find many recipes for vinegar-based glass cleaner, but they all involve a little bit of vinegar mixed with a lot of water. Try two or three teaspoons of white vinegar in a quart of warm water. You can also add a pinch of baking soda or liquid detergent. If you want a scented cleaner, add a couple of drops of your favorite essential oil.

Clean your windows with crumpled newspaper, a cotton cloth, or a microfiber cloth to avoid dealing with wads of lint. If you don't have a microfiber cloth, try a clean coffee filter. It's lint free and cheap. To avoid streaks on the glass, don't clean your windows while they're warm or when the sun is shining directly on them.

Little-known use for cornstarch. Want to clean your windows with something better than expensive commercial cleaners and fight dirt at the same time? Try this formula using ingredients you probably already have in your pantry.

Get out your box of cornstarch and start mixing. You know it as a great thickener for gravy and pie filling, but cornstarch is a timesaver all around your house. This natural kitchen staple works to clean glass and furniture, shampoo carpets, and even starch your shirts.

The Argo company, a well-known maker of cornstarch, offers this recipe for a window-cleaning solution. Mix one-half cup white vinegar and one-half cup ammonia into a bucket of warm water. Blend two tablespoons cornstarch into a few tablespoons of cold water until it's thoroughly mixed, then add to the bucket. Be sure the cornstarch dissolves completely.

Apply the mixture to your windows with a clean cloth, and wipe dry with a lint-free cloth or paper towel. When you wash glass with cornstarch, you won't have to deal with streaks and spots, and you can use it to clean both the inside and outside of your windows. What's more, cornstarch helps reduce static, which attracts dirt.

Bubble wrap windows for cheap insulation. Save the bubble wrap that protects fragile items during shipping, and use it for easy and cheap window insulation. Some do-it-yourself fans say they can do the job in an hour or two and make back their costs in a couple of months. Here's how.

- Cut a piece of bubble wrap to fit the inside of your window. Any size bubbles will work, but wrap with larger bubbles lets you see through the glass a little better.
- Use a spray bottle of water to apply a light mist on the window.
- Apply the bubble wrap, bubble side facing the glass, while the window is wet. Smooth it in place.
- Use tape to secure the bubble wrap to the window frame if the water doesn't hold it.

Apply bubble wrap to your windows at the beginning of winter, then take it down in the spring. Mark the pieces of wrap so you'll know which windows they fit, and you can reuse them again next year.

HANDY HINT

Stop window box soil splatter

Keep your windows clean and the soil in your flower boxes where it belongs. When you plant flowers in your window boxes, add a layer of gravel, marbles, or pebbles on top of the soil. It will keep the dirt from splashing out of the box and onto the glass when it rains or when you water your plants. Plus, it gives a nice, clean look to your window boxes.

WOOD FLOORS

Beauty underfoot

Wise ways to clean wood floors. Advertisements may encourage you to buy all sorts of fancy products and special cleaners to clean your wood floors. But all you really need is a little water. Try these tips to make your wood floors shine.

- Dampen your duster. You should use a vacuum or dust mop to clean your wood floors at least once a week. But a dry mop merely stirs up the dust. Don't just push the dust around. Turn your mop into a dust magnet. Lightly spray the bottom of your dust mop with water. The damp mop will sop up all the dust and grime. This works best for wood floors with a polyurethane coating and should not be used on wax-finished floors.
- Vanquish dirt with vinegar. For more thorough cleaning, look no further than your pantry. A natural disinfectant, vinegar makes a gentle and effective wood floor cleaner. Mix a quarter-cup of white vinegar with four cups of warm water. Dampen a rag or sponge with the solution, and wipe it on your floor. Make sure to wipe the floor dry as you go. You can also just spray straight vinegar on your floor, then wipe it with a soft cloth.
- Avoid common troublemakers. Steer clear of oil soaps, ammonia products, or floor cleaners that contain wax, paraffin, silicone, or mineral oil. They can damage or dull your floor's finish. So can pretreated dust mops.

Take steps to preserve your floors. Your wood floors look great now. The trick is to keep them looking that way. Make your wood floors last longer by taking good care of them. Follow these precautions, and your floors will require less maintenance.

- Clip the claws. Keep your pets' nails or claws trimmed so they don't scratch up your floor.

- Hold the heels. Don't walk on your wood floors while wearing high heels, which can cause dents and scratches. Don't wear cleats or golf shoes inside, either.
- Ditch the dirt. Put mats or throw rugs by each door to catch any dirt or grit that may otherwise be tracked through your home. These tiny particles can scratch your floor.
- Lift to shift. When moving furniture or other heavy objects, lift the item rather than sliding it across the floor. This way, you avoid scuffing the floor's surface.
- Focus on furniture. Place plastic or felt pads under the legs of tables, chairs, and other pieces of furniture to guard your floor against scraping or scuffing.
- Swab spills swiftly. Wipe up any spills right away with a slightly dampened towel.
- Shield the sun. Sunlight speeds up the fading of your wood floor. Use curtains, blinds, shutters, or other window treatments to block the sun. You may also want to rearrange area rugs and furniture regularly so the floor ages evenly.
- Hook up a humidifier. Using a humidifier during the winter months can help cut down on gaps or cracks.

Sporty solution for scuff marks. Erase scuff marks like an ace. All you need is a clean tennis ball. Carefully cut an "X" into the tennis ball, then slip the ball over a broomstick or mop handle. Rub the tennis ball back and forth over the scuff marks on your wood floor, and they should disappear.

Save time and money by screening. Your wood floor has seen better days. Wear and tear has taken its toll. But before you undertake a complete refinishing project, try something less drastic. For light damage, screening and recoating should do the trick.

Screening may be a better, cheaper – and less messy – alternative to sanding and refinishing. With screening, you use a special pad and a low-speed buffer to remove just the top layer of your floor's polyurethane surface. This gets rid of scratches and allows you to apply fresh coats of urethane.

Unlike sanding, this process doesn't produce too much noise or dust. It's also an easy and quick do-it-yourself project. You should be able to complete a room in less than a day. Clean up the dust with a vacuum or rag. Apply a clear finish, and your work is done.

Remember, screening only works for light surface damage. But it can be a great way to repair, refresh, and extend the life of your wood floor.

Refinishing advice from the experts. Sometimes, the damage to your wood floor is just too much. For deep scratches and damage that has worn through the stain to the bare wood, sanding and refinishing may be your best option.

Don't undertake refinishing lightly. It's a tough, messy, extensive project. You will need to use a drum floor sander, which must be handled carefully or else it can gouge your floor. The sander is very noisy and makes quite a mess. You'll need ear protection, a dust mask, and safety goggles. You'll also need to put up plastic sheeting to protect your home from all the dust. Block any vents, so dust doesn't get in them. Cleanup will likely require a heavy-duty shop vacuum.

After sanding the floor down to the bare wood, you must apply a new coat of stain and a few coats of finish. When applying the stain, keep in mind that many products produce harmful vapors or are flammable. Make sure to work in a ventilated area.

Consider all your options before resorting to sanding and refinishing. Also consider how many times – if any – your floor has been refinished before. Each time you sand the floor, you remove some wood. Look around the floor edges or near heating registers to make sure there's enough wood remaining.

If the damage is limited to a small area, consider getting replacement boards instead. That way, you can avoid refinishing the entire floor. You may also need to replace boards if your floor feels spongy or the floorboards have warped or buckled.

While you can rent the equipment to sand and refinish your hardwood floor yourself, you may want to hire an experienced professional to make sure the job is done right.

It may be quite a hassle, but once you sand and refinish your floor, it will look as good as new and add value to your home.

WOOD FURNITURE

Great looks on display

Furnish your home for free. Furniture can be expensive – but it doesn't have to be. In fact, you can find some amazing bargains. How amazing? Here's how to get gorgeous, gently used furnishings for free.

- Go online. Thanks to the Internet, free furniture may be only a few clicks away. The Freecycle Network, an online community made up of nearly 5,000 groups totaling more than 8 million members, is dedicated to reducing waste and keeping good stuff out of landfills. It's a great resource for free stuff, including furniture. Visit *www.freecycle.org* to search for a group near you. Once you join – membership is free – you can browse listings. Everything offered is absolutely free. When someone posts an item you want, respond to that post with an email saying you want the item. If the owner agrees to give it to you, simply work out an arrangement to pick it up. Similar websites include *www.freesharing.org* and *www.freeuse.org*.

- Go for a drive. If searching the Internet seems too high-tech, you can always just hop in your car. Drive through a well-to-do neighborhood, and keep an eye on the curb. You'll be shocked to discover what some people throw away. You may find perfectly fine furniture ready for the garbage truck. As the saying goes, one man's trash is another man's treasure.

- Ask your friends. You don't need to depend on the kindness – or wastefulness – of strangers. Your friends may also come through with offers of free furniture. Before they donate a dresser or table to goodwill or throw it away, perhaps they'll ask if you want it. Especially if you let them know you're on the lookout for furniture. You'll save them the hassle of trying to get rid of their old stuff, and they will help you save money. That's what friends are for.

Clever ways to camouflage scratches. Over time, your wood furniture will likely get scratched. But you don't have to leave those unsightly scratches for everyone to see. Try these simple tricks to hide scratches and keep your furniture looking great.

- Invest in iodine. To conceal scratches on darker wood, brush on some iodine, then buff with a cotton swab. For lighter wood, thin the iodine with an equal amount of denatured alcohol before applying. Furniture scratches disappear like magic when you swipe them with this simple formula.

- Go nuts. It may sound crazy, but these crunchy snacks make furniture scratches disappear like magic. Break a walnut or pecan in half, and gently rub the nutmeat directly into each scratch. The scratches will be gone. Make sure to stay within the scratch or else you'll darken the surrounding wood as well. Brazil nuts and almonds may also work.

- "Shoe" scratches away. Find shoe polish that matches the color of your furniture, and apply it to small scratches with a soft cloth or a fine brush. The shoe polish will give furniture scratches the boot.

- Color it with crayons. Dip into the box of crayons you keep for your grandchildren, and look for a matching color. You can even blend colors to find the perfect shade. Heat the crayon with a hair dryer, rub it into the scratch, and buff the area with a soft cloth.
- Break out your makeup kit. Rub an eyebrow pencil over tiny scratches. This beauty aid can make your scratched wood furniture look more attractive.

Repair dings in wood furniture with a beauty supply. Nail polish can add a touch of glamour to your fingers and toes. But it also comes in handy around the house.

Fill small gouges or shallow chips in your wood furniture with some clear nail polish. A dollop or two should do the trick. The key is to apply enough so the dent becomes even with the rest of the finish.

Perk up old cabinets with paint. Want updated cabinets without paying a lot? Try these painting techniques. Your boring wood cabinets will look new and improved, but your pocketbook won't take a pounding.

Here's a low-cost method for giving your cabinets a stylish crackle finish. Paint the surface with a base coat of paint, and let it dry completely. Then apply some plain white glue. You can thin the glue with a little water, but you don't have to.

Brush on a thicker coat of glue for bigger cracks. A thinner coat will produce finer cracks. You may want to vary the thickness of the glue in spots for a more natural effect.

Wait a few minutes, but don't let the glue dry completely. While the glue is still tacky to the touch, apply a top coat of paint. Let it dry thoroughly. As the paint dries, you'll see cracks forming in the finish. Once it's dry, you can apply a coat of wax to give it an even more aged look.

Crackling isn't your only decorative paint option. You may prefer these other creative ways to inject new life into old cabinets.

- Glazing. Cover a base coat of paint with a thin, translucent film of color for a rich, antique finish. You can buy tinted glazes or tint your own by mixing it with paint.
- Stippling. Achieve a sandy, textured look with this technique, which consists of dabbing dots of paint onto a painted surface. The two paint colors should be similar for a subtle effect.
- Stenciling. Add a custom pattern to your cabinets to give them some character. Just tape a stencil to the surface and apply paint carefully.

You can also consider color washing, rag rolling, and sponging. Ask about these and other techniques at your local hardware store.

Hot tip for degreasing cabinets. Kitchen cabinets located near your stove can become grease magnets when you fry food. Here's an easy way to cut through the grease.

Slightly dampen a sponge, and pop it in the microwave for 20 to 30 seconds. Spray a citrus cleaner on your cabinets, then wipe them with the hot sponge. The heat from the sponge helps remove the grease. Just be careful handling the hot sponge. Wear rubber gloves to protect yourself.

Dynamic duo fights dirt. Oil and vinegar make a pretty tasty salad dressing. But these ingredients also form an effective and economical wood furniture cleaner. Put two tablespoons of light olive oil and three cups of white vinegar in a spray bottle and shake well.

Spray the homemade mixture onto your wood furniture, rub it with a damp cloth, then wipe it dry with a lint-free cloth. The vinegar pulls dirt from the wood, while the olive oil moisturizes it so it doesn't dry out. You could even substitute lemon juice for the vinegar. It also does the job, while leaving a pleasant scent.

Get rid of glue with vinegar. Out with the old, and in with the new. Before replacing a broken or loose dowel on your wooden chair, make sure to remove the old glue first. Leave any residue, and the new glue won't hold as well. To soften and remove glue from wood, use a mixture of vinegar and hot water. Rubbing alcohol should also do the trick.

Wipe out white marks. Moisture from cold drinks and steam from hot dishes can leave white marks on your wood tables. Get rid of these white watermarks with the following household items.

- Mayonnaise. Don't hold the mayo. Just spread some of this oily condiment on the mark. Rub it in and let it sit a while, perhaps even overnight. Then wipe it off – and wipe the mark away.
- Petroleum jelly. Rub some petroleum jelly into the mark, and leave it overnight. Wipe off the excess with a paper towel and buff with a soft cloth.
- Toothpaste. Brush away the mark with nongel toothpaste, which acts as a mild abrasive. Rub toothpaste into the mark, then wipe it off with a damp cloth.
- Baking soda. Make a paste of baking soda and water, and rub it into the mark. You can also use a mix of equal parts baking soda and nongel toothpaste. This is a slightly stronger abrasive than toothpaste alone, but it's still mild enough to use on your wood furniture.
- Salt. Gently apply a paste of salt and cooking oil. Either olive oil or vegetable oil should work. Leave the paste on the mark for an hour or so before wiping it off with a dry cloth. You can also try a salt and water paste, similar to the baking soda and water paste.
- Oil and vinegar. Mix equal parts olive oil and vinegar, and rub it onto the mark. Make sure to rub with the grain. Use a soft, dry cloth to wipe it off.

HANDY HINT

Craft your own coasters

Coasters can protect your wooden furniture from water rings or heat damage. Make your own tile coasters for parties, special occasions, or just everyday use. Here's how to do it.

- Pick out some square ceramic tiles. They can be fancy designer tiles or plain ones. You can even paint the plain tiles.
- Trace the outline of a tile on a cork board, then cut out the cork square with a utility knife. Do this for each tile in the set.
- Attach the cork squares to the bottom of the tiles with a hot glue gun.
- Let your coasters dry before using them.

Find new uses for old items. Who says a dresser has to go in the bedroom? Rethink the rules, and put it to use somewhere else. This strategy, called "repurposing," can save you money and spruce up your home.

You may not need to buy a new piece of furniture. Look around your house, including the garage, basement, and attic, and see what items could be used in another room in a new way.

A dresser has the most potential for repurposing. Move it to your dining room to store linens and silverware. It can also go in the bathroom to hold towels and other toiletries. Put it in your kitchen to hold pots, pans, cutting boards, and random kitchen tools. In the living room, it can act as a TV stand and a place to keep your board games. You can even use it as a potting bench and storage for gardening supplies.

Use your imagination, and you can repurpose several other pieces of furniture. Armoires can be turned into storage for toys, linens, or office supplies. Transform living room end tables into bedroom night stands, make doors into tabletops, and use bookcases for handy closet storage.

Unstick drawers with ease. Dresser drawer sticking? Don't give up hope – just reach for some soap. Rub the runners and bottom of the wooden drawer with a dry bar of plain soap. That should provide enough lubrication to make the drawer slide in and out smoothly. Candle wax or beeswax will also do the trick.

If these lubricating methods don't work right away, sand the bottom and sides of the drawer with fine sandpaper. Then apply the soap or wax again. Your drawer should slide in and out with no problem.

MYTHBUSTER

'Keys' to cleaning your piano

Toothpaste helps keep your teeth pearly white. So you might think it would be ideal for cleaning your ivory piano keys. But that's not necessarily the case. While some people recommend using toothpaste and a damp cloth or cotton swab to clean piano keys, piano experts disagree.

Here's what they suggest — use only a damp, soft cloth. At most, add a little mild soap. Never apply any liquid directly to the keys. Put it on the cloth, then wipe the keys with it. Steer clear of chemicals, acidic substances like vinegar, and anything containing bleach. You also want to avoid products that contain alcohol because alcohol-based products can dull ivory and melt plastic.

Unless you have an antique piano, chances are you don't have ivory keys anyway. But the same cleaning precautions should be taken with plastic keys.

Chapter 4

MAJOR APPLIANCES

Major appliances can turn into major headaches if you don't pay attention to minor details. You rely on your air conditioner, furnace, hot water heater, humidifier, and washer and dryer, so you want to keep them running smoothly. Get the lowdown on installing, maintaining, cleaning, repairing, and replacing these important items. You'll also find out how to conserve energy, save money, boost performance, and sidestep danger. And that's a major relief.

AIR CONDITIONERS

Staying cool & collected

Save cash with a spring checkup. Don't wait until that first scorching summer heat wave to discover there's something wrong with your air conditioner. Find out how turning on your air conditioner in spring can actually save you money. Your wallet will thank you.

When temperatures hit the 70s, give your air conditioner a test run. If you notice something amiss, schedule a service call. By acting quickly, you can catch small problems before they become major catastrophes. And major catastrophes come with major repair bills.

You can also save money by making sure your unit is operating at top efficiency. That means lower monthly utility bills. As an added bonus, you'll avoid the longer waits and higher prices of the peak summer season. You can schedule an appointment at your convenience and even take the time to comparison shop when you're not acting out of desperation.

With some basic home maintenance, you may be able to avoid calling a repairman at all. Before picking up the phone, take these simple steps.

- Check the filter. It may need to be cleaned or replaced. Vacuum and wash dirty filters in warm, soapy water.
- Vacuum the coils and fins. Use an upholstery brush attachment.
- Seal any leaks around the unit.
- Give it a break. After shutting off the unit, wait at least five minutes before restarting it. This puts less stress on the compressor.
- Check your circuit breakers and fuses. Double-check the thermostat as well.

- Make sure the vents are open and no furniture is blocking them.
- Clear any debris, leaves, and grass from the outdoor unit.

Stay safe. Remember to unplug your air conditioner and turn off the power before performing any maintenance.

Guide to selecting the right size. Think like Goldilocks when shopping for a window air conditioner. Not too big, not too small – but just right. If the unit is too big for the room, it will cycle on and off too frequently, wasting energy and taxing the electrical components. If it's too small for the room, it will wheeze and struggle to cool it. Pick one that's just the right size. Here's how to do it.

- Measure your room and calculate the square footage. To do this, multiply the length of the room by its width.
- Check the power. An air conditioner's power is measured in British Thermal Units, or BTUs. The more BTUs, the more powerful the unit. Pay attention to this important number when buying an air conditioner.
- Go by these guidelines. As a general rule of thumb, you need at least 20 BTUs for each square foot of living space. But you can make some adjustments to this basic formula. Add or subtract 10 percent if the room is extremely sunny or shady. More people means more BTUs, too. Figure on an extra 600 BTUs for each additional person who will spend time in the room. If you plan on putting the unit in the kitchen, tack on an additional 4,000 BTUs.

If this seems like too much math, you can find online calculators and charts at the websites of stores like The Home Depot and Lowe's to help steer you in the right direction.

You also need to take into account the measurements of your window to make sure the unit will fit. And make sure your home's electrical system can handle the unit's power requirements.

HANDY HINT

Get more for your money

Saving energy helps you save money. That's why it's important to make sure your window air conditioner is as efficient as possible. One way to do that is simply buying a more efficient model. While you'll spend more money upfront, you should save money later.

Look for an air conditioner's energy efficiency ratio (EER). The higher the EER, the more efficient the unit. You want a unit with an EER of 10.0 or higher. Say you have an air conditioner from the 1970s with an EER of 5. Upgrade to a new model with an EER of 10, and you will cut your cooling costs in half.

Even if your unit is just 10 years old, it uses 35 percent more energy than new, energy-efficient models. Making the upgrade can save you an average of $250 over the lifetime of the unit. Look for the Energy Star label when shopping for a new unit.

Just keeping your air conditioner's filter clean can reduce your energy consumption by 5 to 15 percent. Regularly clean or replace your filter to keep your system running smoothly.

Where you place the unit can also make a difference. If possible, install your window air conditioner facing north or east. Windows that face south or west get more sun, which will make your unit work harder.

Hush a noisy window unit. Your window air conditioner helps keep the temperature down. You just wish it would keep the noise down, too. Try these tips for silencing a noisy air conditioner.

- Clean the unit more often.
- Oil the moving parts.
- Tighten any loose nuts and bolts.
- Tighten the screws on the front panel.
- Make an airtight seal by using caulk or putty around the edges of the window frame.
- Replace any cracked window glass. Keep loose glass in place with putty.
- Lighten the burden on the window and frame by installing window-mounting brackets to support the unit's weight.
- Place wood shims between the unit and frame to fill any gaps.
- Inspect the insulation. Replace any torn or missing insulation inside the unit. Pack it tightly to quiet the whir of moving parts. Make sure there's no loose insulation stuck to the fans. That could cause a grinding noise.
- Fix the fan blades. Check if any are bent or uneven, and carefully bend them back into place. A bent fan blade can bang against the inside of the air conditioner.
- Straighten any damaged coil fins, which can cause a loud hum. They're usually located at the back of the unit.
- Peek at the power cord. If it's twisted or frayed, it may not supply steady power. This could lead to occasional stoppages, then noisy restarts. Replace the cord if necessary.

Keep in mind that some units are just noisier than others. But these tips should help minimize rattles, hums, clanks, squeaks, and other annoying noises.

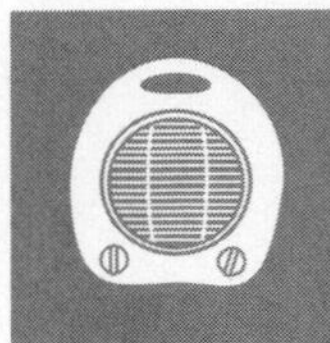

HUMIDIFIERS

A breath of fresh air

Easy way to clean your humidifier. Regular cleaning keeps your humidifier free of mold, mildew, and mineral deposits. Fortunately, you can do your regular cleaning with a regular household product – vinegar. Just follow this step-by-step guide.

- Mix equal parts vinegar and warm water in a spray bottle.
- Unplug your humidifier and take it apart.
- Empty the tank, and spray it with the vinegar and water mixture. Let it sit for a while, then scrub it clean with a sponge, cloth, or old toothbrush.
- Soak the filter in a mixture of vinegar and water for about an hour.
- Pour a little vinegar into the base, and let it soak at the same time.
- Scrub the filter and base clean.
- Thoroughly rinse and dry all the parts.
- Refill the tank with cool water.
- Put your humidifier back together.

Get rid of odors with a lemon. Let your humidifier pull double duty as an air freshener. Just add a few teaspoons of lemon juice or vinegar to the water. You'll get rid of any odors in your humidifier and also keep the air smelling clean and fresh.

Simple way to defeat mold

Your dehumidifier comes in handy during hot, muggy, or damp weather. But don't forget to empty, clean, and dry the reservoir regularly. Otherwise, it can become a breeding ground for mold. Keep your dehumidifier working smoothly by emptying the water from the reservoir as it fills up. This may be as often as once a day during humid conditions.

If that sounds like too much work, look for a dehumidifier with a larger reservoir. It will work better and need emptying less often. Some models are also designed to drain automatically.

10 tips to improve indoor air quality. You may be the king or queen of your castle – but that can be a royal pain if your castle's air is polluted. Indoor air quality can be up to 100 times worse than outdoor air. According to the Environmental Protection Agency, here are 10 steps you can take to improve air quality in your home.

- Get some fresh air. When the weather cooperates, open windows and doors. Or run your air conditioner with the vent control open.
- Make sure bathroom and kitchen fans vent directly outdoors.
- Change or clean the filters in your central heating and air conditioning system regularly. That way, the filters will keep working to trap dust and other pollutants. Dust and vacuum your home regularly, too.

- Keep humidity between 30 and 50 percent to minimize mold. You can find a moisture or humidity gauge at the hardware store. A humidifier or dehumidifier can help you achieve the right balance.

- Test your home for radon. This cancer-causing radioactive gas can seep into your home through cracks and openings in floors and walls in contact with the ground. You can use a do-it-yourself radon kit. Call a pro if you have high levels.

- Open windows and use extra fans when painting, remodeling, or using household cleaning products. These products may release harmful chemicals called volatile organic compounds. Store these products safely, too.

- Don't smoke or allow others to smoke in your home.

- Make sure furnaces, fireplaces, and gas stoves are properly vented. Check that your chimney is properly sealed. Fully open the flue damper when using the fireplace.

- Consider a mechanical ventilation system, which uses ducts and fans to bring fresh air to your whole house.

- Install carbon monoxide detectors in living spaces.

FURNACES

Warding off the big chill

Slash utility costs. Utility costs go up and down with the seasons. But with dozens of clever tips, you can keep them down longer – even all year round.

Start with these eight ways to make your house super energy-efficient.

- Fix leaky air ducts. Sealing leaks can save you up to 20 percent on heating costs.
- Install a programmable thermostat. This lets you easily adjust temperatures throughout the day. Set it for lower temperatures overnight or when no one is home, then set it to warm up in the morning or when you come home.
- Close the heating and air-conditioning vents in unoccupied rooms. This can shave 5 to 10 percent off your energy bills.
- Clean or change your furnace filter regularly. A clogged filter lets less air through, making your furnace work longer to heat your home.
- Add insulation. If you have an older house, chances are it doesn't have enough insulation. Properly insulate your home to save 10 percent on heating and cooling costs. Your attic is a good spot for extra insulation.
- Close the fireplace flue when the fireplace is not in use. Otherwise, heat will escape up the chimney.
- Use ceiling fans to push warm air down. It will help heat the room more evenly.
- Strategically use drapes and shades. Open them on cold days to let in the sunshine and make your room warmer. Close them at night to keep heat in. On hot days, close the drapes to keep the sun out and your room cool.

But don't stop there. Try these other moneysaving tricks to keep your heating and cooling bills under control.

- Plant a shade tree on the west or southwest side of your house to block the sun's heat. As it grows, your cooling bills will shrink.

- Move your thermostat to an inside wall away from windows and doors. That way, drafts won't cause the heating system to cycle on unnecessarily.

- Open windows on a breezy day rather than using your air conditioner.

- Try a dehumidifier instead of cranking up the AC. With less humidity, you may be comfortable at a higher temperature.

- Blow hot air out of your kitchen with an exhaust fan while you're cooking. The cost of running the fan is less than that of cooling down your home.

- Go up or down a degree. Each degree makes a difference. Lowering your thermostat one degree can reduce your heating bill by up to 3 percent. Raising your thermostat one degree can lower your cooling bill by 2 percent.

- Keep doors closed as much as possible. Every time you open a door, you let in cold air or heat.

- Insulate air ducts and pipes so you don't lose heat.

Flip through the rest of this book to find even more helpful suggestions on how to save money on your utility bills.

Find air leaks with a flame. Shed some light on saving energy. All you need is a candle. If you've got one of these, you won't believe how much lower your utility bill can be.

You can save 10 percent or more on your heating bill just by stopping air leaks in your home. Find out where your warm air is going by holding a lit candle next to windows, doors, ducts, plumbing, electrical outlets, and light fixtures. A stick of burning incense will also do the trick. Smoke drifting to the ceiling means nothing is blowing in, and you'll stay warm and cozy. But horizontal smoke means you have a draft.

Once you find an air leak, you have to do something about it. Applying caulk or weatherstripping should fix the problem. Although you could hire a professional to do the job, the cost of these materials is small, and sealing your home is not a difficult do-it-yourself project. While the process may take some time, it's time well spent. In fact, weather-stripping old windows and doors may reduce your energy costs by 15 to 30 percent.

WARNING

5 danger signs from your furnace

Your furnace may be trying to tell you something. Pay attention to these telltale signs of trouble. They could indicate it's time to call a professional or even replace your furnace.

- Yellow or flickering flame. Your burner flame should be blue. If it's yellow or flickering, it could mean your furnace is producing poisonous carbon monoxide.
- Rust. If you notice rust on and around your burners and heat exchanger, your furnace's days may be numbered.
- Soot or corrosion around your furnace or vents. Also, watch out for scorch marks by the door — a sign the flame is escaping the furnace.
- Strange noises. Banging, popping, rattling, or squealing noises could be cries for help. If the blower runs excessively or frequently turns on and off, your furnace may be on its last legs.
- Scary symptoms. If you or your family experience frequent headaches, nausea, sluggishness, a burning feeling in the nose or eyes, disorientation, or flu-like symptoms, act quickly. Air out the house and call for help. These symptoms could indicate a carbon monoxide leak.

Boost efficiency with your vacuum. Want to keep your heating system running smoothly? Then you must get rid of dust. It can blunt your heating system's efficiency by 10 percent or more. For an extremely dirty duct system, you may need to hire a professional.

But you can also defeat dust with your trusty vacuum cleaner. Vacuuming your vents, registers, and air ducts will help improve the efficiency of your system. Make this step a regular part of your housecleaning routine. You should also make sure furniture and drapes don't block airflow.

HANDY HINT

Save energy with body heat

Party guests bring more than good cheer. A crowded house also generates a lot of body heat. In winter, save energy by lowering your thermostat a few degrees before your guests arrive.

The lowdown on high-efficiency filters. High-efficiency furnace filters come with high price tags. But is the extra efficiency worth the extra cost? On one hand, a high-efficiency filter traps smaller airborne particles of dust and dirt. It would come in handy when you're doing a project that results in a lot of dust, like sanding.

But the filter's ability to catch small particles also makes it harder for air to get through once the filter gets clogged. So your furnace has to work longer to heat your home, driving up your heating costs. That's why it's important to change high-efficiency filters regularly.

When shopping for filters, look for the Minimum Efficiency Reporting Value, or MERV, rating. The higher the rating, the more efficient the filter. But unless you run the furnace fan all the time – which adds to your energy bill – you won't get much bang for your buck.

A cheaper solution may be to stick with a less-efficient filter, but take steps to minimize dust. That means removing footwear at the door, banning smoking and pets from your house, and regularly vacuuming. And, of course, cleaning or changing the filter regularly.

WASHERS & DRYERS

A whole new spin on clean

Surprising way to get your clothes cleaner. Here's a soap opera worth watching. Find out how to get your clothes cleaner by using less soap in your washing machine. This moneysaving tip makes your washer last longer, too.

Experts say most people use too much soap when doing laundry. Rather than making your clothes cleaner, this has the opposite effect. It leaves your clothing stiff, faded, and with a residue that attracts more dirt. The extra soap also takes its toll on your machine. Detergent buildup can lead to odors, mold, and mildew. It can also cause wear and tear that shortens the life of your appliance.

To protect your clothes and your washer, cut back on how much detergent you use. Start by paying attention to the instructions on the bottle and the lines in the cap. Don't fill the cap to the brim – just to the appropriate line. You can probably get by with even less than the recommended amount. A tablespoon or two may do the trick. If you have a high-efficiency machine, use a detergent designed especially for them.

Even if you don't currently use too much detergent, you can still cut back and end up with cleaner clothes. Just add a half-cup of borax to each load. Borax boosts the effectiveness of detergent, so you can get by with less – about half the amount you normally use. Borax also helps remove stains, whitens and freshens clothes, and softens hard water.

HANDY HINT

Speedy system for sorting laundry

Laundry takes up enough of your time. Speed up the process with this timesaving trick. As your clothes get dirty, put them in one of three laundry baskets — one each for darks, lights, and whites. If you sort your laundry as it accumulates, you won't waste time rummaging through a big mound of dirty clothes later. You can just grab a basket and throw a load in the washing machine.

This trick also lets you keep better tabs on your laundry. When you notice a basket is full, you know you have enough laundry to do a full load of wash when you have some spare time.

Hot tips help save energy. The more, the merrier. When doing laundry, don't stop at just one load. Dry several loads in a row to take advantage of the leftover heat in your dryer. This one easy laundry tip will lower your electric bill. That's because your dryer won't waste energy heating up between loads.

You can also save money – about $60 a year – by using just the cold-water wash cycle. Your clothes will still get clean, but your washing machine won't gobble up your hot water.

Save on your electric bill and add humidity for free. Just try this ingenious solution. Instead of throwing your wet laundry in the dryer, hang it indoors. Either hang your damp clothes from a clothes rack or from your shower curtain rod. As the water evaporates, the moisture will fill your dry home. With this trick, you don't need to run your dryer or your humidifier.

Simple fix for a costly problem. When a hose goes, the water flows – and that costs you dough. Washing machine hoses often leak or break, leading to costly water damage. Luckily, a simple fix can prevent this problem.

Periodically, check the rubber fill hoses that carry water to your washer. Look for bulges, cracks, blisters, and bare spots. It's a good idea to replace these hoses every three to five years – their average life span.

For even more protection, replace cheap rubber hoses with stronger stainless steel ones. They will cost more, but they will also last longer and save you money in the long run.

Minimize mold in your washer. Your laundry should come out of the wash smelling fresh and clean. But every time you open your washing machine, you get a whiff of mold. Try this easy fix to freshen your machine. Run the empty washer through a cycle with a cup of bleach. The bleach should eliminate the mold wherever it lurks. Do this once a month to keep mold away.

You can also help prevent mold by leaving your washing machine door open in between loads. That way, the inside of the machine will dry completely. Mold needs moisture to grow, and a damp, closed machine could be an ideal environment. Leave the detergent dispenser cover open between loads, too.

Banish buildup with vinegar. Your washing machine cleans your clothes – but sometimes it needs to be cleaned, too. Soap scum and mineral deposits can clog the hoses and hamper your washer's performance.

To clean the hoses and the inside of your washer, put a cup of white distilled vinegar in the detergent compartment and run the machine on empty using hot water. Do this a few times a year to clear any buildup and keep your machine running smoothly.

Fabric softener sheets pull double duty

Used dryer sheets can still be put to good use in your laundry room. Before you throw them away, use them to clear lint from in and around your dryer. They also come in handy for wiping up any liquid detergent spills around your washing machine.

Reduce your risk of a dryer fire. Dryers can be dangerous. In 1998, the U.S. Consumer Product Safety Commission reported 15,600 dryer-related fires. But you can minimize your risk by minimizing lint.

Lint buildup clogs ducts and blocks airflow, resulting in excessive heat and potential fires. It also affects your dryer's performance. When ducts are clogged, your dryer uses more energy to dry each load. Longer drying times put extra wear and tear on your machine and your clothes. Your dryer may even overheat or fail.

One precaution you probably already take is to clean the lint filter after each load. But that's only part of the problem. Lint slowly builds up in the exhaust ducts, too. Prolong the life of your dryer – and possibly yourself – by cleaning your dryer exhaust vent every year or two. Here's how to do it.

- Unplug the dryer. If it's a gas dryer, turn off the gas.
- Pull it away from the wall and disconnect the vent tubing.
- Reach in and pull out any lint from the back of the dryer, as well as from the tubing.
- Use a vacuum hose to suck up any lint you can't reach. You can also try using a long-handled brush.
- Make sure to check and clear the vent on the outside of the house, too.

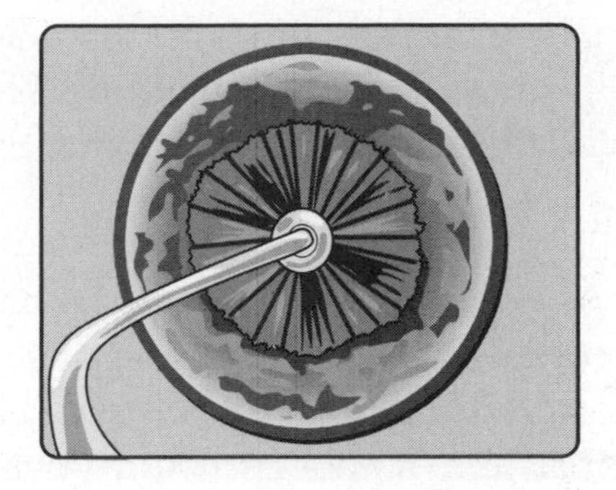

You can buy dryer vent cleaning kits to make this task easier. Kits include special brushes, flexible rods, and adapters for your vacuum and dryer. Hook the rods and brushes to your cordless drill, and the rotating brushes will scrape the ducts as your vacuum or dryer blower blasts air to clear the lint. These kits typically cost around $20, but you can find them for as little as $11. Of course, you can also hire a professional to do the job, but it will cost more.

However you decide to clean your dryer exhaust vent, just make sure you do it. You will extend the life of your dryer, improve its performance, and help prevent a potentially deadly fire.

Dryer dilemma — repair or replace? Your dryer is on the fritz. Should you repair it or buy a new one? That depends on how serious the problem is – and how much it will cost to fix it. Follow these guidelines when deciding what course of action to take.

- Stick with it. Unlike washing machines, dryers do not vary greatly in the amount of energy they use. So you won't reap big savings by upgrading to a newer, more-efficient model. It makes sense to hang onto your dryer for as long as it lasts, which is usually around 12 or 13 years.

- Consider repair costs. Common repairs include replacing the drum drive belt, blower wheel, or drum support rollers. These fixes may be enough to keep your old dryer in business. But if repairs get too costly, consider shopping for a new machine. One general rule of thumb is to replace your dryer if the repair costs more than half the price of a similar new model.

- Choose wisely. If you decide to replace rather than repair your dryer, look for one with a moisture sensor. This feature automatically turns off the machine when the load is dry rather than relying on a timer. Not only does this save energy – and money – it also minimizes shrinkage and wear and tear on your clothes.

As with any new purchase, comparison shop and read product reviews to pick the dryer that's right for you. Also consider delivery and installation costs, as well as the cost to dispose of your old machine. If your current dryer is getting old, you may want to start keeping an eye on prices before something goes wrong. That way, you'll be prepared to make your decision when the time comes.

WATER HEATERS

Some like it hot

Must-have water heater accessory. On chilly nights, you may wrap yourself in a blanket to stay warm. Do the same thing for your water heater, and you'll save money on your water bill.

Insulating your water heater reduces standby heat loss – the heat lost through the walls of the tank – by 25 to 40 percent. This translates to a savings of 4 to 9 percent on your water heating bill.

For around $10, you can buy a blanket of fiberglass insulation made just for this purpose. Follow the directions carefully, especially for a gas heater. You want to make sure not to cover the exhaust vents and air intakes. And never cover the temperature relief valve.

Insulate your hot water pipes, too. That way, the water in the pipes stays warmer longer. You won't waste as much energy and water waiting for the hot water to reach the tap.

Trim costs with a timer. Timing is everything. You can save energy – and money – by installing a timer on your electric water heater. With a timer, you can shut off your water heater at night while you sleep or during peak demand times. Then set it to turn back on so you have hot water in time for your morning shower. A timer costs about $30, but you should save at least that much on your utility bills during the first year.

Check your utility company's electricity rates. Some companies charge higher rates during "on-peak" times – when there is the most demand on their system – and lower rates during "off-peak" hours. You can set your timer accordingly to take advantage of the lower rates. Timers do not work as well with a gas water heater because of the pilot light.

Even if you don't use a timer, you could just switch off your water heater when you don't plan to use it for long periods of time.

Flush your tank in four easy steps. Poker players know you can't beat a royal flush. If you don't want to gamble with your hot water heater, you should think along the same lines. Flush your water heater tank annually to keep your water heater in tiptop shape.

Over time, sediment, dirt, and mineral deposits naturally build up inside your water heater tank. This gunk can make your water heater's heating element less efficient, and it takes up space your water heater would normally use for water.

Fortunately, fixing the problem is simple. You can flush your tank with these easy steps. Just remember to check the manufacturer's instructions before you begin.

- Grab a bucket, turn off the water heater circuit breaker or gas valve, and shut off the incoming water.

- Find the drain valve near the bottom of the tank, place the bucket beneath it, and open the valve. If it has been awhile since the tank was flushed, attach a garden hose to the drain valve and run the hose outside or to a drain in your floor.

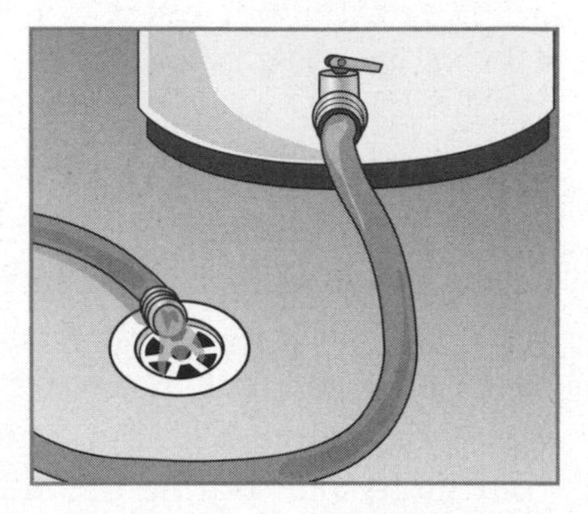

- Let the water drain into the bucket until it runs clear. If the water is still dirty when the tank empties, allow the tank to refill with a few gallons of water before draining it again.

- When you are done, turn off the valve, restore the incoming water, and turn on the water heater circuit breaker or gas valve.

Now your water will heat faster, and your water heater will last longer. For best results, flush your tank at least once a year. You may need to flush it more often if you have hard water.

Chapter 5

THE BATHROOM

Perhaps someday, someone will invent the self-cleaning bathroom, the uncloggable sink, and a toilet that fixes itself. But until that day comes, you can use the tips and tricks in these chapters to speed up your cleaning, make inexpensive cleaning products, and win the war against clogs, stains, odors, and other common bathroom problems.

SINKS & FAUCETS
Just go with the flow

Stop drain clogs and odors with H_2O. Pour a kettle of boiling water down your drain once a week to melt the buildup that contributes to drain clogs. This fights odors while helping prevent clogs. But even if you get a clog, you can still handle it yourself, cheaply and naturally, with homemade remedies like these.

- Pour one-half cup of baking soda into the drain. Follow with one-half cup of white vinegar. Immediately cover the drain. After several minutes, uncover the drain and pour in a kettle of boiling water. The baking soda and vinegar should break down the clog, and the hot water should wash it away. Just remember, you cannot use this clog fighter if you have already used a commercial drain opener or if the drain opener is still in the standing water caused by the clog.

- Bring six cups of water to a boil. Pour one-half cup of salt and one-half cup of baking soda down the drain, then follow with the boiling water. Let it sit for eight hours and then flush with water.

- If your drain is slow, but not yet clogged, combine a cup of baking soda, a cup of salt, and three-quarters cup of white vinegar, and pour the mixture into your congested drain. Let it soak in for about 20 minutes, and rinse with a gallon of boiling water.

Clean your bathroom with three cheap ingredients. Don't spend money on toxic cleaning products like ammonia. Find out how to use vinegar and other natural alternatives. With just three ingredients, you can have an inexpensive cleanser for everything in your bathroom.

- Toilet bowl. Sprinkle baking soda generously in the basin, pour in one cup of vinegar, and let sit for several minutes. Scrub vigorously with a toilet brush and rinse.

- Chrome. Polish your chrome with vinegar.

- Tile and grout. Sprinkle baking soda over flat tile surfaces and rub with a damp sponge. For vertical tile, apply baking soda to a damp sponge and wipe. To clean grout, make a paste of three parts baking soda to one part water and scrub it into the grout.

- Bathtub. To clean unsightly film off your tub, wipe it down with vinegar, then baking soda, and rinse clean.

- Sink. Sponge it down with baking soda for regular cleaning, and use vinegar to remove hard water deposits.

- Windows and mirrors. Clean with equal parts vinegar and warm water for a streak-free shine.

- Shower head. Thoroughly wet a towel with vinegar, and wrap it tightly around your shower head to help remove mildew and mineral deposits. If you're not happy with the results, fill a resealable bag with vinegar and completely submerge the shower head. Use a rubber band to attach the bag to the shower head so it can soak in the vinegar overnight. Remove the bag in the morning, and use an old toothbrush to scrub it clean.

- Mold and mildew. Apply a mixture of four parts hydrogen peroxide and one part water directly on mold or mildew. Let sit for several minutes and scrub. Wear rubber gloves to protect your hands.

ALTERNATE USES

Shine your faucets with toothpaste

You can make your dingy faucets shine like new in no time. Just dab a little toothpaste on a soft cloth and give your faucets a quick rubdown. Wipe off the toothpaste with a damp cloth, and your faucets will gleam again.

Restore the shine to a stainless steel sink. Has your kitchen sink lost its stainless steel shine? Try using the common household items listed here to buff your basin.

- Vinegar. Dampen a cloth with white vinegar or apple cider vinegar. Polish your sink and dry it with a clean cloth.
- Olive oil. Rub your sink with olive oil and those annoying streaks will go away.
- Club soda. Pour a little club soda on a cloth and wipe down your sink. Dry with a clean cloth.

Make your own cleaning wipes. You broke down and bought some cleaning wipes, but you are still horrified at the price. Don't worry. You can turn this spending negative into a positive. When you run out of wipes, save the container and fill it with homemade wipes. To make these wipes, you need one roll of high-quality paper towels and a bottle of pine cleaner.

Cut the roll of paper towels in half so you end up with two short rolls. Put aside the other half to use as a refill later.

Check the label on your cleaning wipe container to see how much liquid it can hold. If it's listed in ounces, divide by 8 to determine the number of cups. Mix one part pine cleaner to four parts water, but don't make more than half of what your container can hold.

Pour this in your container and add the half-roll of paper towels. Let it sit for several hours, so the cleaning solution can thoroughly dampen the paper towels. Remove the cardboard roll from the center. This should pull up the innermost paper towel in the roll. If not, pull up one corner of the paper towel, since it will be the first one you use. Close the lid on your container, and use the wipes as needed.

If you prefer not to cut your paper towels in half, use an old square or rectangular baby wipe container and buy paper towels that are perforated to tear off by the half-sheet. Fold each half-sheet to fit the baby wipe container, put the sheets in, and pour in the pine cleaner and water. Just remember, don't fill the baby wipe container more than half full with liquid.

Wipe out sink stains with a lemon

Cut a lemon in half and use it to rub out stains on porcelain, fiberglass, cast-iron, or stainless steel sinks. Scrub with the lemon half if the stain doesn't come up easily.

For rust and other stubborn stains in a stainless steel sink, clean with a combination of lemon juice and borax.

Easy way to clean a porcelain sink. Ugly stains in your white porcelain sink will vanish when you do this. Mix three-fourths cup of bleach with four cups of water, and apply to the stain on your porcelain sink. Let sit for 20 seconds, and rinse.

For stubborn stains, soak paper towels in bleach, and place them over the stains. Saturate several paper towels with water, and put them over the paper towels with bleach. Let sit overnight, and rinse clean in the morning. The stain should be gone.

If you don't want to use bleach, sprinkle cream of tartar on a damp cloth and rub it into the stain and rinse clean. This works well for light stains. For heavier stains, put on gloves and make a paste from cream of tartar and hydrogen peroxide. Use this to clean the stain, and then rinse.

To protect your hands, it's a good idea to wear rubber gloves when you're cleaning with hydrogen peroxide or bleach.

ALTERNATE USES

Silence a leaky faucet

Your bathroom faucet started leaking at midnight, so you can't call a plumber until morning. Meanwhile, the plop of dripping water is keeping you from sleeping. Here's a simple solution.

Cut a strip of dental floss several inches longer than the distance from the faucet to the drain. Loop the floss around the faucet head and tie it so it trails to the drain. Position the floss right where the water is dripping. Now, the water can slide silently down the floss.

Protect your pipes from freezes. Don't just worry about your hose and outside pipes when a big freeze comes. Some of your indoor pipes may also be in danger, especially the ones that run through unheated areas, such as your bathroom cabinet, kitchen cabinet, basement, crawl space, garage, and attic. Insulate pipes in these unheated areas, even the pipes for hot water. You can do this with self-sealing pipe sleeves from your local home improvement store.

During a freeze, open kitchen and bathroom cabinet doors to allow warm air to reach the plumbing. During a severe freeze, let cold water drip slowly from any faucet attached to pipes in unheated or exposed spaces. This could make the difference between a pipe that freezes and one that doesn't.

If you expect to be out of town during a freeze, don't turn off your furnace or heater. Instead, turn it down to 55 degrees, so your pipes will have a fighting chance against the cold.

Secret boost helps clear clogs. If your sink plunger doesn't clear a clog on the first try, air from the sink's overflow hole may be the problem. Look for the overflow hole slightly below the top of the sink's rim, and stuff it tightly with a damp rag. When you try the sink plunger again, it will be more effective.

You may run into a similar problem if you have a double sink in your kitchen. If one sink basin is clogged, stuff the drain of the other sink with a wet rag. This should give an added boost to your sink-plunging efforts, and that may be just what you need to clear the clog.

Remarkable way to keep shower tiles clean. Imagine making your ceramic tile walls resistant to hard water spots, soap scum, mold, mildew, and even dirt. Some people do this by polishing their tile walls with paste car wax. Before you try this, clean the tile with your favorite soap scum and hard water spot removers. Then choose a good car wax and apply a light coating to your tile, following the directions on the package.

Buff with a dry cloth for maximum shine that lasts a long time. This should cause soap scum, hard water mineral deposits, and dirt to simply slide away instead of sticking to your tile. When your tile needs cleaning, choose a gentle cleanser so you won't strip off the wax. This helps keep your tiles sparkling clean for months.

And here's a word of caution – never apply car wax to floor tiles because it can make them more slippery than a banana peel.

New use for old toothbrushes. Don't throw out old toothbrushes. They can be great scrubbing brushes for grout or hard-to-reach spaces, like the area around your faucets. But before you use an old toothbrush, make sure it's clean and disinfected. Boil the toothbrush, soak it in bleach and hot water, or run it through your dishwasher on the top rack.

MYTHBUSTER

Stop spending money on ceramic tile cleaner

You don't need to spend money on floor wax for your ceramic tile floors, say the experts at Merry Maids. They recommend routine sweeping and mopping and suggest you mop with either water alone or water combined with a squirt of liquid dish soap. Just be sure to change the mopping water when it gets cloudy, and avoid using harsh scrubbers on your floor.

Say bye-bye to stubborn grout stains. Grout stains can make a beautiful tile floor look dingy. Try these tricks to make it look beautiful again.

- Make grout stains disappear using a pencil eraser.
- Fold sandpaper and use the edge to rub out a grout stain.
- Consider using powdered oxygen bleach, like OxiClean. It's better than chlorine bleach for several reasons. It's less likely to discolor your tile or grout, it's safer than chlorine bleach, and it's surprisingly tough on stains. To clean grout with oxygen bleach, follow the package directions for mixing the powder with water, apply to your grout, and let stand for 20 to 30 minutes – then scrub and rinse. If the grout stains are not completely gone, repeat this process. Be sure to rinse both the grout and the surrounding tile afterward.

TOILETS
Get this potty started

Disinfect your bathroom without the awful smell. It's easy. Just reach for hydrogen peroxide. It's odorless and considered a broad-spectrum disinfectant, which means it's effective against many kinds of germs. Commercial-strength hydrogen peroxide is powerful enough to be used in hospitals, but even household hydrogen peroxide is considered a low-level disinfectant. It's useful for sanitizing surfaces and cleaning items used in home health care.

To put this inexpensive disinfectant to work in your house, fill a spray bottle with 4 ounces of hydrogen peroxide, spray on kitchen and bath surfaces, let sit for 10 minutes, and then wipe with a clean paper towel. Make sure you let the hydrogen peroxide work for 10 minutes. Research suggests this can make a significant difference in how well this sanitizer works.

Be aware that hydrogen peroxide may not be safe for all surfaces. It may be corrosive to aluminum, zinc, copper, or brass if left on too long. It also has bleaching power that may cause discoloring or fading. Play it safe and test hydrogen peroxide on a small, inconspicuous area before using it on an entire surface.

MYTHBUSTER

Plumbing secret from the experts

Just because the package says its wipes are flushable doesn't mean you should flush them. Cities have reported sewer clogs where flushable wipes played a role. Some experts recommend against putting these wipes in the toilet — even if the package label promises it's safe.

If you have had problems with clogs, try tossing these wipes in your bathroom trash instead. Other items that should never go in the toilet include paper towels and facial tissues.

Simple way to lower your water bill. A soda bottle can help you curb your utility costs. Fill a two-liter soda bottle or half-gallon milk jug with sand, pebbles, or gravel. Put the cap back on and close it tightly. Remove the lid from your toilet and gently lower the jug or bottle into the tank. Flush the toilet once to make sure the jug or bottle does not interfere with any of the toilet's moving parts.

Put the lid back on the toilet tank, and keep an eye on the toilet to make sure it continues to flush properly over the next few days. If it does, you will soon have a lower water bill and here's why. Because the jug or bottle takes up a half gallon of space, you'll use less water every time you flush. Even if you only flush this toilet four times a day, you could cut your water usage by about 120 gallons every month.

Keep in mind this tip won't work for the new low-flow or high-efficiency toilets, so don't try it if your toilet was bought or made after 1992. Also, be very careful with toilets made between 1980 and 1991. Using the bottle or jug may not work as well for these toilets as it does for older toilets, so monitor them carefully. If you have to flush twice or if the toilet develops problems, remove the bottle or jug from the toilet tank right away.

WARNING

Cleaners you should never use in your toilet

You might think you can use drain cleaners and cleaning tablets in toilets, but guess again. Chemical drain cleaners, like Drano and Liquid Plumr, may be great for sink and other drain clogs, but don't use them to clear a clogged toilet.

In fact, they shouldn't be used in toilets at all unless the label specifically says so. Most of these products contain caustic chemicals that produce enough heat to melt a greasy or soapy clog — but that much heat can cause cracks in your toilet. You'll be far better off if you attack a toilet clog with a plunger.

Also, avoid using drop-in bleach tablets that help keep the toilet clean. Over time, these tablets cause parts in your toilet tank to wear out long before they should. So you not only pay for the cleaning tablets, but for extra repairs as well.

5 penny-pinching ways to make your toilet shine. You don't have to spend extra money on a commercial toilet bowl cleaner. Just use one of these instead.

- Get rid of that toilet bowl ring once and for all with borax and lemon juice. Combine enough borax and lemon juice to make a paste that can cover the entire ring. Flush the toilet once, apply the paste, and let it sit for several hours. Scrub the ring, and flush to rinse.

- Pour one-fourth cup of bleach into the toilet bowl, let it sit for a few hours, and then flush. Don't use this if you already have a cleaner tablet hanging in the toilet bowl tank. Combining bleach with a tank cleaner that contains ammonia may release toxic fumes.

- Pour three cups of vinegar in your toilet bowl before bed and let it sit overnight. In the morning, clean the bowl with your toilet brush, and then flush to rinse.

- Sprinkle baking soda over a faint toilet bowl ring and scrub.

- Mix one-fourth cup of baking soda with a full cup of vinegar and immediately pour into the toilet. Wait a few minutes, scrub, and flush.

Unusual toilet bowl cleaners that really work. You won't need to hold your nose or wear gloves to clean your toilet if you use one of these.

- Coke. Pour one can into the bowl. Let the acid in the Coke do its thing for a while and flush.

- Tang. Sprinkle one-half cup of the powdered drink mix in your bowl, wait an hour or two, and then flush.

- Alka-Seltzer. Drop in one or two fizzy tablets, let them fizz a bit, and flush to rinse.

- Denture cleaning tablets. Drop in several tablets, wait a few minutes, scrub, and flush.

Get more power from your plunger. Flushing was not enough to move the clog, so you need something stronger. That's where your plunger comes in. It helps you push and pull the water around the clog more powerfully, making underwater waves that shift and dislodge the clog. But some stubborn clogs may not budge unless you get the maximum power from your plunger. Here's how to start.

- Get the right plunger. Don't use the cup kind made for sink and drain clogs. Those are too shallow. Instead, look for a plunger with a taller dome, such as a flange plunger. This plunger looks like a sink plunger, but with a smaller rubber circle attached at the end. This kind of plunger can give you more pushing and pulling power.
- Before you use the plunger, line its rim with petroleum jelly. This helps maintain a tight seal between the plunger and the toilet surface, so you can put more pressure on the clog.

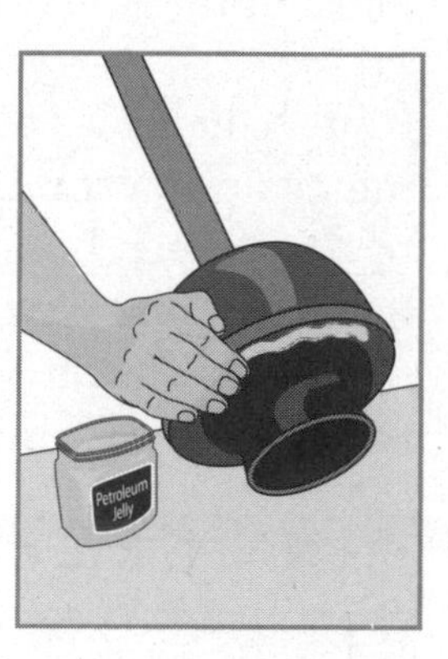

TUBS & SHOWERS

Making a splash

Clean your shower less often. Prevent soap scum buildup and pesky clogged drains with one simple switch. You won't believe the difference. All you have to do is switch from bar soap to liquid soap and here's why.

Certain ingredients in bar soap naturally bind with the calcium and magnesium in your shower water. This combination forms soap scum. Liquid soaps don't contain the bar soap ingredients that contribute to soap scum. That's why switching soaps may mean you don't have to clean your shower as often.

Soap scum also contributes to drain clogs, especially if you have old pipes. When you slash soap scum, you help prevent clogs, too.

Prevent water spots and soap scum. Stop water spots and soap scum from forming on your shower door, and you'll never have to clean them. Just wipe down your glass shower door with Rain-X, the same stuff you put on your windshield to improve visibility in the rain.

Rain-X helps because it changes the way water behaves. A water molecule is a combination of hydrogen and oxygen held together by "hydrogen bonds." Although glass is mostly silica, it contains hydrogen and oxygen, too. This fools the hydrogen bonds in water, so they try to cling to the glass. This makes rain cling to your windshield, so it becomes harder to see through.

But Rain-X forms a slick barrier between the windshield glass and rainwater, preventing the water from clinging. As a result, the water simply slides away.

Rain-X has a similar effect on shower door glass. It forces water to keep moving so it can't deposit soap scum or water spots. This may keep your shower doors clean for months, especially if you wipe down the door after each shower.

If you'd like to try Rain-X, keep these thoughts in mind.

- Rain-X should not be used on plastic, only on glass or fiberglass shower doors.

- Avoid getting Rain-X on your shower floor. It can make it slippery.

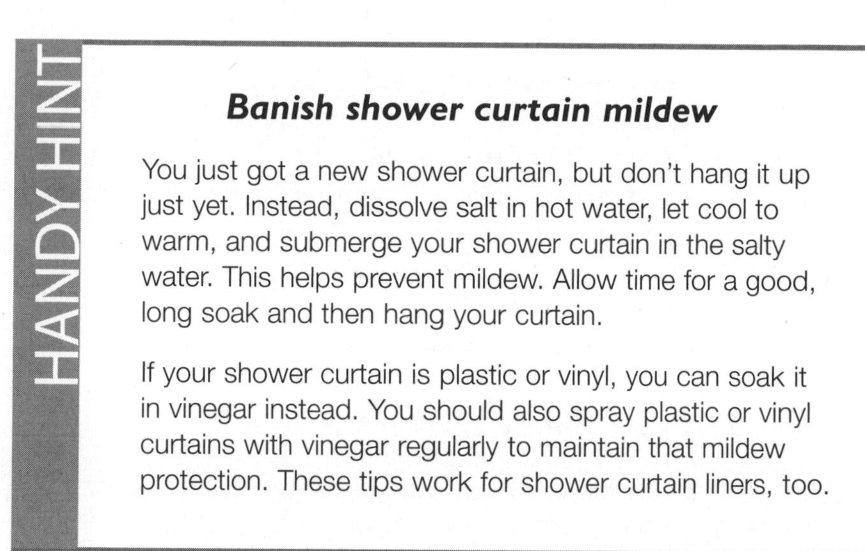

HANDY HINT

Banish shower curtain mildew

You just got a new shower curtain, but don't hang it up just yet. Instead, dissolve salt in hot water, let cool to warm, and submerge your shower curtain in the salty water. This helps prevent mildew. Allow time for a good, long soak and then hang your curtain.

If your shower curtain is plastic or vinyl, you can soak it in vinegar instead. You should also spray plastic or vinyl curtains with vinegar regularly to maintain that mildew protection. These tips work for shower curtain liners, too.

Three shower door cleaners hiding in your kitchen. You ran out of shower door cleaner, and you don't want to go to the store. No problem. Check your kitchen for one of these handy shower door cleaners.

- Vinegar. White vinegar is cheap, but it can still dissolve that nasty soap film on your glass shower door. Just pour enough vinegar on a sponge to dampen it well, and rub the vinegar over your entire door. Bathe the track of your sliding shower door with full-strength vinegar to make it like new. Let the vinegar sit in the track for a few minutes and then rinse.

- Dishwashing liquid. The same dishwashing liquid you use to hand wash dishes can cut soap scum and bring the shine back to your shower door – even where other bathroom cleaners have failed. All you have to do is clean the door with a mixture of warm water and dishwashing liquid.

- Lemon juice. Dampen a sponge with lemon juice and wipe down your shower doors. This won't cost much, but your shower doors may end up looking like a million bucks.

Make your own shower scum fighter. Say sayonara to shower scum. Stir one tablespoon of borax and two teaspoons of dishwashing liquid into three cups of hot water. After the borax dissolves, add one-half cup of white vinegar. Pour this potion into a spray bottle, shake, and use it to clean your shower.

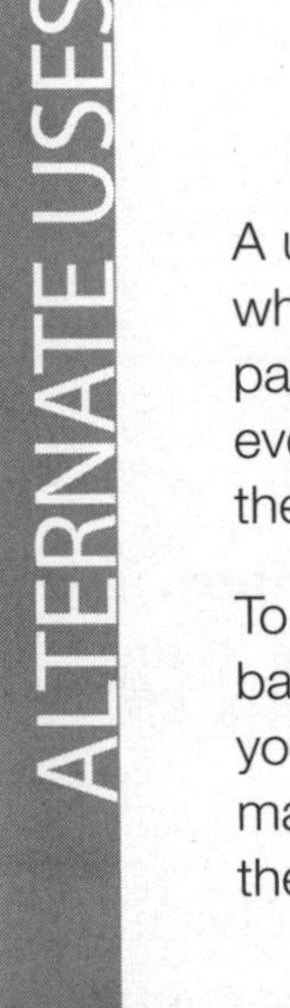

Get a handy shaker for free

A used shaker-top jar makes a good baking soda shaker when you need to scour your bathroom, so check your pantry. A jumbo spice shaker from the warehouse store or even an old sugar or cheese shaker may be perfect for the job after their contents are used up.

To try this, clean a shaker-top jar thoroughly, pour in some baking soda, and see how well it works when cleaning your bathroom. If the first jar is a flop, try another one. You may need to experiment with different containers to find the one that works best.

Scrub your tub with baking soda. Baking soda can get your tub and shower sparkling clean without fumes or toxic chemicals, and it costs less than a brand-name bathroom cleaner.

According to the Arm & Hammer company, baking soda is safe for tile, chrome, steel, enamel, and plastic, so use it as a gentle scouring powder for your tub, shower, sinks, and bathroom counters.

Simply dampen a sponge, sprinkle baking soda on it, wipe the surface, and rinse with warm water. Just be sure to put some extra baking soda on your sponge before attacking that bathtub ring.

4 ways to fight mildew without bleach. Sure, bleach will kill bathroom mildew, but who wants to breathe those fumes in a tiny room? Try these kinder, gentler mildew removers instead.

- Spray grout and tile mildew with a mixture of water and white vinegar and wipe clean. For more stubborn mildew, apply undiluted vinegar by hand, let sit for a while, then scrub and wipe clean. Once you have restored your dirty tile, protect it from future mildew invasions. Mix one-half cup of rubbing alcohol, three cups of water, and one tablespoon of liquid laundry detergent in a spray bottle. Spray this mixture on your tiled bathroom walls after each shower.

- Mix four parts hydrogen peroxide with one part water. Put on gloves, apply this mixture directly to the mildew, let sit for five minutes, and scrub. You'll kill the mildew fast, and your shower and tub will be sparkling in no time. Best of all, you can make this simple, two-ingredient cleaner yourself – for just pennies.

- Make a paste of water and borax, apply to mildew, and scrub clean. Wear gloves for this one. It packs some power.

- Wash your mildewed shower curtain in hot soapy water and rub lemon juice on the mildew. Let the curtain dry in a spot that gets full sun most of the day. You've just rescued your shower curtain from its date with the trash can.

Zap mold and fungus with baking soda. Kill molds and other types of fungus without using harsh and toxic bleach. Use baking soda, instead. It's cheap, it's an effective cleaning powder, and you probably have some in your kitchen right now. Mix baking soda with water to form a paste, and apply it to the mold. Don't rinse off.

Remember, mold can be very hazardous, especially if you breathe it in, so wear gloves and a mask when getting rid of it.

HANDY HINT

Stop mildew before it starts

The bottom of your shower curtain acts like a magnet for mildew and mold, but don't bother cleaning it. Instead, just trim off that part and you may never deal with a scummy shower curtain again.

14 tips to cut your water bill Your water bill may be a lot higher than it should be. "Easy-to-fix leaks in the average American home waste enough water each year to fill a backyard swimming pool," said Peter Silva, assistant administrator for the Environmental Protection Agency's Office of Water.

That's why you should check for leaks in your appliances, faucets, toilets, and outdoor sprinkler system, or any other device that uses water. Find and fix hidden leaks and you'll be surprised at how much your water bill drops.

Here are 13 more ways to trim your water bill.

- Install high-efficiency toilets that use 1.6 gallons of water per flush instead of the three gallons or more used by toilets made before 1992.
- Wash only full loads of dishes and laundry.

- Take shorter showers and never take baths.
- Stop dollars from going down the drain during your shower every morning. Put a bucket in the shower while you wait for the water to warm, and collect water from the faucet while waiting for it to reach the right temperature. Use this water to give your potted plants a drink instead of running extra water from the tap.
- Put mulch around your plants to retain moisture, so you won't have to water as much.
- Install low-flow faucet aerators.
- Rinse with water from a cup instead of running the faucet while brushing your teeth.
- Replace your ancient washing machine with a water-saving ENERGY STAR machine.
- Compost more so you can use your garbage disposal less.
- Use drip irrigation to water your garden.
- Choose plants for your yard that are well-suited to your climate and soil, and emphasize plants that are drought-resistant or don't require much water.
- Collect water from your downspout in a rain barrel, so you can water your outdoor plants for free.
- Don't use your dishwasher's pre-rinse cycle or pre-rinse the dishes by hand.

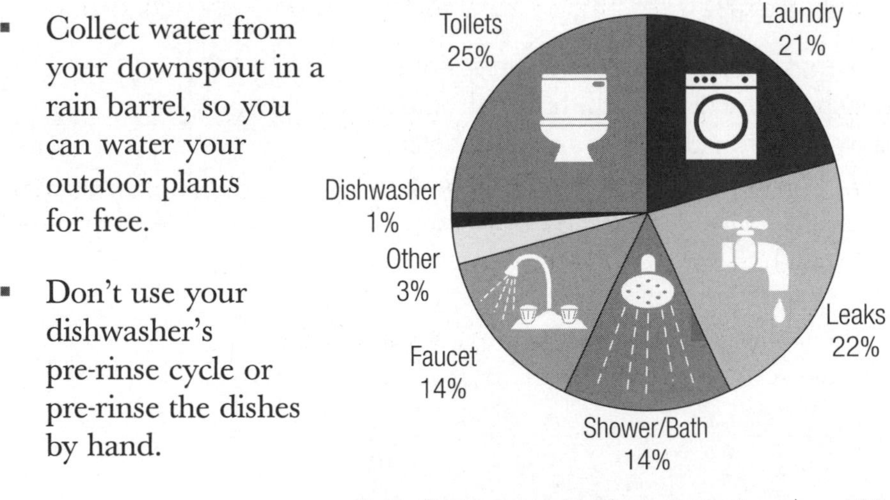

Lazy way to remove rust stains. Make sure your tub or sink is clean and dry, and then cover the rust stain with a very thick layer of salt. Gently wet the salt with lemon juice so the salt becomes soggy, but stays in place over the rust. Let it sit overnight. The citric acid in the lemon juice can work on the rust stain while you sleep. Just rinse thoroughly with hot water the next morning.

For a tougher stain, put on a pair of gloves and make a paste from cream of tartar and a little hydrogen peroxide. Scrub this into the stain using a toothbrush.

Sometimes the stain is on the side of your tub or sink, so the rust remover refuses to stick. In that case, sponge the rust with white vinegar. When you rinse the vinegar away, the rust stain should wash away, too. If you have a more stubborn rust stain, apply kerosene to a cloth, rub the kerosene into the rust, wash with soapy water, and rinse.

Put soap slivers to good use. You hate throwing away leftover soap slivers, but sticking them to the new soap doesn't work. Try this instead. Put a small pile of slivers into an old sock, one leg of knee-high panty hose, or one cutoff leg of regular pantyhose. Loop the sock or hose into a knot and use it as a soapy sponge in the shower. You can also slit a sponge and push in the soap slivers.

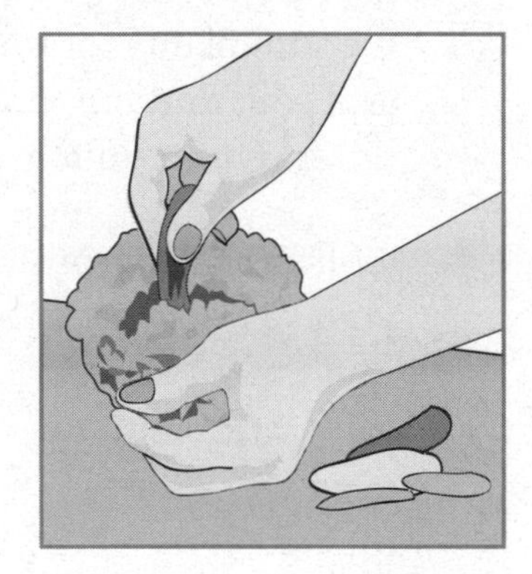

Or make a super soaper from an old washcloth. Fold the cloth in half and sew up two sides. Sew strips of Velcro on the open side so you can close it, and slip in your soap slivers.

Chapter 6

ELECTRONICS

Electronics constantly make your life better. Cellphones help you manage emergencies and keep in touch. Computers and printers help you shop online, compose documents, and print copies. DVDs save information and offer convenient entertainment, while digital cameras help preserve treasured memories. Yet, these electronics can become nuisances if they stop working or meet with an accident. Prevent problems by taking smart steps to protect your gadgets.

CELLPHONES
Hang up on bad connections

Help your cellphone battery last longer. Extend your cellphone battery's life and go longer between charges with these tips.

- Shut off your phone when you don't need to use it, like right before you go to bed.
- Turn off your phone or put it into airplane or standby mode if you expect to be in an area of poor reception for more than a few minutes. Your phone uses extra power when it searches for a signal from a cellphone tower, especially when the signal is weak. Regularly check your "bars," the indicator for good or bad reception, so you become familiar with "dead zones" you enter frequently.
- Turn off your phone's backlight unless you expect to use it often.
- Avoid storing your phone in hot places, such as inside your car or in direct sunlight. Heat speeds up the aging of your cellphone battery and shortens its life.
- Charge your phone for at least 30 minutes after the low battery indicator appears. Do this as soon as the indicator appears, or you may discharge your phone battery too much. Many cellphone batteries die from this problem. For best results, charge your phone before it reaches "empty" at least three out of every four times you charge.
- Check the battery indicator when your phone rings. That helps you recognize when you are running out of power and need to keep a call short.
- Look through your phone's instruction manual to discover any features, such as Wi-Fi, that use extra power when you

are not actively using them. Learn how to turn those features off and on so you can temporarily disable them anytime you don't need them.

- Avoid using "vibrate" and ring tones at the same time. Choose ring tones most of the time, and only turn on the vibrate option when the situation calls for it.

- Set your screen's brightness a little lower or, if you have the option, set it to "auto" so it can adjust to use lower light when less light is needed.

- Choose wallpaper that is not animated, preferably something still and black.

WARNING

Rescue your battery from a fiery doom

Your car's glove compartment may seem like the best place to hide your cellphone while you enjoy some fun in the sun, but don't do it. The inside of your car is even hotter than the outside temperature, and that broiling heat can overheat your cellphone battery — and might even fry it to death. Find a cooler storage spot for your cellphone, such as your picnic basket or beach bag.

How to save a wet cellphone. Your cellphone just made a big splash, but you can still save it – if you hurry. The key is to dry it as quickly as possible.

Snatch the phone out of the liquid and remove the battery and Subscriber Identity Module (SIM) card, the little card that stores information. Wipe the water off the card, the battery, and the phone. Shake out the phone and unscrew the back. Use a vacuum cleaner or shop vac – not a blow dryer – to remove water from inside the phone, but don't let the vacuum cleaner touch the phone. If possible, gently clean the phone's insides with a cleaning spray made for electrical contact.

Gather some silica gel packets, the kind used in some vitamin and pill bottles to keep the contents dry. Place a layer of these in a box, place your phone on top, and close the box. If you don't have enough silica gel packets, use dry, uncooked rice grains instead. Let the phone dry in the box for at least 48 hours before you turn it on. If the phone doesn't power up, replace the battery and try again.

The Consumer Product Safety Commission warns against using a water-damaged phone because the circuitry may slowly corrode and pose a safety hazard, even if the phone seems to work normally after it dries. That's why you must dry your phone quickly instead of letting it dry naturally. The longer moisture stays in your phone, the higher the odds that corrosion will occur.

COMPUTERS

The school of hard drives

Save money on printer ink. The font you choose for a document can make a surprising difference in how often you need to buy printer ink or toner cartridges. A recent study by Printer.com revealed that documents printed in Times New Roman typeface use significantly less ink than the same documents printed in another font at the same font size. Research by *Consumer Reports* confirms these results.

Printing in Century Gothic requires even less ink than Times New Roman. However, you may use more paper because Century Gothic is a wider font. Other cost-saving fonts include Ecofont, Courier, and Courier New. Some of these fonts are already on your computer, but you may need to visit *www.ecofont.com* to download the Ecofont demo software.

Meanwhile, beware of expensive ink hogs like Verdana, Tahoma, Arial, and Franklin Gothic Medium. Estimates suggest you could save up to 60 percent on ink just by switching from these ink-guzzling fonts to Times New Roman or Century Gothic.

Times New Roman	Uses less ink
Verdana	Uses more ink

Unusual way to protect yourself against ID theft. Before you make a photocopy of your tax return, consider this. Many of today's copiers record an image of your copy on a digital hard drive. If the copier owner fails to erase the hard drive before selling the machine, the new owner can view an image of your tax return and use it for identity theft. In fact, a CBS news report confirmed this.

This does not mean you should never make a copy of anything again. Instead, take these steps to protect yourself.

- Avoid copying private information on public copiers, like the ones you find at libraries or grocery stores. Also be careful about providing paper copies of sensitive information to copy centers, like Kinko's, where you may not be the person who makes the copy.

- If you must copy private information on a public copier, at a copy center, or even on your employer's copier, ask questions first. Find out whether the copier has a hard drive. Not all of them do. If the copier doesn't have a hard drive, make your copy.

- If the copier has a hard drive, ask if the copier owner has a policy or procedure to either erase or protect old copies so they can't be viewed. If no policy is in place, make your copy elsewhere.

- Buy a combination copier-scanner-printer so you can make your copies at home. Check your manual, call the manufacturer, or visit the maker's website to find out how to remove recorded images from your home copier.

MYTHBUSTER

Discover new and improved recycled printer paper

Experts warned years ago that using recycled paper in your printer was an invitation for trouble. They reported that recycled paper could contribute to poor printing results, printer jams, and maintenance problems. But times have changed.

Today's improved recycled paper can easily compete with brand new, unrecycled paper. You no longer need to worry about jams or maintenance problems from recycled printer paper. What's more, using this paper will not void your laser or inkjet printer warranty.

The only real difference between new paper and recycled paper is that recycled paper may be less bright, less thick, and may make text and graphics slightly less sharp. Fortunately, these differences are so small most people probably won't notice.

Using recycled printer paper saves trees and keeps paper out of landfills. Compare the price of recycled printer paper to the paper you use now. You may find making the switch is easier than you ever imagined possible.

Unleash the extra ink in your printer. Your laser printer has just warned you it's running out of toner, the ink your printer uses. But don't rush to change your toner cartridge just yet. It may still have plenty of ink. Check your printer manual for instructions on how to remove the toner cartridge. After you remove it, shake it from side to side several times, and put it back into the printer.

This trick may not work for every kind of printer and cartridge, but shaking some cartridges redistributes the toner. It's possible you could continue printing for weeks before you really need to change the cartridge.

Banish germs and filth from your keyboard. Your keyboard may contain more than 3,000 germs per square inch, according to a University of Arizona study. Those germs can come from spills, crumbs, people with colds or flu, people who don't wash their hands after using the bathroom, or even sticky fingers after lunch. That's why you should clean your keyboard regularly.

Check for keyboard cleaning instructions in your computer's or keyboard's instruction manual. Follow those directions or use these.

- Shut down your computer and unplug your keyboard. If your keyboard has both a power cord and a data cable, disconnect both.
- Make sure you have a soft, lint-free or microfiber cloth and some rubbing (isopropyl) alcohol available. You also need a can of compressed air with a straw nozzle or a vacuum cleaner with a dusting brush and nozzle attachment.
- If you bought a can of compressed air, use the instructions on the can to blast crumbs and other debris from your keyboard. If you prefer a vacuum cleaner, carefully vacuum your keyboard with the hose attachment and dusting brush.
- Flip the keyboard over so the keys face downward. Shake it a few times to dislodge crumbs and other hidden debris.
- Turn the keyboard upright, dampen your cloth with rubbing alcohol, and wipe down the keyboard – including its underside.
- Let the keyboard dry completely.
- Reconnect the keyboard to the computer, and turn the computer back on.

If you spill a drink on your desktop keyboard, turn off the computer and clean the keyboard right away. Disconnect the keyboard, turn it over, and shake out any liquid that has pooled beneath the keys. Dampen a cloth lightly with rubbing alcohol, and wipe down any keys that are sticky. Let the keyboard dry before you reconnect it to your computer.

To make your keyboard even easier to clean, you can buy a flexible plastic cover. It slips over the key tops and tightly hugs the sides of each key. This means crumbs and dust accumulate on top of the cover instead of burrowing under the keys – so you no longer need to clean the spaces between keys.

Make a free keyboard protector in seconds. Protect your keyboard from dust bunnies, pet hair, and spills when you are not using it. Slide a plastic grocery bag over the cord-free end and tie the bag handles loosely around the end where the cord is attached. If you don't have a grocery bag, use a plastic place mat or a shoe box lid. You can even customize the shoe box lid by using a hole punch to make an opening for the cord.

Replace a missing manual for free. You need the user manual for your computer or printer, but you can't find it – or perhaps you got your computer secondhand and never had a manual. Luckily, you can get that manual for free in just a few minutes. Make sure you have the brand name or manufacturer, product name, and model number of the item. Then go to your computer and visit *www.retrevo.com*.

Scroll to the bottom of the page and click on the "Manuals" link. Navigate through a few menus and you will find your manual. Fortunately, the site doesn't just provide computer manuals. You may also find manuals for many other electronic devices – including cellphones, televisions, dishwashers, and more.

If you can't find the manual on Retrevo, don't give up hope. Visit the manufacturer's website and click on the link for "Support." Then look for links that say "User manuals," "User guides," "Documentation," or something similar. After a little hunting, you will usually find a link to download the manual for free.

No matter where you find your manual, the document is usually in PDF format. This means you need to download the free Acrobat Reader program from *www.adobe.com* before you can read the manual. This is easy to do and will be useful when you download other manuals in the future.

WARNING

What to do before you donate your computer

That computer you are about to donate or recycle could end up in the wrong hands, putting you at risk for identity theft. Even if you delete all your old passwords, tax returns, email, financial information, and other private files, you may not be protected.

When you put files in the Trash or Recycle Bin, you only remove the directions to find the files, not the files' content. This is similar to what would happen if someone removed all the street signs from your neighborhood. Finding your house would take longer, but people would still find it eventually. Likewise, identity thieves can still find private information even if you "delete" it. So back up the files you want to keep, and then try one of these options instead.

- Clean your hard drive using software that wipes the drive many times instead of just once. This ensures that no trace of your private information is left behind. Both commercial and free software is available to help you do this.
- Remove the hard drive before putting the computer out to pasture. You can either do this yourself or pay the Geek Squad a small fee to do it for you.

DVDs

No-sweat high tech

How to repair a scratched CD or DVD. You can repair even badly scratched CDs and DVDs, and save yourself 10 bucks or more on a replacement. Just hunt for the scratch and try one of these clever tricks.

- Buff out the scratch with toothpaste. It's just abrasive enough to do the job. Use regular toothpaste, not the gel kind. Squeeze a little toothpaste on to a soft, lint-free cloth or cotton ball. Gently rub the cloth over the scratch, starting at the center of the disc and rubbing outward to the edge. Rub each section of the scratch at least eight times, adding more toothpaste, as needed. Rinse off the toothpaste with warm water and let the CD dry completely before you play it. If the scratch isn't fixed, try buffing it with toothpaste again, but this time keep buffing for three times as long. This buff-and-rinse technique may also fix scratches on DVDs.

- Fill the scratch with furniture polish. Douse a microfiber cloth with furniture polish, such as Pledge, and rub the scratch on your CD. For a DVD scratch, spray the DVD with furniture polish and use the microfiber cloth to rub off the polish.

- If a CD is not badly scratched, hold the CD by its edges and the center hole so the scratched side is facing out. Position the CD a few inches from a 60-watt light bulb and slowly rotate the CD so the entire top surface becomes very warm. Play the CD immediately.

Help your DVDs last longer. You spent your hard-earned money on a DVD, so you hate the thought of throwing it out after just a few years. Make sure that doesn't happen. Protect your DVDs from damage and accidents with these tips.

- Hold the disc by its edges and the center rim. This prevents damage to the data portion, the part of the DVD's surface where the movie or other contents are stored.

- Don't tempt fate. Keep your DVDs as far from food and drinks as possible.

- Put your DVDs in their cases when you aren't using them. This prevents scratches and helps protect the discs from dust and damage.

- Store the discs in a cool, dry place. Keep them out of direct sunlight, as well as high heat and humidity.

- Avoid placing a heavy object on top of a DVD.
- Never use a ballpoint pen or a pencil to label your DVDs. Even permanent markers can cause trouble. Use only nonsolvent felt-tip pens, like Sharpies, and be careful to write only on the label portion of the disc.
- Don't bend the disc.

HANDY HINT

Fast fix for faulty DVDs

That DVD from the library or video store may not be as defective as you thought. It might merely be dirty, not damaged. Blow the dust off the DVD and clean it, but make sure you clean it properly.

Dampen a soft, lint-free cloth with a little rubbing alcohol. You might be tempted to scrub or wipe in little circles, just as you would when cleaning other items. But wiping in circles may damage your disc.

Instead, start at the center of the disc and wipe outward to the edge. Gradually rotate the disc so your wiping pattern resembles the spokes of a wheel. Wipe the entire disc. Let the DVD dry completely and try to play it again. You may discover that your formerly defective DVD works just fine now.

PHOTOGRAPHS

Your life in pictures

Preserve your precious old photographs. You want to keep your albums and boxes of old photographs forever, but some of them are beginning to show their age. Even if you own a scanner, you can't imagine how you would find time to correct and scan your endless photo collection. But you don't have to scan for hours – you don't even have to buy a scanner. You can record and repair your photos digitally with help from an online scanning service.

At first, it might sound silly to have someone scan your photographs for you, but scanning services do more than that. They not only scan prints, but also slides, negatives, and more. In fact, they can even retouch the scans of your pictures. For example, a scanning service may remove scratches, correct red-eye, or restore color if a photo has become discolored.

Before you try a scanning service, visit their website to learn how to use their services and discover what features they offer. Some sites provide extensive help sections, learning pages, and tips. The service will probably ask you to start an account, fill out an online order form, and mail your photos to them. A good service provides frequent email on the status of your package or a UPS tracking number. Your photos are shipped back to you after scanning.

The scanning takes roughly four weeks. After that, you can probably review your scanned images online and choose which ones to purchase, but some services and pricing plans may work differently. Double-check to be sure.

You can usually choose how to receive your scanned images. They can be put on a CD, DVD, or an external hard drive, or they can be stored online. Prices often depend on the number of images scanned, the kind of pictures you send – such as prints, slides, or negatives – shipping costs, and any extra features you choose to add.

Popular scanning services include *www.scancafe.com* and *www.scan digital.com*. If you want to try one of these, start with a small number of photographs, perhaps 10 or 20. This makes the order easier to manage. And, if you like the results, you can send a much larger batch the next time you order.

Safest way to rescue wet pictures. Don't throw away your photographs just because they got soaked. You can save them if you act quickly. The sooner you salvage your photos, the less damaged they'll be.

A quick rescue may be tough if you have a lot of wet photos. But remember, if you have undamaged negatives for some of your photos, you can get reprints made. Concentrate on the photos that cannot be reprinted.

Get submerged photos out of the water immediately and gather any other photos that are still damp. If you have photos that are stuck to their frames or glass – or stuck to an album – only remove them if you won't cause any damage.

If you decide to risk extracting the photo yourself, take a picture of the photo or have it scanned in the frame first. The new picture may be useful if part of the old photo remains stuck after you detach the rest of the picture. You should also take pictures of your other photos as soon as you can see a clear image.

Dry loose photos as quickly as possible. According to the Federal Emergency Management Agency, you can gently wash and rinse the photos in clean water first, if needed. But remember that wet photos are very fragile, so only handle them by their edges.

To dry the photos, place them face up in a single layer on a clean, flat surface, such as a cloth, window screen, paper towels, or plastic. Choose a drying area without direct sunlight that's safe from animals and children. To help prevent mold, pick an area with good air circulation or use a fan, air conditioner, or open window to help dry your photos.

These tips will work for most photos, but not all. Your best chance of recovering your pictures is to consult with a photograph conservator right from the start. Keep in mind you may also need professional help from a photo retoucher or photo lab to save or reproduce photos that are moldy, stuck together, or very old.

To find a conservator, contact the American Institute for Conservation of Historic and Artistic Works for a list of conservators near you. Call 202-452-9545 or visit *www.conservation-us.org*.

WARNING

Unstick stuck-together photos with floss

Two of your precious photos are stuck together. You might be tempted to pull them apart, but experts advise against it. Only try to separate the photos if you have a digital copy of each photo, undamaged negatives, or another way to replace them if they become damaged during separation. If the photos are valuable or very important to you, contact a photo conservator for help right away.

If you still want to risk separating the photos yourself, find a Teflon dental floss, such as Glide. Cut a length of the dental floss and ask someone to hold the pictures steady for you. Gently and carefully work the floss between the photos to ease them apart.

Take blink-free group photos. You have yet to figure out a way to keep people from blinking during a group shot. There's good news – the days of closed-eye photographs may soon be over. According to Australia's Commonwealth Scientific and Industrial Research Organization, physicist Piers Barnes has discovered a formula that virtually eliminates the problem.

If your group contains 20 people or less, count the number of people in your shot. Divide that number by 3 if you have good lighting or divide by 2 if the lighting is poor. The result is the number of pictures you must snap to produce one blink-free picture. So if your group contains 12 people, you should take four shots in better lighting or six shots in lousy lighting.

For best results, warn people not to blink and immediately take all your shots as quickly as possible.

Chapter 7

YOUR LAWN & GARDEN

"A garden is never so good as it will be next year," said Thomas Cooper, a 19th century political philosopher. And he was right. Most gardeners are always looking for better ways to garden. If you are one of those gardeners, turn the page to find great tips for attracting birds to your yard; getting more from your garden tools; improving your grass, trees, and shrubs; getting rid of pests; and growing prettier flowers and tastier vegetables.

BIRDS

Backyard buddies

Attract birds to your yard. Birds will flock to your yard if you provide food, water, shelter, and safety. Here's how to start.

- Mount bird feeders on poles, and put baffles on the poles to prevent other wildlife from climbing it.

- Don't waste your money on feeds that contain canary seed, oats, wheat, corn, milo, or red millet. Choose regular sunflower seeds, black oil sunflower seeds, or millets other than red millet. If you like cardinals, include safflower seed.

- Get their attention. Birds are attracted to dripping water. Use a nail to poke a hole in the bottom of a can or milk jug, hang the container a few feet above your birdbath, fill with water, and let it drip. Once birds become accustomed to drinking from your bath, you won't need the dripper. Change the bath water every few days so your feathered friends won't get sick.

- Make your birdbath drown-resistant. It should be no deeper than 3 inches at its deepest point and have a rough surface, like concrete, that helps prevent slipping. If your bath is too deep or slippery, add pebbles or gravel to make it more shallow and improve traction.

- Choose a birdbath that sits on a pedestal if cats or other predators frequent your yard, and place it well away from bushes or hedges. Predators may use shrubbery to sneak up on unsuspecting birds.

- Place the birdbath near a tree with overhanging branches, so birds have a nearby place to shake off water and preen after bathing. Wet birds may be too heavy to fly very far or high.

- Select plants that provide food or cover for birds throughout the year, especially when little else is growing. Plants that produce berries and seeds can be good choices for food sources, while evergreens may provide cover during winter.
- Don't bother cleaning up flower seed stalks in autumn. Let the birds clean the seeds out of them instead.

Create a haven for hummingbirds. Your yard doesn't offer any shade for your hummingbird feeder, and you can't seem to convince hummingbirds to visit. Fix both problems with a single, colorful solution.

Hummingbirds love red, so take an old straw hat or a red plastic plate and decorate it with red silk or plastic flowers. If you use a plate, poke a hole in the center, turn it over, and decorate its underside. Using flowers that have wire stems may make the job easier.

When the decorations are secure, attach the hat or the plate so it's centered above the top of your feeder and shades the feeder on all sides. You may be able to hang the plate from the bar that supports your feeder. Otherwise, try some combination of wire, fishing line, and florist's tape to attach the hat or plate.

The red flowers not only add shade, they help attract the hummingbirds' attention. That may be all it takes to make them regular visitors to your feeder. What's more, experts recommend shade for your feeder because the hummingbirds' food spoils more quickly in sunlight.

Make your own wild bird treats. Forget those complicated winter treat recipes. Instead, make a three-ingredient base and add extras from your pantry. For the base, you need three cups of suet from your butcher shop or supermarket meat counter, three cups of yellow cornmeal, and one cup of chunky peanut butter.

Melt the suet in a pan, mix in the cornmeal and peanut butter, and add extras such as birdseed, raisins, rolled oats, or unsalted nuts without the shells. Press this mixture into pine cones, put in a suet feeder, or use citrus halves.

To use a citrus half, scoop the pulp out of half an orange or grapefruit, poke two holes in opposite sides of the rind. Tie the ends of an 18-inch piece of heavy yarn or wire into both holes for a hanger. Load your bird treat mixture into it. Hang it outside and watch the birds enjoy the feast.

For a summer bird treat, use this no-melt recipe. Melt a pound of lard in a saucepan over medium heat. Add 16 ounces of crunchy peanut butter, stirring until melted. Remove the pan from the heat and stir in six cups of cornmeal, one-half cup of raisins, one cup of sunflower seeds, and five cups of all-purpose flour. Transfer to a pan, let cool, and cut to fit your suet feeder.

HANDY HINT

Fill a hummingbird feeder without spills

You don't need to buy a special spill-proof hummingbird feeder to put an end to your refill problems. You can make any feeder goof-proof for pennies. Take your pick. These options are easy, cheap, and you won't spill a drop.

- Use a turkey baster or squeeze bottle to transfer the liquid from its original container to your feeder.
- Nestle a funnel in the mouth of your feeder and pour in the hummingbird nectar.

Put together a whimsical teacup bird feeder. Teacup bird feeders make great gifts for family and friends – and while you're at it, make one for yourself. To make this bird feeder, you'll need:

- a pretty teacup and saucer from a flea market, garage sale, or thrift mall.

- strong glue, such as epoxy glue, Gorilla Glue, or Super Glue
- 24 inches of three-quarter inch copper pipe.
- a flat-topped pipe cap that fits snugly over one end of the copper pipe.

Choose a location for your bird feeder. Look for a place that's sheltered and easy to see from inside your house. Push the copper pipe into the ground to mark the spot.

Wash the teacup and saucer and let dry completely. Place the saucer on a flat surface and apply glue to the area where the teacup normally sits. Place the teacup in the saucer and press it in place.

Your glue directions should tell you how long to hold it in place to dry. Don't attempt the next step until the glue has dried completely.

Turn the cup and saucer over so the saucer rests on the cup. Apply glue to the pipe cap and press it into the center of the upturned saucer. Hold it in place and let it dry completely.

Take your teacup and saucer out to the copper pipe and slide the pipe cap over the end of the pipe. Fill your feeder with birdseed and enjoy watching your new friends.

Prevent weeds from fallen birdseed. Seeds that fall from your bird feeder can sprout and give you a bumper crop of weeds. Here's how you can stop them from sprouting.

- Bake your birdseed in the microwave before you put it in your feeder. Experts suggest you pour one gallon of seed into a paper bag, and microwave it for five minutes on high.

- Spread the seed on a long, flat pan and bake it in your conventional oven at 300 degrees for 30 minutes.
- Lay a small tarp on the ground under your feeder. Empty it occasionally so a heavy rain won't wash the seeds into your yard.
- Use a shop vacuum to clean up stray seeds several times during the winter when the ground is bare and dry.

GARDENING TOOLS
Dig this

Help garden tools last longer. Lysol and vegetable oil can help keep your tools in tiptop shape for many years. Find out how you can use them to sanitize and store your tools more effectively.

Be ruthless to dirt and germs – clean and disinfect all gardening tools, including shovels and pruning tools after each use. Make sure you get all the dirt and plant debris off when you clean.

Surprisingly, many experts recommend that you disinfect pruning tools after each cut or each plant and disinfect your other tools after cleaning. You can use a mix of one part bleach to nine parts water, but remember that bleach can be corrosive.

If you use it, coat the metal with a thin layer of oil before storing, so the tool won't rust. You can use rubbing alcohol instead of bleach, but it's more expensive. Lysol or Pine-Sol is a better choice.

To protect and maintain those tools, mix sand and vegetable oil in a 5-gallon bucket. Store your hand tools by pushing them into the sand in the bucket. This helps clean and lubricate them. Store your shovel in this bucket between uses during the gardening season and dip it into the bucket once before hanging it up for the winter.

Plant seeds without back pain. Don't let back trouble stop you from planting seeds in your garden. You can sow without bending. Cut a length of PVC pipe between 3 and 4 feet long. Make sure it reaches higher than your waist when you rest one end on the ground. Place the pipe where you want a seed planted and drop the seed through the pipe. Use the end of the pipe to push soil over the seed.

WARNING

What to do before you dig

No matter where you plan to dig in your yard, take a few precautions before you grab your shovel. Contact your local utilities and find out where lines and pipes are located in your yard. The calls and information are free. And make sure you know the locations of wiring and pipes for any landscape lighting, fountains, or water features in your yard, too.

Four outdoor uses for milk jugs. It's a breeze to make any of these nifty garden helpers from an empty, one-gallon or half-gallon milk jug.

- Soil scoop. Cut off the bottom inch from a half-gallon milk jug. Lay the jug on its side with the handle facing up and grab a magic marker. Notice that the handle is on a corner between two sides. On each of these sides, draw a diagonal line that starts near the bottom end of the milk jug and ends an inch or two below the handle. Cut along these diagonal lines and you'll have a scoop that's good for soil and many other things in your garden.

- Portable harvest holder or portable trash can. Cut a hole out of the top corner opposite the handle in a one-gallon milk jug. Use it as a portable holder when you pick berries, cherry tomatoes, or nuts. Cut another jug the same way to create a portable trash can when you are weeding. Cut a wider, deeper hole and you can use the jug as a portable storage bin for small items.

- Plant markers. Cut the plastic sides into strips, label each one with permanent magic marker, and push into the appropriate spot in the ground.

- Cloche or hot cap. Cut off the bottom of a gallon milk jug, place over a young plant, and push down into the ground. This is like putting a tiny greenhouse over the plant to help keep it warm. Leave the cap on to protect against frost. Remove the entire cloche on warm, sunny days so your plant won't get too hot.

Easy care for gardening gloves. Gardening gloves can get sopping wet if you work during the morning dew or right after it rains. Here's a great way to dry them. Remove the bottoms from two small, plastic pots and slip a glove over each one. Set the pots on an old baking rack or dish rack to help them dry.

To store your gloves, clean out a tall, plastic canister or jar with a screw-on or snap-on lid. Good choices include large peanut butter jars from warehouse clubs or a tennis ball canister. Put your gloves in the jar, put the lid on tight, and store your gloves in your garden shed without fear that bugs will burrow inside them.

HANDY HINT

Make a measuring hoe

You're working in your garden, your shoes are muddy, and you need a yardstick that's inside your house. Make sure this never happens again. Paint or notch marks for inches and feet on the wooden handles of your hoes, rakes, shovels, and other tools. The next time you need to measure the planting depth for bulbs or the space between plants, your ruler will be right there waiting for you.

New uses for old rubber gloves. The best thing about buying new rubber gloves is recycling your old ones. Try these tips to help you get started.

- Get organized. Make large rubber bands by cutting the wrist and palm of the glove into strips. Use these strips to bind items together in your tool shed. Or wrap the rubber bands loosely around your string trimmer cord or other cords to keep them coiled up.

- Hang more tools. If the hanging hole in your tool is too small, thread one end of your "rubber band" through the hole. Now one end of the rubber band is behind the hanging hole, while the other end is in front. Use one finger to hold the front end open so you can thread the back end through that loop. Pull it tight so one end surrounds the handle of your tool while the other provides a "hanger" large enough to slip around a hook.

- Make a tool grip. Snip off the glove's fingers at the base and trim the tips. Slip the fingers over the handles of your garden tools.
- End slips and slides. Cut out the palm of the glove. When you bring cut flowers in from your garden, place the palm under your flower vase to provide a nonskid mat.
- Add a garden jar opener. If the lid for your fertilizer or pest control product is too tight, don't run for the jar opener in the kitchen. Instead, keep an old rubber glove with your gardening supplies to use as your garden "jar opener."

GRASS & SHRUBS
Greener acres

Know when to prune for healthy plants. When is the right time to prune your trees and shrubs? It all depends on when they bloom. Use this simple rule of thumb to keep your plants healthy.

Prune spring-flowering shrubs and trees after they flower. These tend to set blooms on branches that were growing during autumn, so pruning before they bloom would remove future flowers. Otherwise, the best time to prune plants that have been dormant during winter is late winter or early spring.

For one thing, it is easier to see which parts of the plant you want to prune before the leaves show up. What's more, if you prune right before the new spring growth begins, the plant recovers from pruning more quickly.

To make pruning easier, find an old shower curtain, frayed vinyl tablecloth, leftover painting drop cloth, or tarp. Place it beneath the tree or shrub before you prune and make sure you keep it positioned beneath the area you are currently pruning. It catches the trimmings, so you spend less time cleaning them up.

Develop a luscious lawn for less. These easy activities are the simplest and least expensive way to keep your lawn looking lovely – and they may mean less work, too.

- Mow at the right height. Winning the war on weeds in your yard begins with this simple strategy. Keep your lawn between 2 and 3 1/2 inches high and never mow off more than one-third of the grass blade. If you mow your lawn too short, more sunshine reaches the ground where the weed seeds are waiting. That extra light helps weeds flourish. Unfortunately, grass that has been scalped reaps less benefit from sunshine, so it is more susceptible to disease, insects, and other enemies. Yet, if you let your grass grow taller, it keeps sunlight off the weeds and develops a deeper root system that helps keep it healthier – even during drought. Best of all, taller grass grows more slowly than short, scalped grass – and that means less mowing.
- Stop bagging clippings. Contrary to popular belief, studies show that small grass clippings do not promote thatch. That means if you never mow off more than a third of the grass blade, you don't need to bag your clippings. Instead, leave those clippings so they can slip down to the ground where they shade the soil and make it hard for weeds to grow. On top of that, your grass clippings may help you save money on

lawn products. "Leaving the clippings recycles nutrients so you'll need less fertilizer," says Marty Petrovic, a turf specialist at Cornell University's Department of Horticulture.

- Keep your mower blade sharp. Sharpen or replace your lawn mower blade at least once a year. A dull blade makes your lawn look bad, makes the grass less resistant to damage and disease, and may cause your grass to need more watering. Keeping the blade sharp leads to a healthier, more gorgeous lawn that may also lower your water bill.

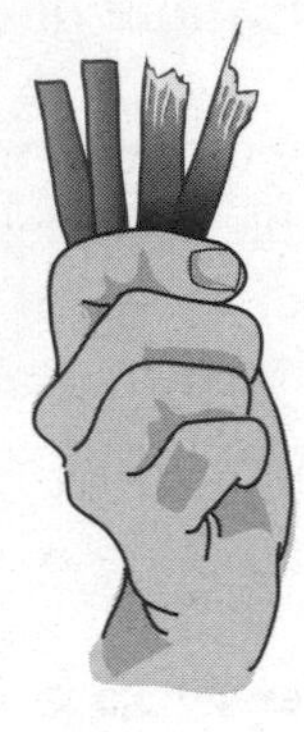

WARNING

Smart way to prevent salt damage to plants

De-icing salt may be absolutely necessary, but it can be very damaging to the plants along your driveway and walkways. The sodium in most regular rock salt de-icers can hamper root growth and limit your plants' ability to absorb the nutrients and water they need. Switch to a calcium chloride de-icer, which is a little less harmful.

For even better results, mix one part calcium chloride de-icing salt with 10 parts sand or kitty litter. This softens or melts snow and ice and provides traction. If any of the frozen stuff is left after you apply this de-icing mix, just sweep or shovel it off your driveway or walkway — but make sure you don't dump it near your plants.

Rescue pond fish from poisonous plants. Before you buy new plants for your garden pond, make sure they are not toxic to the fish that live there. Your fish may eat the roots and other parts of any pond-dwelling plants.

Plants nearby your pond can be dangerous too, especially if they drop anything into the pond. That includes leaves, berries, seeds, sap, stems, or flowers. So keep your fish happy and healthy by avoiding plants like these.

Plants poisonous to pond fish		
amaryllis	anemone	angel's trumpet
apricot trees	autumn crocus	azaleas
bird-of-paradise flower	black walnut	bleeding heart
buckeye	carnation	castor bean
chokecherry	cherry trees	climbing nightshade
columbine	daffodil	daphne
day lily	delphinium	deadly nightshade
Easter lily	English ivy	euphorbia
flowering tobacco	foxglove	gloriosa lily
Christmas rose	hemlock	holly
honeysuckle	jack-in-the-pulpit	java bean
Japanese laurel	jasmine	mountain laurel
lantana	larkspur	lily of the valley
lobelia	milkweed	mistletoe
mock orange	monkshood	morning glory
poppy	potato	peach trees
periwinkle	plum trees	privet
redwood	rhododendron	snapdragon
sweet pea	tiger lily	tomato
trumpet vine	wisteria	yew

Fertilize your lawn with free ashes. The wood ashes from your fireplace may be just the fertilizer your lawn needs, some experts say. Wood ashes provide potassium and phosphorous. They are also very alkaline, so they can help improve soil that is too acidic. But be careful. Don't spread wood ashes close to acid-loving plants, like azaleas or blueberry, and don't use wood ash on alkaline soil.

If you aren't sure whether your soil is alkaline or acid, ask your local cooperative extension agent how to do a soil test and how much it costs. The test is usually very cheap. If you already know your soil is acidic, ask the agent how much ash to spread on your lawn. A little may go a long way.

Defend your shrubs against winter. Instead of buying a whole load of products to protect your shrubs against winter's onslaught, perhaps you can use items you already have. Check with your local cooperative extension agent for the shrub protection tactics that work best in your climate. Then see if these tips can help you save money.

- Create a wind screen. If your shrub is small enough, a teepee of branches tied off at the top may do the job. Use evergreen branches, if they are available. For a larger bush, pound three or four wooden stakes into the ground so their tops are a little higher than your shrub. Grab an old sheet or blanket you no longer want. Make sure the sheet can reach from the top of the stakes to the bottom, then staple it to the stakes so you surround your bush. For a temporary wind shelter, you can use Bubble Wrap instead.

- Place evergreen branches, a thick layer of raked leaves, or another inexpensive mulch around the base of your shrubs. This retains moisture, helps resist foliage browning, and helps prevent root damage from frost heaving.

- To protect shrubs from frost, cover them with unwanted drapes, old sheets, tarps, fabric, burlap, or even an old car cover. Use stakes or a frame to keep your cover from touching the buds, blooms, or leaves. And make sure the bottom edge of the cover rests on the ground, so the plant is fully enclosed. Don't forget to remove your cover the next day if warm daytime temperatures are expected.

HANDY HINT

Simple plan to sow grass seed evenly

This trick works for both fertilizer and grass seed. Mix flour into your fertilizer or grass seed before you spread it. The flour acts like a highlighter pen for your yard, showing where you have already put down the fertilizer or seed. Even if you get distracted, you won't have to worry about missing — or overloading — any part of your yard.

Cut ornamental grasses without the mess. It's time to trim your ornamental grass, and you're not looking forward to picking up cut blades of grass off the ground. But this year will be different because you will do less clean up. Here's how. If your garbage collectors allow you to dump trimmings in your trash can, bring the can near the plants you will be working on.

Before trimming each plant, grab a bungee cord, rope, or some duct tape, and wrap it around the grass above where you plan to cut. Make sure this "holder" won't come loose and then start trimming. When done, you should have a neatly wrapped bundle on the ground, and you can dispose of it easily in the nearby trash can.

Secret to safe off-season pruning. The correct time to prune your favorite tree was months ago, but dead and low-growing branches are a problem now. Fortunately, you may not need to wait. Experts say you should avoid pruning 15 percent or more of the top of the tree except during its correct pruning season. But light pruning – less than 10 percent of the plant – can be done any time of year.

Be careful if the tree is an oak or elm because pruning these hardwoods at the wrong time of year can lead to tree-killing diseases. Play it safe and contact your local cooperative extension agent for advice before pruning these trees.

OUTDOOR PESTS
Banish bugs, slugs & garden thugs

13 natural ways to defeat garden troublemakers. Pest problems? You'll find over a dozen natural kitchen staples that can battle ants, mice, mosquitoes, and more. Just keep reading.

- Vinegar. Spray vinegar or a vinegar-and-water mix anywhere you want to repel ants.
- Hot pepper sauce. Mix two tablespoons of hot sauce and two teaspoons of mild dishwashing liquid into a gallon of water. Spray this mixture on plants to keep deer from eating them.
- Peppermint oil. Soak a cotton ball in peppermint oil or peppermint extract, and place it where mice have been visiting.

- Black pepper. To repel rodents, try sprinkling black pepper around your garden plants and on your compost pile. If you know where they live, sprinkle pepper in and around there, too.

- Cloves. Snip an old pair of pantyhose into sections, tie off one end of each section, fill it with whole cloves, and tie off the other end. Tuck these sachets into drawers and closets to get rid of moths.

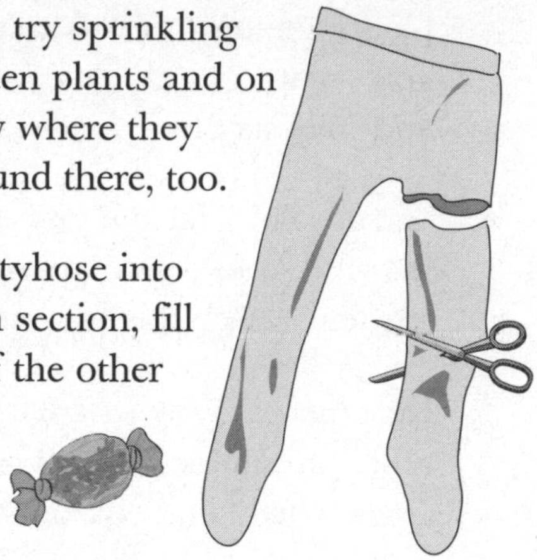

- Dish soap. Mix one tablespoon of mild dishwashing liquid – not dishwasher detergent – in a gallon of water. Apply this to your plants to repel or kill red spider mites, thrips, mealy bugs, and aphids. Like store-bought insecticidal soap, this may burn the leaves on some sensitive plants. Test a small area before applying to the whole plant.

- Salt. If you know how the ants are getting into your house, spread a layer of salt in their path. They will make a U-turn. To fight fire ants, switch to Epsom salts. Pour an inch over their mounds and another inch around the mound.

- Garlic. Put two cups of water and one garlic bulb in your blender. Blend, strain, and pour into a spray bottle. Coat the leaves and stems of plants under attack from whiteflies, beetles, deer, or aphids. This only stops pests for a week, but it may last longer if you add a few drops of mild liquid soap, like pure Castile soap.

- Tea leaves. Surround a plant with a circle of tea leaves and coffee grounds to keep slugs away.

- Crushed eggshells. Crush some eggshells, and spread them around a plant that needs protection from slugs. The slugs can't handle those sharp edges.

- Coffee grounds. Sprinkle coffee grounds on anthills or anywhere you want to repel ants. Deer also don't like the smell of coffee and may stay away.

- Citrus rind. Halve a grapefruit, scoop out the pulp, and place the rind, round side up, near a slug-damaged plant in your garden. Check this trap once a day for slugs.

- Rosemary. Grow rosemary in your yard or in a pot to help repel mosquitoes. Sprinkle rosemary and sage on barbecue coals when you cook outside to keep the annoying pests away.

Squirrel-proof your bulbs. Try one or more of these ideas to keep those digging nibblers away from your tulips and other bulbs.

- Offend their noses. Spray the bulbs with something that smells horrid before you plant them. This can be a repellent like Critter Ridder, Ropel, or Liquid Fence. Squirrels despise the smell and leave your bulbs alone.

- Cage your bulbs. Fashion a cage around your bulbs when you plant. Dig your bulb-planting trench, and lay a long strip of hardware cloth or chicken wire at the bottom. Deposit soil on the bottom strip, followed by your bulbs. Place more soil over the bulbs, and rest the top strip on that soil. Fasten the edges of the strips together using wire, twist ties, or zip ties. Cover both bulbs and cage with soil.

- Leave no trace. Clean up thoroughly after planting bulbs. Make sure no outer shells or portions of outer shells, scraps of bulb bags, or parts of the bulb remain on the ground to alert squirrels that a bulb is below.

- Screen them out. The freshly dug dirt may also catch a squirrel's interest. Squelch it by laying an old window screen over the area until the ground stops looking different from the surrounding dirt. For extra protection, rest a rock on each corner of the screen. For more lasting protection, lay chicken wire over the area where you plant your bulb. Unlike screens, this can stay put until the bulbs begin to emerge.

- Feed the squirrels. Squirrels can be distracted by food that is easier to get. You may be surprised at how well this works.

HANDY HINT

Make friends with rodent-resistant bulbs

You can prevent mice, gophers, and squirrels from digging up or eating your bulbs, particularly if you are ready to switch to new flowers or you are planting bulbs for the first time. Just plant the kind they don't like.

Bulbs that are poisonous or intensely disliked by these four-legged pests include daffodils, narcissus, camassia, fritillaria, alliums, bulb irises, snowdrops, ivy-leafed cyclamen, chionodoxa, magic lily, Spanish bluebells, and Siberian squill.

New way to win the war on moles. Pesky moles may be the enemy of neat yards and undamaged plants, but getting rid of them is tough. So here's how to make them your allies instead.

First, protect your plants with a barrier. This is usually best for beds and rows of plants. You need a sheet metal or hardware cloth that is long enough to surround the area and is at least 25 inches wide. Dig a trench that is 10 inches wide and between 15 and 24 inches deep. Make sure it surrounds the bed or row.

Shape your barrier into a backward "L" that points away from the plants it protects. Rest the barrier in the bottom of the trench so several inches of metal remain above the soil. Refill the trench.

Now you can start reaping the benefits of moles. This old-time gardener's trick still works today. Collect the molehill soil, mix it with some compost, and you may not need to buy potting soil. Not only is molehill soil almost completely weed-free, but mole tunneling also helps loosen and aerate the soil and mixes deep soil with surface materials. The end result is a higher-quality, fertile soil your plants will love.

If you don't need potting soil, you can still put molehill soil to good use. Just spread or scatter the soil over your lawn as a top dressing. Moles may also help if you have a grub or Japanese beetle problem because they will eat up those pests.

HANDY HINT

Win a sweet victory over slugs

Pour your favorite cola into pie tins, jar lids, or some other wide, flat dish with a steep rim. Slugs are lured into your trap by the sweetness of the drink. Once they fall in, they can't get back out.

Scare off gophers, mice, and moles. The Animal Humane Society suggests a spicy sauce remedy to repel these types of rodents. Mix together one tablespoon of peppermint oil, one tablespoon of Tabasco sauce, one teaspoon of chili powder, and two cups of cold water. Soak several cotton balls in the mixture until drenched, and drop them down the mole or gopher hole.

But don't throw out this sauce if you have any left over. Mice also do not like these ingredients. In fact, experts say remedies containing either peppermint oil or chili powder make mice scurry away. So you can imagine what happens when you put these ingredients together. Give it a try and see for yourself.

Solve the case of the vanishing pond fish. The fish in your garden pond can be very attractive to hungry raccoons, herons, and other backyard wildlife. Persuade fish-eating predators to take their appetites somewhere else.

- Create hiding places. Give your fish a place to hide when predators come for dinner. Sink sections of sewer pipe or wide, black PVC pipe into the bottom of the pond. Or build an emergency shelter in the deepest part of your pond. Use bricks for the sides and a large patio paver stone for the roof. Repurpose open weave, stackable, plastic storage crates as underwater stands for potted plants so they can provide an extra shelter. Include plenty of underwater plants for the fish to hide behind, too.
- Fortify the edges. Place loose stones, thick and wide border plantings, or boulders around the edges to make reaching the pond much tougher for predators.
- Block it off. Stretch fine nylon netting over the top of the pond to keep predators from reaching in, wading, or swimming.

- Scare them away. Use blinking Christmas lights or an item attached to a motion detector, such as a radio or a sprinkler.
- Fence them out. Install an electric fence around your pond.
- Make it steep and deep. Give your pond steep sides and make it at least 3 feet deep.

Send spider mites packing. You think your plants have spider mites because they have bronzed, scorched, or distorted leaves – or even webbing. Hold a piece of white paper under a leaf and tap the leaf with a pencil. Examine the paper with a magnifying glass. If small spots appear on the paper and move around, you may have spider mites. Here's how to fight back.

- Add peat moss around the base of outdoor plants and set potted plants on plates of water. Mist or spray the plants several times a day. Spray the undersides of leaves with a strong stream of water to dislodge the mites.
- Move plants out of direct sunlight or shade them during the hot, late afternoon hours.
- Mix equal parts water and rubbing alcohol together and either spray it on the plant or pour it on a cotton ball and wipe down the leaves. Rinse the plants a few hours later. Before using this on the entire plant, test a small area first.

Fight back against rascally rabbits. Try these tricks to help keep rabbits from wreaking havoc in your yard and garden.

- Send old tennis shoes and other old shoes to a happy retirement in your garden or lay down some dog hair. Rabbits may be fooled by the scent and stay away.

- Fence off a bed or small garden with stakes and chicken wire or hardware cloth. The fence should extend 2 feet above the ground or snow level, but it should also reach several inches below the soil.

- Wash out several empty prescription pill bottles. Soak cotton balls in white vinegar and fill the bottles. Poke a hole in each top and put them back on the bottles. Place them around your garden.

- Rabbits love cover, so take inventory of places rabbits can hide. Clean out brush piles and debris, get rid of tall weeds, and remove or relocate any potential hiding place.

- Put a quart of water in a sprayer. Set the sprayer aside. Drop four fresh jalapeño peppers in your blender. Add enough water to make a slushy liquid. Blend the water and peppers, strain, and add your "jalapeño juice" to the water in the sprayer. Add one drop of multipurpose glue, like Elmer's, close the sprayer securely, and shake it. Spray this on plants to protect them from rabbits.

ALTERNATE USES

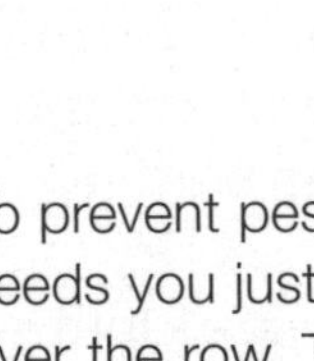

Shield your seeds

To prevent pests from digging up or eating that row of seeds you just planted, lay down some gutter guard mesh over the row. This is the strip of mesh used to keep leaves out of your roof gutters. Hold down each end of your mesh seed protector with rocks or bricks.

Arm tomatoes and blueberries against bird damage. Encourage the birds to eat blueberries and tomatoes somewhere else. To help keep your tomatoes safe, gather enough resealable, plastic sandwich bags so you have one for each tomato.

Unseal each bag, slide it over a tomato from bottom to top, and reseal the bag so that a little opening for air is left around the stem. Snip a lower corner of the bag to allow drainage and air flow. This should help cut your bird-caused tomato losses.

To help protect your blueberries, take your cue from Cornell University researchers. Make this spray to use on blueberry plants when they start to ripen. Heat one quart of water and pour in half of a 5-pound bag of sugar. Make sure all of the sugar dissolves and put the mixture in a sprayer after it cools.

Cornell researchers say this significantly reduced the bird damage to their blueberries. Just don't forget to reapply this solution after it rains, and be sure to use scare tactics, like hanging shiny pie tins nearby, to help shield your blueberries even more.

Tackle your deer invasion. The deer have a local restaurant they love to visit every day – your yard. Try several of these methods to fight back.

- Drop two eggs and one cup of water in a blender. Blend thoroughly and add one cup of skim milk and a few drops of mild dishwashing liquid. Lightly spray plants you want to protect from deer. Spray again after a heavy rain.

- Lay a perimeter of chicken wire or hardware cloth several feet wide on the ground around a particular bed or plant. Don't forget to remove the wire or hardware cloth temporarily before mowing the area.

- Apply milorganite fertilizer to flowers, bulbs, and bushes once or twice a month. Research suggests deer are far less likely to bother plants with this protection because they hate the smell.

- Choose deer-resistant plants. These are the plants deer eat only when they cannot get anything else. Call your local cooperative extension and ask how to get information on deer-resistant plants or visit your state's cooperative extension website. But don't stop there because deer vary in their choice of food. "A flower or shrub that does well in one neighborhood may be little stubs in another," says David Drake, a New Jersey extension specialist in wildlife. He recommends driving around your neighborhood to see which plants have escaped deer damage. Those are the ones you want.

- Surround plants or beds with deer-resistant plants, like garlic or catmint.

- Alternate among these scare tactics so the deer don't realize they have nothing to fear. Hang or scatter human hair or dog hair around your garden and replace it monthly. Leave small blinking Christmas lights on at night. Hang soap bars or pie tins from your trees. Blare your radio or play a recording of a barking dog.

ALTERNATE USES

Spread bug killer more effectively

Buy an old flour sifter at a yard sale, one you won't use for food. Paint the handle a bright color and store it with your garden tools to minimize the chance you'll use it in your kitchen.

When you need to spread small amounts of an insect-killing powder, use the sifter. It can help spread the powder evenly so you're less likely to miss a spot or use too much in one place.

Prevent root maggots. Save your tea bags after you use them. When you plant root crops, such as carrots or onions, tear open an individual-size tea bag, and dump the leaves in the planting hole. This should keep root maggots away.

Prepare planting beds without weeding. Why break your back weeding when you can prepare your entire garden bed for planting in one fell swoop? What's more, you'll improve your soil at the same time.

The secret is an easy, inexpensive process called solarization. This process uses summer sunlight and plastic sheeting to heat your soil. The high, continuous heat causes most weeds, in-ground pests, and harmful soil microbes to die – while helpful soil microbes flourish.

As a result, you may find that seeds sprout more quickly, and your plants grow faster and stronger. If you have a vegetable garden, you may also see your plants produce more vegetables. Here's how you can try this amazing process.

- Schedule your solarization. For best results, plan to solarize for four to eight weeks during June, July, or August. This still leaves time to plant many trees, shrubs, perennials, and winter vegetables during late summer or autumn while the soil is still warm.

- Prepare the area. Mow all the weeds and remove large clods, sticks, and other debris. Rototill your soil or turn it over with garden tools and then rake the soil smooth to get rid of air pockets that could interfere with soil heating. Next, water the soil thoroughly. This helps the sun's heat penetrate more deeply into the soil and helps kill seeds and harmful microbes. Finish by digging a trench, 6 inches deep, around the bed.

- Solarize. Cover the bed with clear plastic that is 1 or 2 mils thick, drop the edges of the plastic into the trench, and bury them to anchor the plastic in place. Wait four to eight weeks in warmer-climate summers or four to 10 weeks in cooler-climate or cloudier summers.

- Uncover and plant. When solarization is complete, remove the plastic and start planting, but disturb the soil as little as possible. Solarization may only reduce weed seeds, weeds, and pests in the first 3 to 6 inches of soil, and you don't want to cultivate heavily enough to bring perfectly healthy weed seeds to the surface. So dig as little as possible, top-dress with fertilizer, and water with drip irrigation or soaker hoses.

Beware of tire planter problem

Before you hunt down cast-off tires to use as a planter, contact your local government to make sure you won't break any laws or ordinances. Some communities restrict or forbid the use of old tires for any purpose.

Clever containers for less. Go shopping for containers in your closets, garage, and any other place you store things you never use. Good ideas for containers include kids' wading pools, hollow cinder blocks, watering cans, five-gallon plastic buckets, wooden barrels or half whiskey barrels, discarded toilets, wooden crates, old laundry tubs, plastic trash bags, rusty strainers, toy wagons, plastic storage containers, driftwood, a bag of potting soil, tea kettles, coffee cans, and tires.

If you don't already have what you need, check garage sales or thrift markets where you can probably find the item for pennies. Just make sure all your containers have good drainage and consider limiting your use of darker-colored containers. Dark colors keep the soil at higher temperatures and that heat may damage young roots or require you to water more often.

Pay next to nothing for garden stakes and trellises. You can get stakes and trellises for cheap or free. Here are some suggestions.

- Use the "waste not, want not" approach and go shopping in your attic, basement, or storage shed. If you need stakes, look for pipes, the slats from old blinds, card holders from flower bouquets, a ruler or yardstick, an old fireplace poker, a curtain rod, or the handle from a broom, mop, or rake you no longer use. If you need a trellis, try an old baby gate, a bed headboard, a flat bedspring from a trundle bed, a wooden ladder, a wire frame Christmas deer that no longer works, or an old swing set.

- Repurpose your old yard sale signs as stakes. Do the same with tree trimmings and fallen branches in your yard.

- Make an unusual trellis for your climbing plants. Remove the fabric from an old umbrella and bury the handle in the ground.

Encourage your roses to go bananas. Your roses will be even more beautiful when you feed them banana peels. Save the peels until they are crisp, and chop them into small pieces. Bury the pieces a few inches deep in the soil around your rosebush, and you'll be offering your roses a yummy potassium snack. That's important because roses can suffer from potassium deficiency.

If a rosebush doesn't get enough potassium, the edges of rose leaves turn yellow or brown and the resulting rosebuds look pitiful. But with enough potassium, your rosebush can produce plenty of healthy leaves – and experts say you can't have gorgeous roses without healthy leaves. Treat your roses with bananas once a month. You may end up with the most beautiful roses you've ever had.

Free fertilizer for your garden. The next time your plants need fertilizer, consider these options before you head to the store.

- Eggshells. Stunted leaves and roots and small or distorted young leaves are signs your outdoor plants or houseplants need calcium. What's more, blossom end rot on your tomatoes means they're low on calcium, too. Add crushed eggshells to the soil to help provide this vital mineral.

- Fish-cleaning leftovers. After you clean fish, bury the scraps near roses or other plants in your yard. Over time, they make the soil more fertile.

- Rabbit droppings. These can add nitrogen and phosphorous to your soil, but they should be composted first – or at least a year old.

- Wood ashes. Lightly sprinkle wood ashes where soil is too acidic, but make sure you don't add them to soils that are alkaline or high in potassium.

- Aquarium water. After cleaning your fish tank, use the old water on your plants to fertilize them. Just don't try this if you have a saltwater aquarium.

Prevent weeds, enrich soil, and water less. Adding a layer of mulch hardly seems like magic, but it can works its charm on your garden in many ways.

- keeps weeds at bay
- retains water in the soil so you water less
- improves your soil quality

- insulates soil and roots against temperature extremes
- prevents frost heaving
- reduces erosion

Before laying mulch, be sure to water and weed, or you could be doing your plants more harm than good. Mulch helps the soil retain water by preventing evaporation, but it also prevents erosion of your soil by making rain enter the soil more gradually than before. If you don't water before mulching, you may expose your plants to a long, dry period.

If you don't weed before mulching, the mulch may provide as many benefits to existing weeds as it does to your favorite plants – helping the weeds thrive.

WARNING

What you need to know about sour mulch

Before you buy or spread hardwood mulch, take a quick sniff and check its temperature with your hand. If the mulch smells like ammonia, vinegar, or rotten eggs or is hot to the touch, it has been stored improperly. This causes the mulch to produce byproducts that can harm your plants within 24 hours and may eventually kill them.

Calculate the amount of mulch for a circular bed. To figure how much mulch you need to buy for your flower clock bed or any other round bed, get out your measuring tape and your calculator. Garden and home improvement stores sell mulch by the cubic yard. To estimate how many cubic yards you need, you must first figure the square footage. Here's how.

Measure from the center of the circle to the edge. Tally your result in feet, not inches, and round up or down to the nearest foot. To calculate square footage from your measurement, use this formula – (center-to-edge distance) x (center-to-edge distance) x 3.14. For example, if the distance were 10 feet, you would multiply 10 x 10 x 3.14 to get 314 square feet.

To turn square feet into cubic feet, multiply your square footage by the depth of mulch in inches. Count on 2 to 3 inches for heavier, finer mulches, like wood chips and gravel, but at least 4 to 6 inches of lighter fluff, like pine needles, straw, and paper. If you needed 2 inches of mulch, you would multiply 314 x 2 to get 628. Then divide this number by 324 to calculate square yards. So 628 divided by 324 comes to 1.938 or roughly 2 cubic yards.

For a square or rectangular bed, measure your garden in feet and multiply the width by the length to get the square footage. Once again, multiply the square footage by the depth of mulch you need. Divide this number by 324 and you'll know how many cubic yards of mulch to order.

Solve mulch problems before they start. Here are three ways to get more value from your mulch.

- Be choosy. Many bagged cypress mulches claim to repel pests, but the Florida Cooperative Extension service reports that only old-growth cypress has pest-repellent powers. The younger cypress trees, which are usually the source of most cypress mulch, can't live up to their pest-fighting claims. That doesn't mean mulch can't battle pests. Cedar mulch contains a natural chemical called thujone, which repels pests like termites and carpet beetles.
- Add nitrogen. Before you mulch, add a source of nitrogen, like grass clippings or commercial fertilizer, to the soil. Many mulches leach out nitrogen as they decompose. Good sources of nitrogen include sawdust, wood ashes, corn husks, and shredded bark.
- Know where to put it. Mulch your fruit trees but make sure the mulch extends about 4 feet away from the tree on all sides or

as far out as the tips of the limbs. Avoid creating a mulch volcano, where a pile of mulch is mounded up against your tree bark, like the sides of a sloping volcano. This puts your tree at risk for damage from insects, rodents, bark rot, and disease. Pull the mulch away from the tree trunk after you put it down.

ALTERNATE USES

Simple way to pull weeds — roots and all

You pulled that weed, but only the leaves and stem came up. The roots stayed firmly in the ground. The next time you find a weed that's too crowded for your hands to grab or one that's too deeply rooted to loosen, grab your needle-nose pliers. No weed survives against those for long.

Put old carpet to work in your garden. To help prevent tomato blight this year, just lay wide strips of old carpet around your tomato plants when you plant them. The carpet should prevent soil diseased by blight from splashing on the plant when you water. But that's not the only way you can use carpet in your garden and yard. Consider these ideas, too.

- To convert a grassy area into a flower bed, vegetable garden, or landscaping island, lay carpet down over the grass. The lack of light kills the grass and weeds after a few weeks.
- Lay carpet in already-prepared beds to help control weeds there, too. When you need to plant, simply cut an X into the carpet and turn in the flaps.
- Use carpet to help make a weed-resistant garden pathway. Lay down carpet first and then cover it with mulch or stone. The carpet prevents weeds from poking through while keeping stones or mulch from sinking into the ground.

For any of these uses, make sure you choose carpet with an open-weave back instead of a rubber back. The open-weave backing allows water and fertilizer to soak through. And remember, any carpet you use in your garden or yard should be carpet-side up, the same way you lay it in your home.

Take control of weeds without toxic chemicals. Here's a simple, inexpensive way to weed-proof your lawn and sock it to those pesky weeds cluttering your sidewalk. All you need is water and one item from your kitchen pantry – vinegar.

Attack the weeds in your sidewalk and driveway cracks first. Just spray undiluted white vinegar on them. Don't be shy about it. Dowse them thoroughly. The weed should shrivel and die in a day or so. If a particularly tough weed survives, pour boiling water on it.

Weeds in your garden and lawn can be a little trickier because you don't want to accidentally spray vinegar on your lawn or garden plants. But if you've got a 2-liter bottle, you won't believe how easily you can kill weeds.

Just cut or remove the bottom section of the bottle and remove the cap. Slip the bottle over the weed, insert your sprayer nozzle in the mouth of the bottle, and wet down the weed. Let the vinegar soak into the ground before you lift the bottle. If the weed is still alive a few days after its first vinegar shower, surprise it with a second.

Free water for your plants. You could get about 30 gallons of free rainwater for your plants from every thunderstorm – if you were willing to pay $90 for a rain barrel. Fortunately, getting a rain barrel may be a lot cheaper than that, and it could be easier than you expect, too.

Contact your local and county governments, water company, and cooperative extension and ask about rain barrel programs. Sometimes you can get a free rain barrel kit to help you make your own – or you can attend an inexpensive rain barrel workshop.

The workshop provides the parts and helps you make your rain barrel, often for less than you would pay to buy one. But even if neither of these options is available, you can still get a free rain barrel instruction sheet.

The most expensive part of making a rain barrel is the cost of the barrel, but you can buy a used barrel for under $20 if you know how. To find a used barrel, check with food service providers, soft drink bottlers, feed stores, recycling businesses, or junk stores. Only purchase a barrel if it's made of heavy-duty, food-grade plastic that does not let in light and hasn't held toxic materials.

If you can't find an appropriate barrel, call your county Extension service or the people who provided your rain barrel instructions. They may recommend a source of used barrels.

ALTERNATE USES

Start seedlings without peat pots

Save the cardboard rolls from your toilet tissue and paper towels. Snip the toilet tissue rolls in half and cut the paper towel rolls into four equal cylinders. Now they can serve as "peat pots" for your seedlings.

Pack your pots together inside a tray or old casserole dish. Fill each pot with soil and a seed. When they're ready, transplant them into the ground, rolls and all. Just make sure the top of each roll is even with the top of the soil and completely covered.

Make your own cold frame. A cold frame can help you harden off seedlings in the spring or grow cool weather crops in autumn or winter. All you need is an old window and materials for a base, like scrap lumber, bricks, or cinder blocks.

A cold frame uses sunlight to keep plants warmer than the outside air, so choose a spot facing south where your cold frame can get direct sunlight for at least half the day.

Once it's built, your cold frame will resemble a box with the front end sunk into the ground so its roof slopes downward. The slope helps rain drain off and allows more sunlight into the frame. Design the size of your cold frame to match the size of the window you use as a roof.

To start, mark off where the south wall and north wall of your cold frame will rest and measure the distance between these marks in feet. Your cold frame must slope toward the south, so dig a sloped bed with the deepest edge at the south end of your frame.

Remember the distance in feet between the north and south wall? That number is also how many inches deep your trench should be. In other words, if the distance between the north and south walls is 6 feet, make the trench 6 inches deep. Dig toward the north wall so you end up with a sloped bed that starts at ground level at the north end and slopes down to the depth of the trench at the south end – a 1-inch drop per foot of distance.

Create a frame from your choice of materials that rests just inside the edges of your sloped bed. If the frame is wood, you may need to assemble it before placing it in the bed. Bricks or cinder blocks can simply be layered along the bed's edges.

Make this frame between 1 and 2 feet deep. If you use cinder blocks, stuff the holes with newspaper or dirt. Place your window on top to complete your cold frame.

MYTHBUSTER

Beware homemade bone meal recipes

Search the Internet long enough and you will find several recipes for making your own bone meal from the bones saved from cooking. The recipes may sound easy and tempting, but the bone meal they produce may not be effective — or safe.

"Cooperative extension does not recommend that homeowners make their own bone meal," says extension agent Stephanie Ray Butcher. "The process required to make a safe product is quite labor intensive, and it is difficult for homeowners to acquire the quantity of material needed to gain any benefit from it in their soils."

Cheap way to preserve extra produce. Your freezer is full, but your vegetable garden keeps producing. Turn those extra vegetables into dried vegetables, and you can enjoy them weeks or months down the road. Drying may even help you take advantage of buy-in-bulk bargains on produce at your farmer's market.

Best of all, produce takes up less space after it's dried, so you can store more in the same amount of space – and you can store most dried produce outside the freezer for several months.

You might think you need a dehydrator to dry produce, but your oven can do the job. Keep in mind oven-drying only works if you can set your oven so it maintains a constant temperature of 140 degrees with the oven door propped open a few inches. Use an oven thermometer to check. For drying racks, use shallow wood or plastic trays with slatted or perforated bottoms.

Although the drying process varies widely depending on what food you use, this is how you dry vegetables.

- Wash in cool water; cut into small, uniform chunks or slices; and blanch.
- Arrange the vegetables in a single layer on each drying tray while the oven preheats.
- Once the oven is ready, put the trays in and check the temperature and vegetables regularly until the vegetables are crisp.
- Cool the vegetables and pack them in clean, moisture-resistant containers, such as glass jars with tight-fitting lids. You can store them in a cool, dry place for months. To reconstitute your dried veggies, soak them in water.

You'll need additional details to successfully dry your own fruits and vegetables, so visit the National Center for Home Food Preservation at *www.uga.edu/nchfp* and click on the "Dry" link or contact your local extension agent for more information.

Create your own vegetable soup mix. A package of dry soup mix costs at least $2, but you can make your own mix for far less if you dry your own vegetables. While your vegetables are drying, measure the other ingredients, such as seasonings, rice, and bouillon granules, and store your mix together with the dried soup vegetables.

When you are ready for soup, toss your dried vegetables into the boiling water along with the other soup ingredients, and the vegetables will rehydrate while the soup cooks. That's almost as easy as using a prepackaged soup mix – but the best part is you get to pick the ingredients. Carrots, corn, okra, onions, peas, celery, chili peppers, tomatoes, and potatoes are good choices.

Sow tiny seeds more easily. Those itty-bitty petunia seeds are tough to see, let alone sow. To make sowing easier, thoroughly clean an old saltshaker, let dry, and find a measuring spoon small enough to fit through the mouth of the shaker.

Use the spoon to help deposit equal amounts of seed and sand in the shaker. When you are done, screw the lid on the shaker, and sow your seeds.

Add a hanging basket for pennies. Turn an old colander into a hanging basket. Any colander can work – enamel, metal, or plastic. All you need is a hanging basket liner and some fishing line.

Clean the colander and, if you like, decorate it or paint with waterproof paint. Once the paint or glue from decorating is completely dry, place the hanging basket liner in the colander.

Choose three holes near the top edge of the colander. Make sure each hole is equal distance apart. Cut three equal lengths of fishing line and thread one length through each hole. Loop each length over the rim and through the hole again a couple of times before you tie the end. Then tie the tops of the lengths together. Fill the basket with soil and plants, and it will be ready to hang.

Bring home freebies from plant and seed swaps. Those new seed and garden catalogs will be a lot less tempting next year if you start saving seeds and dividing your plants now. These extras give you ammunition for plant or seed swaps.

The idea is simple. Everyone invited to a seed swap brings seeds to trade. You find someone who has the seeds you want and offer to trade some of your seeds for some of theirs. Plant swaps work the same way. So if you envy a neighbor's perfect plants, perhaps you can swap to get one of those plants or its seeds. You could even wind up with seeds or plants that are not sold in nurseries.

The easiest way to organize a plant or seed swap is to talk with friends and neighbors ahead of time and offer to host the swap. Just be sure to start planning far enough in advance, so everyone has time to collect seeds or divide plants. Consider scheduling your swap for a weekend during the spring or autumn. Remember that people attending the swap are essentially shopping for new seeds or plants, so try to make yours almost as healthy-looking, portable, and well-labeled as similar products in stores.

If you can't organize a plant or seed swap, hunt for an existing swap you can attend. Contact local garden clubs or ask your cooperative extension agent if any upcoming garden-related events include a seed or plant swap.

If you have Internet access, search for nearby plant and seed swaps in the forums at *www.gardenweb.com*. You can also visit *www.freesharing.org* and check for a plant exchange group in your area.

HANDY HINT

Feed your plants with kitchen trash

Toss your meat and dairy leftovers in your trash can, but save your peels and your leftover fruits and vegetables. Drop these in your blender, add water, and blend until smooth. Use this to water your plants and you'll be feeding them, too.

Double your perennials for free. Dividing your perennials not only gives you more at no cost, it also helps you contain overgrown plants and revitalize tired ones. Most perennials need to be divided once every three to five years.

For best results, divide your spring and summer bloomers in autumn at least four weeks before the ground freezes. Divide autumn bloomers in the spring as soon as you spot new growth.

Before you divide a plant, water it thoroughly, prune the stems and leaves to around 6 inches high, and prepare the planting space.

To divide the original plant, lift its root ball out of the ground. Insert a sharp shovel, flat-edged spade, or spading fork in the soil at least 4 inches away from the plant. Press down until the end of your tool has penetrated below the root level and pull your digger back out of the ground. Use this technique to make a circle around the plant. Slip your shovel under the plant and lift the root ball out.

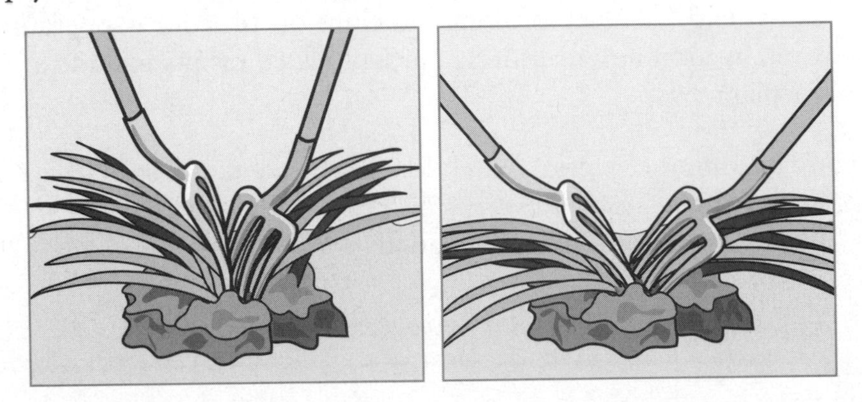

Some plants can be pulled apart with your hands or cut apart with a knife. If your perennial is too big or thick for that, insert two pitchforks in the root ball so they are back to back in the center of the plant. Position them so both handles are vertical. Pull the handles of the pitchforks apart to separate the plant, but be careful to avoid breaking the handles. After dividing, plant your "new" perennials right away.

What you should never compost. Don't add a weed to your compost pile if there is any chance it may contain seeds. Those seeds may survive and sprout after you spread your compost in the garden. And that's not all – don't use bones, grease, meat scraps, or fat. They attract rats and other pests, they stink, and the fats can actually make your compost take longer to break down.

Feel free to toss most other kitchen scraps on your compost pile, including freezer-burned vegetables, coffee filters, bread, and tea bags. You can also use wood ashes, pet hair, uncolored human hair, shredded newspaper, sod, hedge trimmings, sawdust, grass clippings, soil, hay, straw, leaves, chopped corncobs, and most yard waste.

MYTHBUSTER

Rescue your spinach seeds from harm

You may have heard that you should soak spinach seeds in vinegar overnight before planting them, but this may be taking a useful garden trick one step too far.

"The purpose of pre-soaking seeds is to soften the seed coat in an effort to improve germination," explains extension agent Stephanie Ray Butcher. She adds that large seeds, such as the ones from corn, snap beans, or cucumbers, can be soaked in water overnight so they will be ready to plant the next day. But spinach is different.

"While spinach seeds can be presoaked in water without harming the seed, it germinates easily without the presoak, and avoiding this unnecessary step saves time and energy." What's more, soaking spinach seeds in a vinegar solution could harm the seeds, Butcher says.

Whip up homemade fungicides. You can start fending off powdery mildew within minutes if you have baking soda and horticultural oil on hand. To prevent powdery mildew, just mix one tablespoon of baking soda and two-and-a-half tablespoons of horticultural oil into a gallon of water. Pour this fungus fighter into a sprayer and spray your troubled plants.

To prevent other fungal diseases, try these remedies.

- Sprinkle chamomile tea or cinnamon over the seedbed when you plant seeds to prevent damping off.
- Drop several garlic cloves and a little water in a blender and puree. Mix the potent brew with a gallon of water in your sprayer and spray your plants to help prevent fungal diseases like downy mildew and tomato blight.
- Mix four teaspoons of baking soda and one tablespoon of horticultural oil into a gallon of water and spray your plants to avoid black spot or brown patch.

HANDY HINT

Make a watering stake for tomatoes

For every tomato plant you'll grow, cut a 5-foot length of 2-inch PVC pipe. Make a mark 10 inches away from one end of each pipe. Dig holes with a post hole digger near where you'll place a tomato plant.

Drop the first pipe in its hole. Place a 2-inch thick board over the top of the pipe. Hammer the board to push the pipe into the soil until the 10-inch mark is even with the ground. Fill the space around the pipe with dirt. Repeat for each pole.

Plant each tomato plant a few inches from a pipe. To water, turn the hose on low and put the nozzle in the pipe. Fill the pipe and move on to the next one. Check the first pipe. If the water drains quickly, refill it again. As the tomatoes grow, tie them to your PVC stakes.

Chapter 8

IN THE GARAGE

"Experience is what you get right after you really needed it." This old saying applies in the garage like nowhere else. Whether you're caring for your car, working with tools, or getting ready to paint, experience can be a tough teacher. Skip a few classes. Learn clever short-cuts, simple solutions, and savvy storage ideas for every-thing found in your garage.

BATTERIES

Staying charged up

Get more life out of "dead" batteries. Don't throw away dead batteries. Put them to good use. When the batteries die in a device that takes two or more, there's a good chance only one is totally drained. The others may have life left in them.

You can find out for sure which ones are dead with an inexpensive battery tester from your local electronics or hardware store. Alkaline batteries start out with 1.5 volts when new. When they reach 1.1 volts, they're dead.

Test your batteries and save the ones that still have a charge. They'll come in handy the next time the batteries give out in your remote control and you have no new ones on hand.

Clean contacts for stronger charge. Electronics not holding a charge? Don't waste money on a new charger or battery. Try cleaning the terminals instead.

Take the batteries out of your gadget and rub the terminals with a clean pencil eraser. Do the same to the contacts inside the battery compartment or on the charger. Wipe with a soft cloth afterward.

3 types of batteries not worth the money. Some just aren't worth the money, no matter how cheap they seem or how good the advertising.

- Batteries labeled Heavy Duty or General Purpose are a common find in dollar stores. They're usually made from carbon zinc.

They don't last nearly as long as alkaline batteries, even though they cost about the same. Plus, they are more likely to corrode.

- Nickel-cadmium (NiCad) batteries hold less power and typically can't be recharged as many times as nickel-metal-hydride (NiMH) batteries. They also contain toxic metals, which means you can't just throw them out with the trash.

- Lithium (not lithium-ion) batteries were made for use in electronics. Unlike NiMH, however, they can't be recharged. Lithiums also cost more and are toxic, so you have to dispose of them like hazardous waste.

The one place you may want to put lithium batteries – in a smoke detector. They last a long time when not in use. That means they can last for years in a smoke detector. For power-hungry electronics, like digital cameras, consider special alkaline batteries labeled Ultra, Power, or High-drain.

MYTHBUSTER

Skip the cold storage

Storing batteries in your refrigerator won't make them last longer. They'll just take up valuable refrigerator space. The exception — if you live in a hot climate without air conditioning. Batteries lose their charge faster when the temperature is above 90 degrees. Otherwise, simply store them in a dry place at room temperature.

Recycle right around the corner. Lots of places will recycle your rechargeable batteries. Drop off your nickel-cadmium, nickel-metal-hydride, and lithium-ion batteries at your local Home Depot, Best Buy, Lowes, RadioShack, or Staples.

Squeeze more juice from your batteries. Batteries that give out in one gadget may still have enough juice left to power another. When the AAs in your digital camera seem to stop working, try popping them into a remote control. Chances are, they'll work just fine – and you'll save by squeezing every ounce of energy from them.

Make your own D battery. Gadgets that call for D cell batteries can actually run on C cells in a pinch. The next time you run out of D's, grab a couple of C's and a handful of quarters.

C batteries are a little shorter than D's, so you need to fill the extra space. Pop the C batteries into the compartment, then slide a quarter between the negative end of the battery and the springy contact. Keep inserting quarters until they fill up the space between the terminal and the contact. Pop the cover back on the gadget and watch it work.

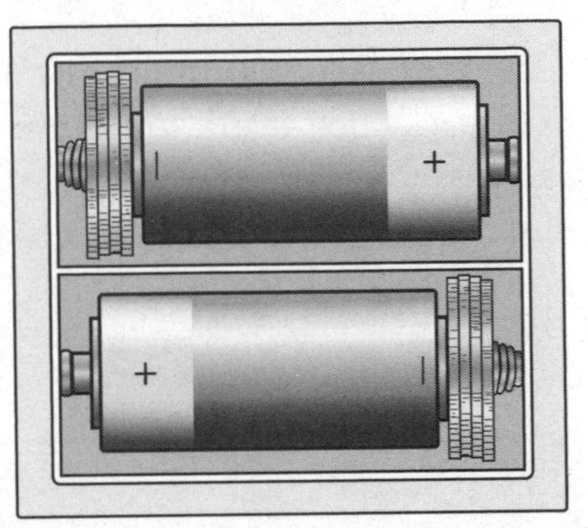

Lengthen the life of rechargeables. Rechargeable batteries aren't cheap, so you want to make them last. These quick tips can tell you how.

- Run down nickel-cadmium (NiCad) batteries in power tools, two-way radios, and medical devices once a month. Drain them to about 10 percent of their power before recharging. Don't leave the battery sitting in the charger for more than two days.

- Nickel-metal-hydride batteries power the same sorts of devices as NiCad. Drain them completely every three months, and don't leave them in a charger for more than two days.

- Don't allow lithium-ion batteries, the kind in video cameras, cellphones, and laptops, to get completely drained before you recharge them. These last longer if you keep them at least partially charged and charge them often.
- Keep the lead-acid batteries in cars, motorcycles, and wheelchairs charged at all times. Never let them drain completely.

CARS
Get it in gear

Slash your tab at the pump. One of the best ways to improve your gas mileage is simply to tighten your gas cap. One in six people drive around with loose or missing gas caps. It's a small thing, but it can cost you big. The Car Care Council says these people lose 147 million gallons of gas each year.

"Most motorists don't realize that it's the little things that don't take a lot of time or cost much that can really make a difference when it comes to saving money at the pump," said Rich White, executive director of the Car Care Council. "Loose or missing gas caps, under-inflated tires, worn spark plugs, and dirty air filters all contribute to poor fuel economy."

Read on for tips that can save you up to 20 cents a gallon on your next fill-up, plus lower your yearly gas costs up to 20 percent.

Go farther on less gas. Driving around with low tire pressure and out-of-alignment wheels is like driving with your parking brake on. All increase resistance, which devastates your gas mileage.

"Conditions that increase rolling resistance ... can cost a mile or two per gallon on a car that normally delivers 20 miles per gallon," according to Rich White of the Car Care Council.

Have your alignment checked periodically, and buy an inexpensive digital gauge to check tire pressure yourself. Don't rely on the gas station's gauge or a pocket-size pencil gauge. Both are often wrong.

MYTHBUSTER

Prolong the life of your tires

Keeping your tires properly inflated improves your gas mileage, makes them last longer, and cuts your risk of having an accident. But if you go by the pressure listed on the side of the tire, you may be over inflating them.

The number on the tire's sidewall is the maximum inflation pressure, not the recommended pressure for your car. For this number, look for a label on the inside of the driver's-side door, or check your owner's manual.

Check your tire pressure at least once a month. "Checking your tire pressure should become a monthly routine," advises Fred Koplin of Yokohama Tire Corporation. "It only takes five minutes. If you're not doing it once a month, chances are you're driving on under-inflated tires."

Test tire pressure before leaving your house, not after you return. Tires need to cool off for three hours before you can get an accurate reading.

Save $1 or more on every gallon of gas. Speeding, hard braking, and fast takeoffs take a serious toll on your gas mileage. Aggressive driving slashes your car's fuel efficiency by one-third on the highway and 5 percent in the city. Driving sensibly, on the other hand, could save you a whopping $1 per gallon on $3-a-gallon gas.

In fact, simply obeying the speed limit can boost your gas mileage as much as 23 percent. Most vehicles get the best mileage traveling between 50 and 60 miles per hour (mph). With $3 a gallon gas, you practically pay an extra 24 cents per gallon for every five miles you drive above 60 mph.

What your tires are trying to tell you

Paying attention to tire wear can help you spot bigger problems, not to mention get more mileage out of your tires. Uneven wear on tires can point to one of three things — wrong tire pressure (under or over), wheel misalignment, or worn parts in the suspension and steering.

Pattern of tread wear		Possible causes
wear on both outer edges		A classic sign of under-inflated tires. If the outer edges wear on a properly inflated tire, however, you may have problems with the steering or wheel alignment.
wear on center treads		This is the hallmark of over-inflated tires. They bulge in the middle, wearing the center down faster.
wear on one side		Too much camber, a problem where the wheels lean outward or inward too far. They may need a simple realignment, but worn out springs, ball joints, or control arm bushings could also be the culprit.
cupping		Scallop-shaped dips that appear along the tire's edge point to an unbalanced wheel or suspension problems. Once fixed, have the tire rotated to a different position on the car and rebalanced.
feathering		One side of each tread rib is sharp, and the other side rounded. The wheel turns either too far outward or too far inward, like the feet on a pigeon-toed or duck-footed person. Run a finger across the tire tread. If you feel sharp edges, you may have feathering.

Lighten your load for better mileage. Clean out your truck, and you'll use less gas. Every additional 100 pounds in your car cuts your fuel efficiency by 2 percent. That's like tacking another 6 cents on to the cost of each gallon of gas. Small cars suffer more than large ones.

WARNING

Douse your risk of gas pump fires

Despite the dire warnings, it seems no one has ever actually caused a fire by talking on a cell phone while filling up at a gas station. Even researchers who tried haven't been able to do it.

Static electricity, on the other hand, can be dangerous. The Petroleum Equipment Institute (PEI) has documented nearly 200 cases of gas-pump fires linked to static shock as of 2010. Play it safe with these tips from PEI.

- Turn off your engine when parked at the pump.
- Discharge static by touching the metal of the car before you start pumping gas.
- Don't smoke while filling up.
- Never climb back into your car while it's refueling.
- Leave the gasoline nozzle in the car if a fire does start. Pulling it out will only spread the fire.

Engine fixes that pay off at the pump. A tuned-up engine takes you farther on less gas. Fixing a car that failed an emissions test or that is noticeably out of tune boosts your fuel economy an average of 4 percent.

Taking care of a serious maintenance issue, like a broken oxygen sensor, can make your car as much as 40 percent more efficient.

That earns you an extra 8 miles per gallon (mpg) in a car that gets 20 mpg. Here are four more engine problems it pays to fix.

- Just one misfiring spark plug can squander 2 to 3 mpg.
- A cooling system thermostat that makes the engine run too cold can waste as much as 2 mpg.
- A slipping automatic transmission can cost you 1 mpg.
- Using the wrong type of motor oil can steal another half a mile per gallon.

Get gas at its cheapest. Experts generally say the best time to buy gas is during the week. Prices tend to rise over the weekend, especially in summer. Some drivers think prices are lowest on Wednesdays, but you'll likely get a decent deal on most weekdays.

Make a new vehicle last longer. An engine needs a little extra care during the first few hundred miles. In general, you should:

- avoid towing a trailer.
- vary your speed often to break in the car's moving parts. Try not to drive at the same speed continuously.

With some cars, you only need to follow these rules for the first 300 miles. With others, you may need to follow them for 1,200 miles or more. Your owner's manual will tell you how long the "break-in" period lasts for your vehicle.

Quick fix for scratched windows. Just buff out scratches gently with a light abrasive, like plain, white toothpaste – not the gel kind. Light scratches should buff out beautifully. For deep scratches, you may need to replace the glass.

Test the depth of your scratch by running a fingernail across it. If your nail catches in the groove, it's probably too deep to tackle with toothpaste. If your nail doesn't catch, then toothpaste may do the trick. Spread it over the scratch, let it dry, then buff away with a soft cloth.

15 quick roadside fixes

Don't let a broken fan belt or blown hose leave you stranded by the roadside. These must-know quick fixes can keep your car up and running until you get to a mechanic.

Car trouble	Quick fix
flat tire	Skip the danger and hassle of changing a tire on the side of a highway. Carry a can of inflator/sealant in your car to temporarily plug a puncture.
broken belt	Keep a roll of Rescue Tape in your car, available at auto part stores. Use it as a fast patch for broken fan or power steering belts.
stuck in "Park"	Take the cover off the gear shifter console, press the brake pedal, and flip the override switch at the base of the shifter. A screwdriver will help you move the switch.
key won't turn	Try a copy of the key. If that one won't work, turn the steering wheel one way, then the other, and turn the key again.
dead battery	Jumper cables are a lifesaver. Keep a good set in your trunk at all times.
leaky radiator	Remove the radiator cap, crack an egg into a cup, and pour it into the radiator. Throw away the shell, replace the cap, and run the car for a few minutes. The egg will cook and plug the leak. Pouring a few teaspoons of ground black pepper into the radiator may do the same thing.
frozen door lock in winter	Heat your car key with the flame from a lighter, then insert it into the door lock. Let thaw a minute before turning.
no traction on ice or snow	Place the floor mats behind the car's rear wheels, with the rubbery side down, to gain traction.

Car trouble	Quick fix
blown radiator or heater hose	Wrap lots of duct tape around the hose for a temporary fix. Even better, try Rescue Tape. It will get you farther and hold the hose together longer.
dragging muffler	Fasteners holding the muffler and exhaust pipe off the ground can corrode or break. Rehang with a wire coat hanger or stainless steel hose clamp.
shot spark plugs	Save old spark plugs after you change them and store in your trunk. If the newer ones go while you're on the road, simply swap in the old ones.
loud exhaust	Patch a hole in the exhaust pipe with an empty soda or soup can. Cut off both ends of the can with tin snips, slide it over the pipe hole like a sleeve, and clamp at each end with hose clamps.
small hole in fuel tank	Place a rubber washer or O-ring over a sheet-metal screw, and turn the screw into the hole so it plugs tightly.
broken antenna	Untwist a wire coat hanger, straighten the hooked end, and bend the hanger into a diamond shape. Gently slide the two ends into the hole for the antenna.
broken window	Cut a piece of heavy plastic slightly larger than the window opening. Tape around the edges with duct tape.

Winter-proof your windshield. Frost-proof your windshield in winter with a homemade solution of vinegar and water. Just mix three parts white or apple cider vinegar with one part water, and wipe on your windows. Vinegar contains acetic acid, which keeps water from freezing. You can even melt the ice on already-frozen windows by spritzing them with this mixture.

During super-cold weather, frost may form on the inside of car windows, too. Wipe the inside of your windshield with a sponge dipped in a saltwater solution of one or two tablespoons salt to one gallon of water. Once dry, it leaves behind an invisible layer of salt that will stop ice from forming on the glass. Don't use saltwater on the outside of your car. Salt can corrode a car's metal.

Banish blind spots with simple trick. Hate checking your "blind spot" while driving? Here's an ingeniously easy way to adjust your mirrors so you don't have a blind spot.

- Tilt your head all the way to the left until it touches the driver's-side window. Now look in the left-side mirror. Angle it so you can see a small piece of your back fender.
- Next, tilt your head to the right about the same distance. Adjust the right-side mirror so you can see the fender's other corner.

These tweaks should nix any big blind spots. When a car passes, you will see it first in your rearview mirror. As it pulls alongside you, it will appear in your side mirror just as it starts to disappear from your rearview mirror. If there's a pause between when it disappears from one and reappears in the other, try adjusting your mirrors again.

Do away with windshield haze. Cigarette smoke, air pollution, and compounds released by vinyl and plastic in your car all help form a hazy film on the inside of your windshield.

It's not just annoying – it's a safety hazard. Light can temporarily blind you when it hits that haze at just the right angle, especially at night.

Glass cleaners may not be powerful enough to clean it off, but this homemade solution will. Mix one part vinegar with one part warm water in a spray bottle. Cover your dashboard to protect it, then squirt the inside of the windshield. Wipe clean with a microfiber cloth or crumpled up newspaper.

As soon as Kathleen West heard about this technique, she couldn't wait to try it. Thanks to a family member smoking in her car, the inside of her windshield was coated in a thin, stubborn film.

"Vinegar, warm water, and a little elbow grease took the haze right off my windshield." Afterward, she wiped it down with old newspaper, which left it streak-free.

WARNING

Money-saving shortcut can make you sick

Don't try to pinch pennies by filling the washer fluid reservoir in your car with plain water. Stagnant water breeds dangerous bacteria, including the one that causes Legionnaire's disease.

The British Health Protection Agency found that people who filled their washer reservoirs with water instead of windshield washer fluid were more likely to catch this illness. *Legionella*, the bacterium behind it, thrives in stagnant water. When sprayed onto the windshield, it becomes airborne and gets sucked into the car through the air vents.

Switching to washer fluid could prevent one in every five cases of Legionnaire's disease in England and Wales, according to the agency. That's because it contains chemicals that keep *Legionella* from growing.

Banish fog for good. Ordinary shaving cream can stop fog from forming on the inside of your car windows. It contains some of the same ingredients as commercial defoggers, for a lot less.

Spray a thin, even layer of foam on the inside of the window. Let sit for a few minutes, then wipe off with a paper towel. The shaving cream will leave behind an invisible, fog-fighting film on the glass.

ALTERNATE USES

Say 'so long' to stuck-on bugs

Dryer sheets make short work of baked-on bugs. Simply wipe away insects with a wet dryer sheet. Experts say it won't harm the paint, but you will need to wash and wax the treated area afterward.

Unstick stuck tree sap. W.E. Thrasher stumbled upon an easy way to take sap off his vehicles. "I struggled to get tree sap off our motor home exterior after having parked the coach under a stand of pine trees," he says. "I tried all the usual commercial 'goo removers,' auto body polishes, and cleaners. No luck with anything!"

Turns out, he had the solution in his medicine cabinet the whole time. Or, rather, his wife did. "When I tried my wife's nail polish remover, the sap came off in a flash! Generic acetone," he adds, "did the same excellent removal job." To make sure it doesn't damage the paint, try the acetone on an inconspicuous part of your car first.

Other people swear by these household sap removers.

- a dryer sheet dipped in water
- a soft cloth dipped in mineral spirits, rubbing alcohol, hand sanitizer, or Avon's Skin So Soft.

Always test them on an inconspicuous area. Some may remove the car's wax, so wash and wax your vehicle afterward.

Act fast to blast away bird droppings. Carry a bottle of no-salt seltzer water in your car at all times, and no bird will ever catch you unprepared.

Bird droppings are highly acidic, so you need to clean them off your car as soon as possible. Otherwise, they can damage the paint. Plus, they're easier to remove while fresh.

No-salt seltzer is simply carbonated water. Shaken up, it doubles as an impromptu water hose to blast away bird droppings without harming your car's finish. Take the cap off, put your thumb over the mouth, and shake. Wash the spot once you get home

MYTHBUSTER

Hidden hazard of 4-wheel drive

Four-wheel drive vehicles aren't as safe as you think on snowy, icy roads. They may take off faster, but they tend to brake slower and get less traction.

All-wheel and four-wheel drives divide the engine's power evenly among all four wheels, which helps you accelerate faster on slick surfaces. It doesn't improve your braking power, however. Your tires, not the engine, are what give you traction to slow down on slippery roads.

When it comes to driving in wintry weather, a front-wheel drive car with four good snow tires brakes faster and handles better around curves than a four-wheel drive with all-season tires.

Get your car ready for winter. Three quick tips can keep you rolling in the worst weather.

- Wax your headlights to keep road slush and mud from sticking to them. You'll have better visibility at night, not to mention less muck to wash off. Ordinary car wax will do it. Simply apply it with a soft cloth every few weeks.

- Stop doors from freezing shut. Spray a little cooking spray on a cloth or paper towel and rub it into the rubber gasket around each door.

- Thaw a frozen lock with a squirt of hand sanitizer. The alcohol in hand sanitizers is also the main ingredient in commercial de-icers. Squeeze sanitizing gel made with at least 60-percent alcohol onto the key and lock.

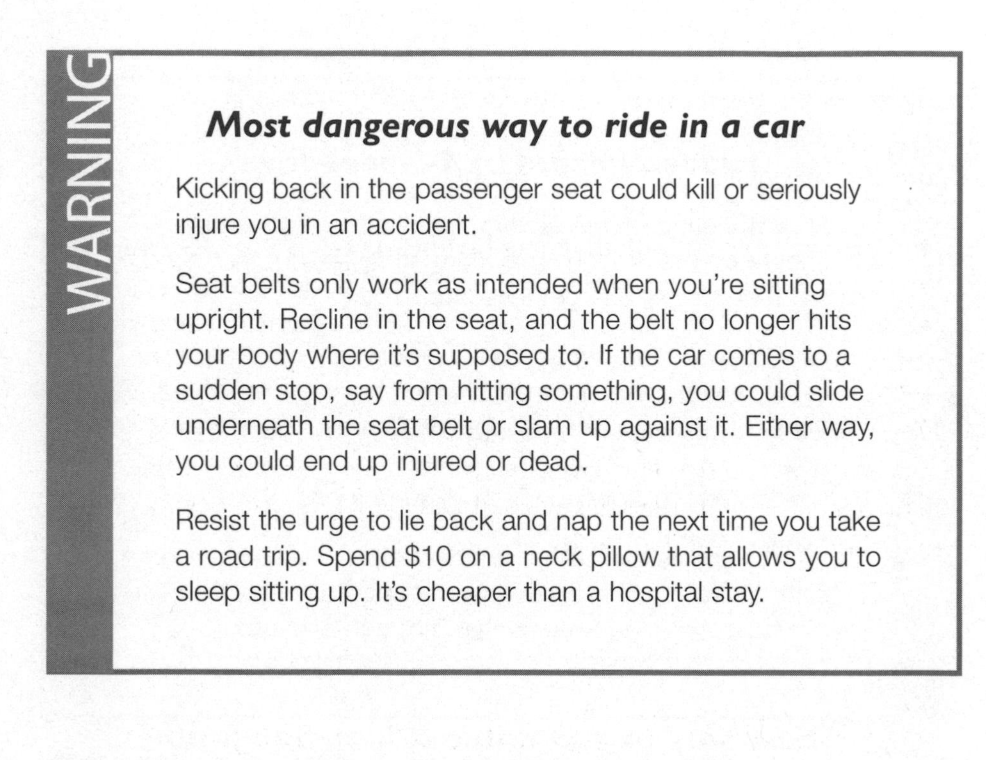
WARNING

Most dangerous way to ride in a car

Kicking back in the passenger seat could kill or seriously injure you in an accident.

Seat belts only work as intended when you're sitting upright. Recline in the seat, and the belt no longer hits your body where it's supposed to. If the car comes to a sudden stop, say from hitting something, you could slide underneath the seat belt or slam up against it. Either way, you could end up injured or dead.

Resist the urge to lie back and nap the next time you take a road trip. Spend $10 on a neck pillow that allows you to sleep sitting up. It's cheaper than a hospital stay.

Cold-weather prep keeps engine humming. Winters are hard on your car. Baby it a little to give it a longer life.

- Warm up the engine. You aren't the only one who moves slower in cold weather. Let the engine idle for five to 10 minutes before driving to circulate oil to all the moving parts.

- Be sure your battery has plenty of charge before winter sets in. Cranking a car can suck three times more power from the battery in cold weather than in warm.
- Keep the gas tank at least half-full. This keeps water from condensing in the tank and the gas line from freezing, plus gives you extra run-time if you get stranded in bad weather.
- Replace a dirty air filter. A clean filter is even more important in winter to keep air flowing into the fuel injection system. A dirty filter also does more harm to your car's performance and gas mileage in winter than summer.

Make your own removable bumper sticker. Forget about scraping stickers off your fender. Turn your favorite bumper stickers into car magnets.

Save the flat refrigerator magnets businesses send you. Lay them out side by side on the table, face up. Next, peel the adhesive backing off a bumper sticker and lay it across the magnets. Press down firmly, and trim away the extra with scissors.

Don't have any magnets lying around? Head to the hardware store and buy a magnetic vent cover, or to the hobby store for a flat, magnetic sheet. Peel off the sticker's adhesive backing, press onto the magnetic sheet, and trim it to size.

HANDY HINT

Easy way to guarantee a spot-free finish

Always wash your car on overcast days or in the shade. Wash it in the hot sun, and the water will dry too fast and leave spots. The temperature difference between the hot car body and cool water can also make the metal contract, shortening the life of the paint and finish.

Level headlights for spot-on aim. You can pay your mechanic to do it, or you can do it yourself for free. All you need is a level place to park, some masking tape, a tape measure, and a flat wall to aim your lights at, like a garage door.

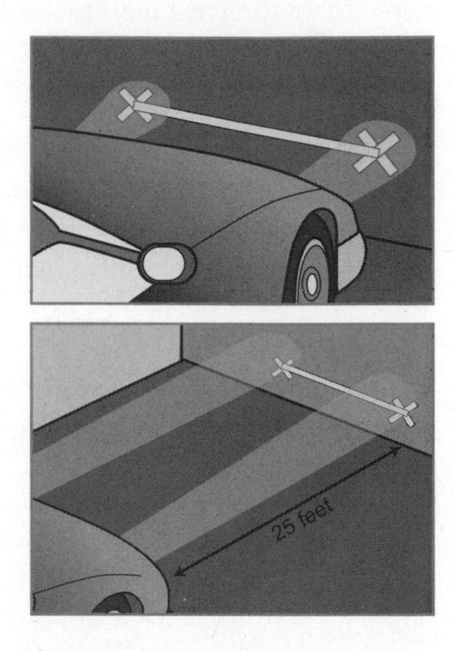

- First, make sure your tires are properly inflated.
- Park 1 foot away from the wall and turn on your lights.
- Find the center of each light on the wall and mark it with an 'X' made with masking tape.
- Take a long piece of tape and connect the center of one 'X' with the center of the other.
- Back up your car so it's exactly 25 feet from the wall, and check the lights again. The center of each light should be 2 inches below and to the right of the original marks.

If yours aren't, you can make some simple adjustments with a screwdriver. Look for a screw at the top of each headlight. Turning it will raise and lower the beam. Another screw on the side of the light will move it right and left. Slowly turn each screw until the lights reach the right position.

In some cars, the adjustment screw is under the hood, behind the headlight. Your owner's manual will tell you where to find yours.

Clear away headlight haze. Car headlights tend to haze over after a few years, dimming the light and making nighttime driving more dangerous. You can buy expensive kits to clean the plastic covers – but why, when you can do it yourself for free?

Simply squirt a little white toothpaste onto the plastic headlight cover. Rub in circles with a soft cloth, working your way across the cover and into all the corners. Work each cover for several minutes, then rinse well. Your headlights should sparkle once again.

Troubleshoot leaks the easy way

Spot the cause of mysterious leaks yourself, just by color and smell. Lay one or two large pieces of wrapping paper under your car, with the white side facing up. Leave it there overnight. In the morning, you'll have a map telling you what's dripping and where. Then check this chart to diagnose the problem.

Leak description	Most likely cause
green, slimy, sweet-smelling, and under the radiator or engine	Coolant coming from the radiator, hoses, or engine. In some cars, coolant is red or greenish-yellow.
dark brown or black, slippery, and under the engine	Motor oil. Exact location of leak will tell you if it's coming from the oil filter, oil drain plug, crankcase, or oil pan.
black and thick, like molasses; sulphur-smelling	Gear oil leaking from the manual transmission, differential, axle, or steering gears.
pink, red, or pinkish-brown	Automatic transmission fluid or power steering fluid. If found near the driver's-side front bumper, probably power steering fluid. Transmission fluid is pink when new but becomes browner with age.
blue	Windshield washer fluid. Washer fluid in winter may be pink, yellow, or orange.
clear	If watery, condensed water from the air conditioner. If oily and under the driver's-side front bumper, power steering fluid.
clear or light yellow	Brake fluid from master cylinder, brake lines, or brake cylinder, depending on location of leak.

WARNING

Safeguard a new paint job

Don't wax your car right away if you like the new paint job. Freshly painted cars need to cure anywhere from 30 to 90 days before waxing. Some professionals even recommend waiting three to six months.

A brand new car, however, can be waxed right away. That's because cars painted at the factory come already cured. The factory paints the car before any of the rubber, cloth, or plastic bits are installed. This allows them to bake on the paint in super-hot ovens that cure it quickly.

Body shops can't do that because such high temperatures would melt the rubber gaskets, plastic dashboard, and electrical wiring. They cure the paint at much lower temperatures. The finish will continue to cure for weeks, if not months. Until then, avoid waxing it.

Instant order for messy truck beds. Put an old shower curtain rod to work organizing the bed of your truck. It will keep things from sliding around or falling over the edge. Stretch the rod across the width of the bed, with one end against each side. Twist to lengthen it until it wedges tightly between sides.

3-cent solution for rust-free tools. Just toss a 3-cent item in your toolbox for a lifetime of rust-free tools. Keep a piece of charcoal or blackboard chalk on each shelf of your toolbox. Both absorb moisture from the air, helping tools stay high and dry.

To cut down on coal dust, drop the charcoal into the foot of a nylon stocking or old sock and tie the end closed. Or save those packets of silica gel that come in shoe boxes and pill bottles, and store them along with your tools.

Keep tools looking as good as new. WD-40 is an excellent anti-rust varnish. Spray it on your metal tools to stop rust, then wipe off the excess before storing them.

WD-40 helps remove rust, too. Spray it on the tool and scrub off the rust with fine steel wool. Don't try to take it off with sandpaper. This will scratch the metal. Next, wipe away any oil still on the tool with a clean, soft cloth.

You can follow this up with a coating of automotive paste wax, if you like, for a long-lasting finish. Or simply wipe down your tools occasionally with another coat of WD-40.

4 ways to remove a stripped screw. These handyman secrets can remove the toughest screws, even if the slot is completely stripped.

- Grab a hacksaw to deepen a stripped slot or create a brand new one. Then reach for your screwdriver and take out the screw.
- File down two sides of the screw to make them more square. Now grip the squared-off screw with a wrench to remove it.
- Drill out the screw with a thin drill bit. Position the bit in the middle of the screw's head and drill through its center. The screw should eventually come free.
- Pick up an inexpensive screw extractor from your local hardware store to make short work of stripped screws. Drill a small hole in the screw's head, insert the extractor bit, and twist. As the bit twists, the screw will back out.

Permanent fix for perpetually loose screws. Stop fiddling around with loose screws. Tightening them doesn't always last, but there's one sure way to make them stick. Unscrew them part of the way and dab a little clear nail polish on the threads and under the head, then tighten them again. The polish will keep the screw from backing out, plus prevent rust.

Free the worst stuck screws. Rusty and just plain stubborn screws can bring your project to a screeching halt. Get back in gear with these three tricks.

- The acids in some everyday items can help loosen a stuck screw or bolt enough for you to turn it. Soak a rag in Coca-Cola and lay it over the bolt or screw. Let sit a few minutes and try loosening it again. Soda water, lemon juice, and hydrogen peroxide may do the trick, too.

- Spray the stuck screw with a penetrating oil, like WD-40. Next, insert a screwdriver, and tap the end with a mallet or hammer while turning it. Tapping helps break the rusty bond. Let the spray soak in, then try removing the screw.

- Sometimes it's more a matter of arm strength and torque – or lack thereof. Try this trick on slotted screws. Insert the largest flat head screwdriver that will fit. Clamp a wrench around the flat head, and lean on the screwdriver while turning the wrench.

Guard wood, walls, and trim from hammer damage. When prying out nails, place a sponge or wood block under the hammer head to keep it from denting the surface. A scrap of carpet or rubber spatula will also work. Easier still, grab the baseball cap you're wearing, and slide the bill under the hammer as you pull.

To hammer in a nail without ruining trim, try this trick. Cut a piece of pegboard a few inches square, large enough to cover the trim where you plan to hammer. Get the nail started, then slide a hole in the pegboard over the nail head. Hammer away until you get the nail in as far as you can.

Remove the board, and finish knocking the nail in with a pin punch or nail set. A nail set has a narrow end that you place against the nail head and a wide end you hammer on. It's perfect for getting nails flush in delicate trim.

ALTERNATE USES

Sort nails and screws with ease

Do something useful with those extra Tupperware lids stashed in your cabinet. Large, upside-down lids make a great place to pour loose screws and nails as you sort through them. And their lip keeps hardware from rolling off the edge and onto the floor. Find what you need, then fold the lid in half and funnel the bits back into their container.

The key to opening a stuck lock. First, try lubricating the lock with a little graphite. Grab a soft pencil and run it up and down the tops of the teeth on your key. Once you've built up some graphite on the teeth, insert the key in the lock and turn it back and forth to work in the lubricant. You can also pick up a tube of powdered graphite from your local hardware store.

If that doesn't do the trick, check your key for rough edges. Use a nail file to gently remove any burrs.

You may need to take the lock apart in order to clean it more thoroughly. Knobs often have hidden screws, so don't panic if you can't find them at first. Look for a small hole on the underside of the knob, where it connects to the door. Insert a thin, straight screwdriver into the hole, and tug on the knob to remove it. Then slide a butter knife or flat head screwdriver under the face plate to pry it off.

You can clean the inner moving parts with a cotton swab dipped in rubbing alcohol. Once you reassemble it, squirt a little powdered graphite in through the keyhole. Insert the key and turn it back and forth to lubricate the lock.

Get instant small-tool storage. Don't waste money on fancy tool storage systems. These three are fast, easy, and – best of all – free, since you probably have these items lying around.

- Bungee cords make storing small tools neat and easy. Stretch one along the edge of a shelf, and staple it at each end. Continue stapling it to the shelf about every 2 or 3 inches. Slide pliers, screwdrivers, and other hand tools into the bungee "pockets" between staples.

- An old belt works the same way. Nail it along the edge of a shelf or workbench. Put a nail through the belt every 2 to 3 inches, leaving enough slack between nails to form a pocket for small tools.

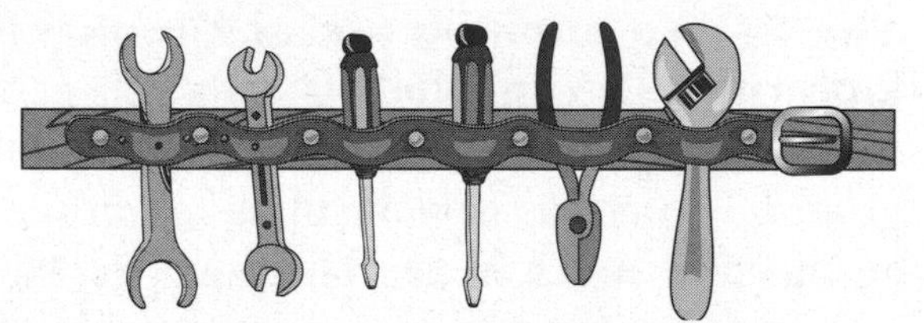

- Fill a bucket or small trough with sand, then pour in one-quarter cup of motor oil. Stir together well, and stick the metal ends of rust-prone tools into the sand. They'll stay sharp, clean, and rust-free.

No dust, no fuss paintbrush holder. Lay your hands on a magnetic strip, the kind used to hold knives in the kitchen. Tack it to the wall or the side of your workbench, and use it to hang paintbrushes. Stick the metal apron that binds the bristles against the magnet. Hang the brushes to dry with the bristles facing down so they collect less dust.

These strips are perfect for holding small metal tools, too, like screwdrivers and wrenches. The more powerful the magnet, the heavier the tool it can hold.

Keep tall tools in line and out of the way. Tall tools were once tricky to store, but not anymore. Set cup hooks into two exposed wall studs in your garage. Stretch a bungee cord across the space between the beams, and hook each end onto a cup hook. Now you can stand rakes, hoes, brooms, and other long-handled items between studs.

Not all workshops feature exposed studs. If yours doesn't, then improvise. Turn an old bar stool upside down and place it in the corner. Stand tall tools in it, handles down, for super-simple storage.

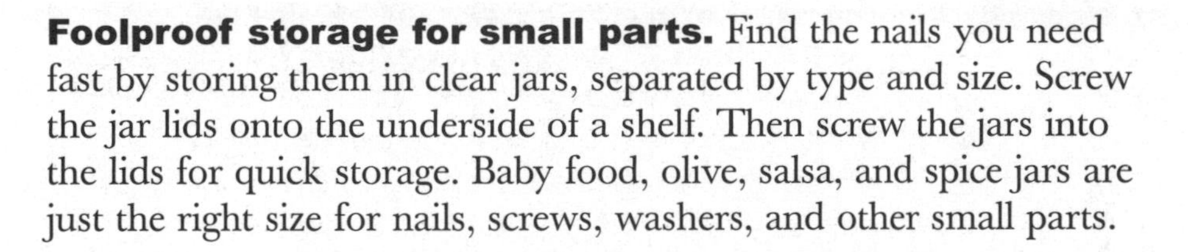

Foolproof storage for small parts. Find the nails you need fast by storing them in clear jars, separated by type and size. Screw the jar lids onto the underside of a shelf. Then screw the jars into the lids for quick storage. Baby food, olive, salsa, and spice jars are just the right size for nails, screws, washers, and other small parts.

No clear jars? No problem. You can put these parts in opaque containers, too. Simply tape one of the items in the container onto the outside so you can see at a glance what's in it.

Guard the blade on sharp saws. Recycle a leaky, old water hose and get a free blade guard for your saws. Cut a piece of hose the same length as your saw blade. Slit the hose down the middle on one side, and slide it over the saw teeth. This trick works on axes and other sharp blades, too.

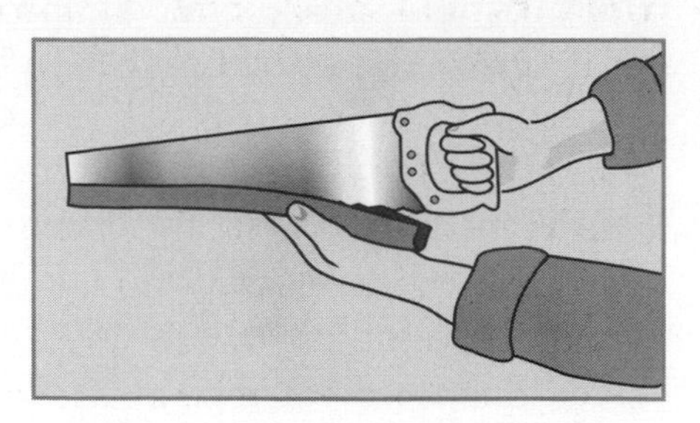

An old tire inner tube can serve the same purpose on a miter or circular saw. Just slit it open and slide over the round blade.

Surefire way to stop losing drill bits. Store drill bits in a block of Styrofoam, rescued from a shipping box, or a piece of green floral foam. Push the bits in, but leave the shank sticking out.

You can store screwdrivers, chisels, and other small, pointed tools this way, too. Push these all the way to the bottom of the foam, so the block doesn't grow top heavy and topple over.

HANDY HINT

Dust-free secret to drilling in drywall

Make drilling into drywall a zero-mess chore. Instead of letting the fine white dust from the hole drift everywhere, capture it as it falls. Tape a brown paper lunch bag or plain envelope below the spot where you plan to drill the hole. Make sure the mouth of the bag or envelop is open to catch dust as it falls, then start drilling. Throw away the dust-filled container when you finish.

Drilling into a drywall ceiling? No problem. Poke a hole in the bottom of a small paper cup, slide it over the drill bit with the cup's mouth facing the ceiling, and start drilling. The cup will catch the dust as you work.

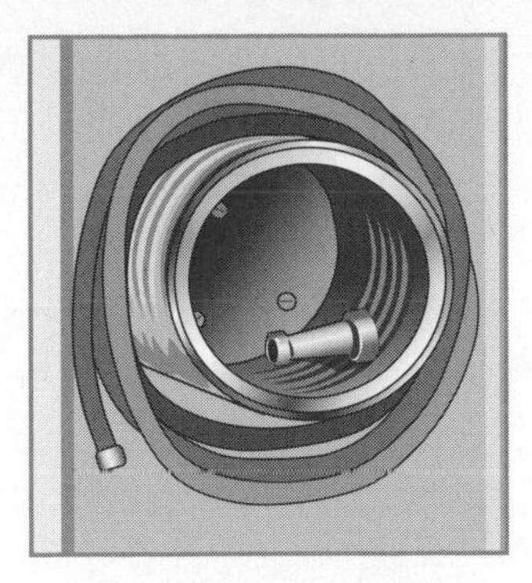

Keep hoses kink-free. Save a sturdy metal coffee can and put it to good use in your garage. Drill a few holes in the bottom and bolt or screw it to the garage wall. Wrap your garden hose around it in winter, or hang bulky outdoor extension cords over it to keep them tangle-free and off the floor. Store the hose nozzle or other small parts inside the can so you can find them easily later.

PAINT

Color your world beautiful

Renovate a room with color. Play around with wall colors to get the effect you want.

- Make a long, narrow room appear wider by painting the long walls a light color and the short walls a darker one.
- Raise the roof, or at least make the ceiling seem higher, by painting it a lighter color than the walls.
- Bring a cozy, intimate feel to open spaces by painting the walls with colors that seem to come toward you, like red, gold, orange, or brown.
- Open up a small space with receding colors such as green, blue, and violet.
- Make a room look more formal and sophisticated by using deep, rich colors and dark neutral tones.

In general, light colors make spaces feel bigger and tend to boost your mood. Whites, in particular, make a room feel clean and full of light.

Reach high ceilings without climbing a ladder. Push brooms often have a handle that unscrews from the main head. Remove the handle and screw it into the base of your paint roller to get another few feet of reach.

Need something longer? Try a golf ball retriever. You can't screw the roller onto the retriever handle, but you can duct tape the roller handle and the end of the retriever together.

Pick the right paint color the first time. Remember that the light in a room plays a huge role in how color comes across. Paint may look like one shade in the store under bright fluorescent bulbs but completely different under the soft incandescent or natural sunlight in your home.

Buy a small sample of paint to test on your walls. Brush it on, then watch over the next 24 hours. See how it looks during the light of day and in the glow of lamps at night.

Key to making brushes last a lifetime. Take good care of high-quality brushes, and they'll last for decades.

To clean off a water-based paint like latex, start by filling a container with warm water and gentle dish soap. Swish the brush around to remove most of the paint, and rinse under running water. Run a metal brush comb through the bristles to loosen any stubborn, dried paint. Even a hair comb will do. Then shake excess water out of the brush.

Bob Carey, longtime do-it-yourselfer, is a fanatic about cleaning his paint brushes. It pays off, says his wife, Angela. "He has brushes that look new decades later!"

His secret – wrap clean, wet brushes in a heavy-duty shop paper towel. Fold it around the bristles to give the brush back its original shape. "He wraps the brush carefully, so the bristles won't have any bends or dry in a weird way. Then he hangs them up wrapped that way. His old, expensive brushes still look like new."

Rescue a petrified paintbrush. Soften up hardened brushes by soaking them in vinegar. This kitchen staple can help salvage brushes crusted with dried paint. Bring a cup of white vinegar to a boil, pour into a glass jar, and soak the brush overnight.

Don't just plop the brush in. Resting the bristles against the bottom of a jar can bend them out of shape. Rig up a simple hanger, instead. Slide a straightened wire coat hanger through the hole in the brush handle. Lay the straight piece across the mouth of the jar and let the brush dangle in vinegar.

Pattern your walls with a simple technique. Tape your roller, not your walls, to create a pleasing pattern of squares. It's more affordable than wallpaper and a whole lot easier. This clever idea comes courtesy of Lowe's.

- First, paint the entire wall the color you want your squares to be.
- Next, find a fresh roller cover, and wrap bands of blue painter's tape around it. Alternate by wrapping one band loosely and the next band tightly, so it compresses the fuzzy nap.

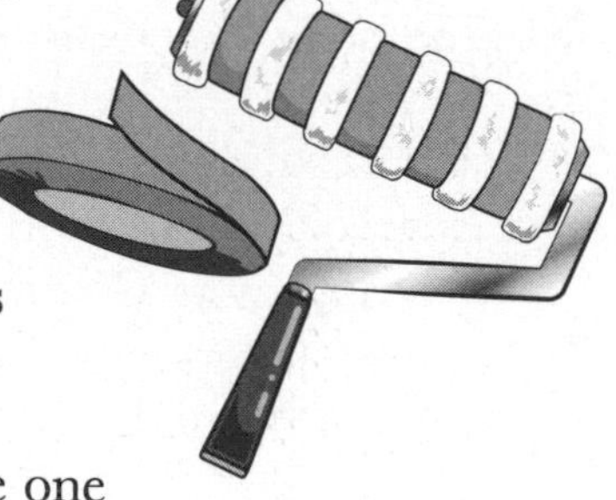

- Pull off the loosely wrapped painter's tape, revealing the nap.
- Roll it in your second paint color, the one you want as the background for your pattern.

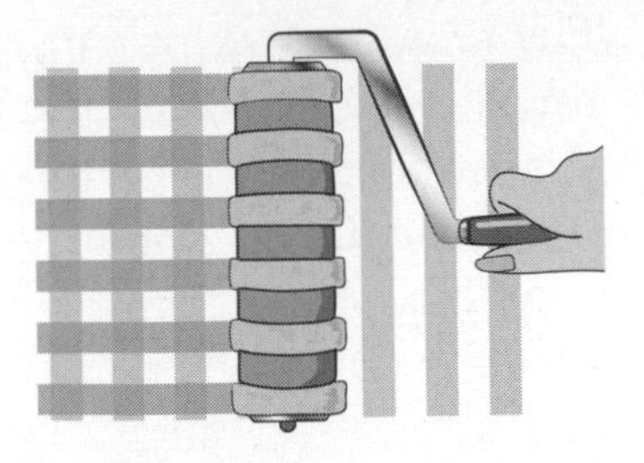

- Start at the top of the wall and roll straight down. Use a level to pencil in a vertical guideline, if needed.
- Paint the horizontal lines next. You don't have to wait for the vertical lines to dry.
- Go in with a small brush to create squares in corners and other places your roller can't reach.

The pattern doesn't have to be perfect. In fact, the variations give the room its cozy, cottage feel. Just be sure to wipe up any obvious smudges with a damp cloth before they dry. For larger squares, buy the wider 1.5-inch or 2-inch painter's tape.

Paint a room without all the fumes. There's nothing better than a freshly painted room, and nothing worse than the smell. Banish paint odors with these clever tricks.

- Vanilla can mask the odor of stinky paint, it won't discolor most paint types, and it's something you probably already have in your pantry. Add a few drops of vanilla extract to a gallon of paint. This simple tip will help keep paint odors under control.
- Peppermint oil has a similar effect, and it shouldn't affect how the paint looks once on the wall.
- Charcoal can suck smells right out of the air. Activated carbon charcoal works best, but regular cooking charcoal will get the job done, too. Crush it into smaller pieces and place in a bucket with a damp paper towel or rag. Leave it in the center of a freshly painted room overnight.
- Water helps absorb strong smells, too, although not as well as charcoal. Leave a few buckets of water in the room overnight, then empty in the morning.

Newly painted rooms stink because of the volatile organic compounds (VOCs) in paint. These toxic ingredients, including benzene, formaldehyde, kerosene, and ammonia, give paint its odor. The more VOCs a paint contains, the stronger it smells.

That's why it's important to open the windows, run fans, and air out the room as paint dries. Try to paint on days you can open the windows. Do this throughout the house, not just in the room you're painting. If possible, put a box fan in one of the room's windows and draw the air outside.

HANDY HINT

Invest in fume-free paint

The surest way to cut down on toxic paint fumes is to buy paints labeled "VOC-free," "no-VOC," or "zero-VOC." They can help you fight indoor pollution and beautify your home.

These paints have virtually no chemical solvents or preservatives, which translates into very little odor. They're also more natural, sometimes made from milk protein, clay, or citrus and other plant ingredients.

At the very least, choose latex over oil- and alkyd-based paints. Latex contains fewer volatile organic compounds (VOCs).

Use color to boost your mood. Set the mood with the right palette of paint colors.

- Create a peaceful, relaxing retreat with "cool" colors, such as blues, greens, turquoise, and violets. These colors may also aid concentration.

- Encourage cheerfulness, playfulness, and conversation with "warm" colors like bright red, orange, and yellow.

- Combine warm and cool colors in the same room to create a sense of balance.
- Cultivate harmony and peace with taupe. Not too warm, not too cool, it's the perfect neutral.

No-sweat way to wash off paint. Ordinary shaving cream takes off more than hair – it removes the latex paint from your hands. Squirt a little foam in your palms, rub it in, then rinse. For oil paint, rub baby oil, butter, or margarine into your hands. Wipe them dry, then wash with soap and water.

Say "so long" to dusty woodwork. Want to dust your woodwork less often? Apply a coat of paste wax. It's great on both painted and varnished baseboards and chair rails. It creates such a slick surface that dust won't stick, and the finish makes trim less likely to suffer scratches.

Look for "finishing wax" when treating painted wood. It's the least potent. Rub wax into the trim with a lint-free rag, let dry, then buff until you see a sheen on the surface. Don't wax spots where the paint has chipped and the bare wood shows through.

You'll still need to dust occasionally, but not nearly as often. Simply wipe a damp cloth or chamois across the wood to clean it.

Painter's secret for perfect windows. Stop spending a fortune on painter's tape. Use wet newspaper to protect window panes. Cut the newspaper in strips about 4 inches wide. Dampen them in the sink or with a spray bottle, and stick the strips to the window. The paper will cling on its own. The sturdier paper used for advertising circulars may work better than newsprint.

Make your own milk paint. It's the original, all-natural, nontoxic paint, and you can make it yourself. Milk paint was a hallmark of Colonial America, since nearly every household owned a cow or goat. Even cave men loved it, painting their walls with milk-based paint 20,000 years ago.

That means plenty of time to perfect the recipe. Try this homemade paint yourself.

- Allow milk to warm up to room temperature.
- Add two cups of white vinegar or the juice of four lemons to one gallon of skim milk to make it curdle.
- Let the mix sit overnight at room temperature to finish curdling.
- Pour the mixture through cheesecloth to strain the curd. Rinse the curd with water and set it aside.
- Combine 3/4 cup of hydrated lime with 1 1/2 cups of water and stir until creamy.
- Add in the curd and stir until it dissolves. Break up large pieces if necessary.
- Combine lime-proof powdered pigment, available at art supply and hobby stores, with a little water and stir until creamy. Then add it to the lime mix.
- Strain again, this time pouring the mixture through the foot of a nylon stocking.

It's ready to use. Apply it with a cheap, natural-bristle brush. The first coat will go on thin, but the second coat will deepen the color and consistency. Store leftover paint in a sealed container in the refrigerator up to a few days, until the milk sours.

This paint won't cover up wall blemishes like latex or oil paint. It's too thin. Be sure to get your surface smooth before you begin.

Sound too complicated? Buy ready-to-use milk paint from a supplier like Old-Fashioned Milk Paint at the website *www.milkpaint.com* or by calling 866-350-6455. Simply mix it with water and paint away.

Homemade spackling saves the day. Patch up cracks and holes in your walls with a paste made of everyday kitchen supplies. That's right, hidden in your kitchen, you'll find a cheap way to repair your walls.

- Mix together four tablespoons of white flour and one-third teaspoon of salt, then add in enough paint or primer to make a doughy or putty-like texture.
- Smooth it over small cracks and dents with a putty knife. Let dry until the surface is completely hard before painting or sanding.

For oil- or lacquer-based paints, leave out the salt. Don't make a batch bigger than you can use in one day.

This flour mixture works best for small cracks and dings in the wall. For bigger imperfections, pick up some Plaster of Paris at your local hobby store. Mix one-quarter cup of vinegar for every pound of plaster. This will keep it from drying before you finish applying it. Then add enough water to make a paste.

Block paint smudges with petroleum jelly. Wipe a thin coat of petroleum jelly on doorknob faceplates, hinges, and other metal hardware to prevent paint smudges from drying on the metal. Then wipe off the jelly when finished. It's a lot easier than cleaning up dried paint.

A thin coat of petroleum jelly will protect window panes, too. Apply along the outer edge of panes, against the paint line. Paint will stick to the jelly, not the glass.

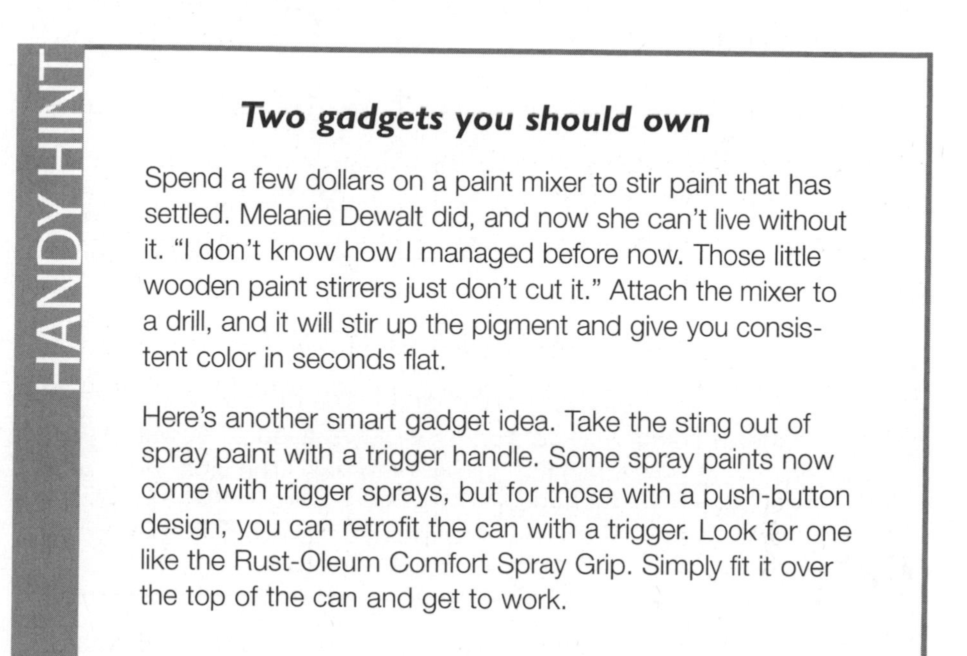
HANDY HINT

Two gadgets you should own

Spend a few dollars on a paint mixer to stir paint that has settled. Melanie Dewalt did, and now she can't live without it. "I don't know how I managed before now. Those little wooden paint stirrers just don't cut it." Attach the mixer to a drill, and it will stir up the pigment and give you consistent color in seconds flat.

Here's another smart gadget idea. Take the sting out of spray paint with a trigger handle. Some spray paints now come with trigger sprays, but for those with a push-button design, you can retrofit the can with a trigger. Look for one like the Rust-Oleum Comfort Spray Grip. Simply fit it over the top of the can and get to work.

Smart ways to store paint. Pop off the lid and stretch a piece of plastic wrap across the mouth of the can. Tap the lid back on securely. The plastic helps seal the paint can so air can't get in. Store paint cans upside down, so the paint creates a tight seal against the lid. This keeps air out, lengthening the paint's shelf life.

Leave the original label on the lid, with the paint's name and ID number on it. Grab a permanent marker and write the date you opened the can and the room you painted on the lid, too.

Keep the cans in a dry area that doesn't get too hot or freezing cold. Don't, however, put them in the same room as a furnace or water heater. A spark or pilot light from these appliances could ignite the paint.

Latex paints can last 10 years if stored properly, while oil-based paints are good for 15 years. Here are two easy tricks to tell if paint is still good.

- Open the can and stir. If the color mixes easily, it's probably still good.
- Brush it across an old newspaper. If you see lumps, the paint has gone bad.

WARNING

Little-known paint danger

Never use an exterior paint on the inside of your house. Exterior paints may contain a mercury-based preservative, aimed at preventing the growth of fungus. The label will tell you if your paint does.

Make cleanup a snap. Spend less time cleaning up and more time enjoying your handiwork with these amazing tips.

- Avoid paint dribbles down the side of the can. When you pour paint into a roller tray or other container, use a paint stirring stick to guide the flow. Hold it across the can's opening as you pour, and the paint will run down the stirrer instead of the side of the can.
- Don't wipe the extra paint from your brush on the inside lip of the can. This gunks up the rim. Instead, tie a piece of twine from one handle to the other

across the mouth of the can. Make the line taut, and wipe your brush against it while painting.

- Tap a small finishing nail through the rim in several places, leaving small holes that let paint drain back into the can. It's a neat way to keep paint from building up in the rim.

Easier way to paint baseboards. Give your back and knees a break when painting baseboards. Rather than kneeling and crouching, borrow your grandson's skateboard or your husband's mechanic's creeper – the thing he uses to roll under the car. Sit on it while painting and scoot yourself along as you finish each section.

Give the slip to stuck-on stickers. The best way to remove a sticky label – fight oil with oil. The adhesives on most stubborn stickers are oil-soluble. That means oils can break the bond that makes them sticky.

Try spraying the label with a lubricating spray, like WD-40, the cooking spray PAM, or a petroleum-based laundry stain remover. Even vegetable, mineral, and baby oil can help. Then rub off the label gently with a scrubbing sponge or paper towel, or lift it off with a putty knife.

Oil doesn't work as well on vertical surfaces. It tends to slide off before it has a chance to soak in. Cover the oiled label with a piece of plastic wrap to help trap the liquid, and let it sit for a while. Or rub a thin layer of mayonnaise into the sticker. The vegetable oil in mayo will help break down the adhesive, while its creamy consistency will keep it in place.

Heat does the trick, too. Aim a hair dryer set on high heat at the label. The heat will soften the glue, so you can peel it off with ease.

For especially stubborn stickers, try a solvent such as lighter fluid. It contains naphtha, and a few drops should take care of a stubborn sticker. Mild solvents like vinegar and rubbing alcohol will remove them, as well, with a little elbow grease.

ALTERNATE USES

Super solvent cleans almost everything

WD-40 ought to be the eighth wonder of the modern world. This one surprising solvent will wipe away everything from crayon marks to road tar, and clean anything from smudges on stainless steel and chrome to stickum left behind by labels or tape.

Wipe rusty tools with WD-40 and very fine steel wool, and watch the rust come right off. Rub a light coating of it on saw blades and other metal parts to prevent rust in the future. It also loosens stuck screws, takes tar off your hands, cleans the gunk off safety goggles, and lubricates garage door runners.

Visit the official WD-40 website at *www.wd40.com* for thousands more uses.

Make permanent marker disappear. Permanent marker doesn't have to be permanent. These techniques can easily remove it from doors, floors, and even skin.

- Dip a cotton ball or swab in acetone-free nail polish remover and scrub off the marker.
- Rub the stain with a soft cloth dipped in vegetable oil. Then wipe clean with a damp cloth.
- Dampen a cotton ball with rubbing alcohol and work it into the mark.
- Spritz the stain with hairspray. Let dry and wash it off.
- Scrub with white toothpaste, not gel, and a damp cloth, working in a circular motion. Rinse with water.
- Write over the stain with a dry erase marker. Let the new ink dry, then wipe off. The permanent marker should come off along with the dry erase.

15 uses for empty coffee cans. Or any other can with a plastic lid, for that matter. Give these canisters a second, or third, life with one of these handy ideas.

- Seed bald spots in your lawn. Punch small holes in the bottom for grass seed to pass through. Snap the lid over the bottom, and fill the can with seed. Remove the lid when you're ready to shake out some seed.
- Guard seedlings against harsh, windy weather. Cut out the bottom with a can opener and set the sleeve over your seedlings. Push it into the dirt to keep the can from shifting.
- Collect kitchen scraps for the compost heap. Cut an "X" shape in the plastic lid and push peels and scraps through it. Empty in the compost pile when full.
- Make glittering outdoor votive holders. Fill the can with water and freeze solid. This helps support the sides of the can. Punch

patterns through the sides with a ball peen hammer and assorted nails, or with a drill. Drop in a votive candle and light.

- Store twine for tangle-free access. Poke a hole in the can lid. Drop the twine inside, and pull it through the hole as needed.

- Bake small batches of quick bread. Remove the lid, place the batter inside a clean can, and bake as usual.

- Use as a container for holiday cookies and other edible gifts. Place goodies inside a clean can, then decorate with wrapping paper and ribbon for a sweet, homemade gift.

- Store ready-made burger patties. Place a piece of wax paper in the bottom. Drop in a shaped patty, then another piece of wax paper. Keep alternating until the can is full, and freeze for later.

- Make a bird feeder. Punch several holes around the bottom edge with an old-fashioned bottle opener. To help hold in the seed, don't push down the tin all the way. Drill two holes at the top, one on each side of the can. Fill with sunflower seeds and pop on the lid. Slide a chain or rope through the top holes and hang from a nearby tree.

- Stash extra plastic grocery bags in them. Cut an "X" in the lid and pull a bag through as you need one.

- Coil your belts and tuck them safely inside the can, then set on your closet shelf. Belts will stay neat and dust-free.

- Turn it into a makeshift piggy bank. Cut a slot in the lid to slide change and dollars through. Make it your rainy-day fund for doing something fun.

- Create free instant pots for plants. Drill a few holes in the can's bottom and add a layer of gravel for drainage. Fill with potting soil and a small plant.

- Pour in fat, used oil, drippings, and anything else you can't dump down the drain. Toss the whole can when full.
- Paint out of a clean coffee can instead of a big paint bucket. Pour in your color and carry the can around for light touch up or trim work.

10 must-have fix-it items

These 10 things lying around your house can fix and clean literally hundreds of items.

Item	Quick fix
WD-40	removes tool rust, frees stuck screws and zippers, blasts gum and grease on laundry, lifts away stuck-on stickers
white vinegar	defrosts frozen windshields, prevents mildew in the shower, removes sweat and grass stains, softens laundry and hardened paint brushes
baking soda	saves pans from burned-on food, fights grease stains, takes tarnish off silver, whitens clothes, makes bathtub rings disappear
dryer sheets	remove bugs and tree sap from cars, clean window blinds, banish stinky shoe odors
white toothpaste	buffs out CD, DVD, and windshield scratches; cleans ceramic cook tops and scuffed-up sneakers
nail polish remover	cleans sap off cars, unsticks Super Glue, removes permanent marker
vegetable oil	wipes off permanent marker, lubricates gardening tools, lifts off labels
rubbing alcohol	cleans computer keyboards and DVDs, gets gunk out of stuck locks, lifts ink from clothing
nail polish	keeps thread from fraying, tightens loose screws, lengthens the life of costume jewelry
shaving cream	stops fog from forming on car windows, washes latex paint off hands

Solve Super Glue mishaps fast. Super Glue is super strong, but it can be removed if you know the secret. The makers of this famous glue admit it has one weakness – acetone, a compound found in some nail polish removers.

Simply dip a cotton swab in nail polish remover, then rub it against your glued-together fingers or other accidentally stuck items. Wash your skin with soap and water afterward, and rub on lotion to combat the chemical's drying effects.

Acetone will dissolve the glue without harming your skin. It can, however, discolor fabrics and laminate countertops, so test it in an inconspicuous area first. If you don't have acetone, try soaking your skin in warm, soapy water.

Read the label on your nail polish remover to make sure it contains acetone. You'll need the real deal to remove Super Glue.

Scrub away dirt and grime with oatmeal. Keep a canister of dried oatmeal by your workshop sink. Reach for it the next time your hands get so dirty you're afraid to touch anything. Pour a little oatmeal in your palm, add a small amount of water, and rub the mixture into your hands. The oatmeal's abrasiveness will gently scour away the toughest dirt.

Pick the right gloves for workshop chemicals. You may think household latex gloves do a good job protecting your hands, but think again. Some common workshop chemicals require special gloves for safe handling.

Take paint stripper. Rubber gloves absorb its main ingredient, methylene chloride, like a sponge, holding it against your skin while you work.

Check the following chart of common chemicals to find the best gloves for handling them.

Household chemical	Type of glove to wear
pesticides and liquid fertilizer	nitrile
paint strippers containing methylene chloride	polyvinyl alcohol (PVA) or viton (fluorocarbon)
turpentine and mineral spirits	nitrile
kerosene, linseed oil, or tung oil	neoprene or nitrile
lacquer thinners	neoprene
VM&P naphtha (Varnish Makers and Painters' Naphtha)	nitrile or neoprene
shellac made with denatured alcohol	nitrile
methyl ethyl ketone (butanone), used to thin lacquer, varnish, and other finishes	butyl
toluene, used as a paint thinner and stripper	viton or PVA
epoxy-based glues	butyl gloves for water-based epoxy; nitrile gloves for solvent-based epoxy
epoxy paints for use on bare metal	nitrile
paints (epoxy-based wood sealers) for use on wood floors	nitrile
concrete etcher or masonry cleaner containing hydrochloric acid	nitrile gloves for short periods of contact; neoprene gloves for longer periods
acetone	latex, if working with acetone for less than 10 minutes; butyl gloves for longer periods of contact

Now that you know how to choose the right gloves, learn how to care for them. PVA gloves are water soluble, meaning they break down in water. Clean them with mineral spirits, not soap and water, when you finish using them.

Check gloves for tears and pinholes before each use by filling them with water, rolling the cuff closed, and watching for leaks. A punctured glove won't protect you from caustic chemicals.

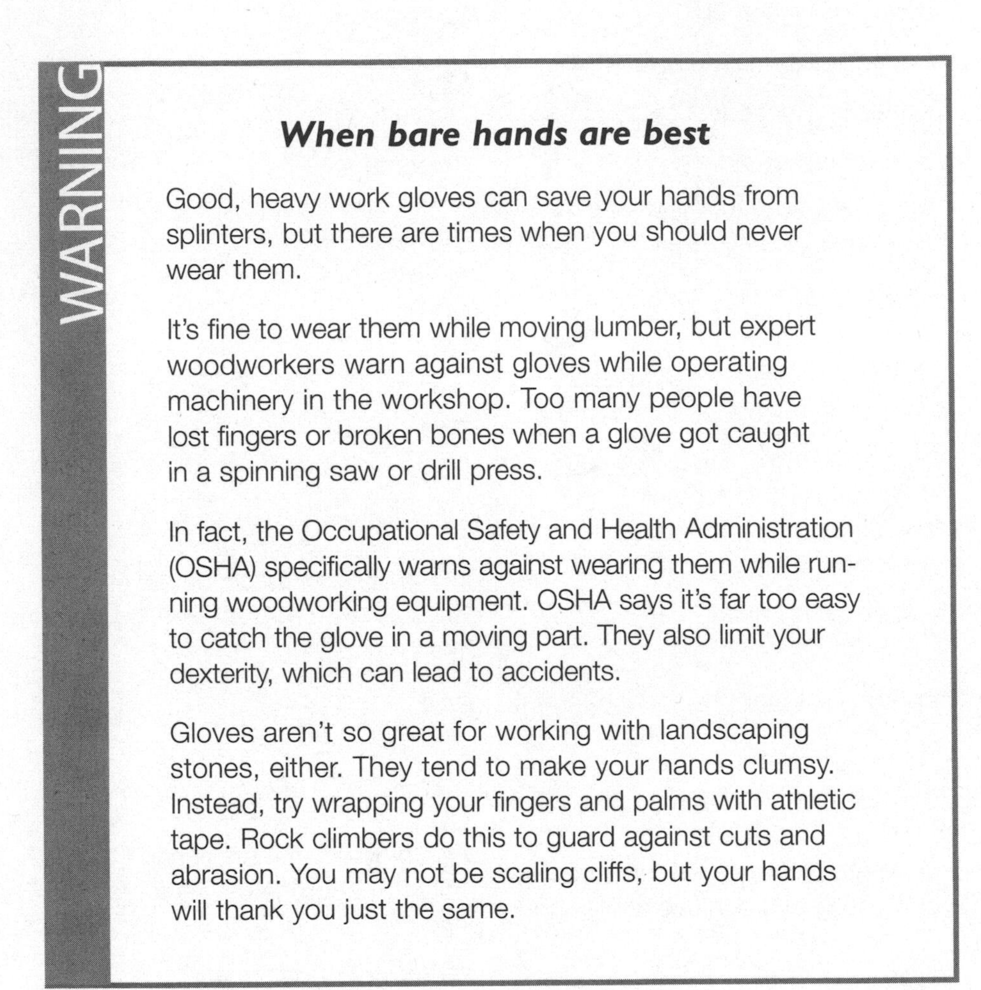
WARNING

When bare hands are best

Good, heavy work gloves can save your hands from splinters, but there are times when you should never wear them.

It's fine to wear them while moving lumber, but expert woodworkers warn against gloves while operating machinery in the workshop. Too many people have lost fingers or broken bones when a glove got caught in a spinning saw or drill press.

In fact, the Occupational Safety and Health Administration (OSHA) specifically warns against wearing them while running woodworking equipment. OSHA says it's far too easy to catch the glove in a moving part. They also limit your dexterity, which can lead to accidents.

Gloves aren't so great for working with landscaping stones, either. They tend to make your hands clumsy. Instead, try wrapping your fingers and palms with athletic tape. Rock climbers do this to guard against cuts and abrasion. You may not be scaling cliffs, but your hands will thank you just the same.

Dodge common DIY mistakes. Tackling your own projects can save big bucks, or it can cost you. Watch out for the most common blunders by do-it-yourselfers.

- Being unrealistic about how long, how hard, or how expensive a project will be. It will almost always take twice as long and cost twice as much as you expect. Plan on that from the start, and you won't get caught out of time, unfinished, and over budget.

- Taking on projects beyond your skill level. There's a saying, "If you have a saw in your hand and a question about what you're doing, you probably shouldn't be doing it." Knowing your own limits will help you budget more realistically and save you from making dangerous mistakes.

- Forgetting to measure twice, cut once. It's an even older adage, and one that's still true today. Double-check every measurement, angle, and fit. You'll save money by not having to scrap materials and start over, and you'll finish the job faster by avoiding a redo.

- Failing to get the right permits. Just assume you need one if your project is anything bigger than hanging wallpaper or painting a room. You may need a permit to ensure your home insurer continues to cover you. And your local code enforcer may shut you down mid-project if you don't have the proper permits posted.

- Using the wrong materials or tools for the job. Install regular wood instead of pressure-treated, for instance, and you can kiss your porch goodbye. Ask lots of questions when buying materials and tools to make sure you get the right ones.

Clever cover keeps workbench clean. Protect your workbench from glue mishaps and oily spills. Attach an old, vinyl, pull-down window shade to one end of your workbench, and put a hook on the other. Pull the shade out over the bench and hook it at the other end when you need to tackle a messy project. Wipe off any gunk when finished, and let dry before rolling it back up.

Tidy up wood with hidden storage. Make the most of all that unused overhead space in your garage. Unfinished ceilings with exposed joists offer the perfect place to store lumber, pipes, and other long materials. Just screw in several two-by-fours perpendicular to the joists, then store your items on top of them, between joists. The same technique also works outside for under-the-deck storage.

Never lose another work glove. Hang up your work gloves as soon as you finish. They'll dry faster and always be easy to find.

Take one of the clips off a wooden clothespin and drill a small hole through the top. Screw it into the workshop wall and reassemble the clothespin. Clip your gloves up after working. They will come free with a single tug.

Keep safety glasses sawdust-free. Rub them with a dryer sheet before cutting wood. The sheet's anti-static properties will literally rub off on the glasses, repelling sawdust that tries to stick to them. The glasses will stay clean longer, and you'll stay safer while working with saws.

A used dryer sheet can make short work of cleanup, too. Just swipe one across your workbench to collect leftover sawdust.

Put the squeeze on slipping garbage bags. Cut an old garden hose into several 6-inch pieces. Slit the hose sections down the middle. Line the can with a trash bag, and slide the hose over the edge of the can and bag to hold them in place.

For recycling and other less-smelly waste, try this trick. Take a trash can with a snap-on lid and cut out the lid's center. This leaves the rest of the lid snapped onto the can, holding the bag in place. Set the cutout portion on top as needed.

Quick fix for sagging shelves. A saggy wooden shelf dragging you down? Flip it over, so the bow faces down. It's not a permanent solution, but it will hold until you can replace the shelf with sturdier wood or add another support bracket.

No-sweat tip to spot dropped objects

Dropped a small screw and have no idea where it went? Flick on your flashlight and lay it on its side on the floor. Anything on the floor, no matter how small, will cast an easy-to-see shadow leading you right to your stray screw.

Shave stuck doors down to size. Figuring out exactly where your door is sticking can be the hardest part of fixing it. First, try tightening the screws that hold the hinges in place. This may pull the door in tightly enough for it to swing freely again.

If that doesn't do it, find where the door rubs against the frame. Take a piece of colored chalk and run it along the inside of the door frame. Now close the door and open it again. You'll see chalk marks along the edge of the door where it stuck. Sand down these areas and seal afterward with paint, varnish, or urethane to keep out wood-warping moisture.

Keep tape close at hand. Turn an old toilet paper or paper towel holder into a handy tape dispenser. Just mount it on the side of your workbench and slide on a few rolls of duct tape, masking tape, or electrical tape.

Chapter 9

OUTSIDE THE HOUSE

Ah, spring time. The birds are singing and your grill is calling. So are your deck, gutters, and roof. Never fear. These tips from the pros will make outdoor chores a breeze and have you ready to entertain in no time.

DECKS & PATIOS

Great outdoor spaces

Fix up your home for a faster sale. Some home improvements virtually pay for themselves when you sell your home. Others are a waste of time and money.

Luckily, *Remodeling* magazine can help you decide. Each year, it compares the cost of projects with how much value they typically add to a home, then publishes the results in its Cost vs. Value Report. Take a look at the eight most cost-effective upgrades for 2011.

Project	*Percent return at resale*
Replacing front door with new steel door	102.1
Installing new garage door	83.9
Upgrading to fiber-cement siding	80.0
Finishing minor kitchen remodel	72.8
Building wood deck	72.8
Installing wood replacement windows	72.4
Updating with new vinyl siding	72.4
Converting attic into bedroom	72.2

Unfortunately, not all improvements pay off at resale. According to the Cost vs. Value Report, these five home improvements aren't worth the effort or the money.

Project	Percent return at resale
Adding garage	59.2
Adding bathroom	53.3
Adding sunroom	48.6
Installing backup power generator	48.5
Remodeling home office	45.8

These numbers are based on national averages. Your return may differ by region and even neighborhood. Have a local real estate agent or appraiser take a look at your home and tell you which projects offer the biggest payoffs in your area.

10 easy tricks to boost your home's value. Try on these 10 not-so-extreme home makeover tips. They'll increase your home's value without costing a fortune.

- Quit hiding your home from potential buyers. Cut back plants to let in more light and reveal the features of your house. Trim shrubs to below window level.
- Give your front door a fresh coat of paint to make an excellent first impression.
- Make your home look snazzy for drive-by buyers. Keep grass cut and edges edged, especially in your front yard.
- Set potted flowers and plants by your front door for a cheerful pop of color that says, "come on in."
- Ditch the old doorknob on your main entry for a solid-feeling handle lock set. It looks more substantial without costing substantially more.
- Dust spider webs away from outdoor lights and wipe down the fixtures. Replace burned-out bulbs and broken fixtures.

- Get windows gleaming inside and out, and give shutters a good cleaning.
- Repaint your mailbox instead of buying a new one. A can of glossy black spray paint costs one-fifth the price of a new mailbox.
- Clear everything off your front and back porches, and sweep them clean. Haul away junk in your back and front yards, or offer it free to a metal scrapper willing to pick it up.
- Weed the flower beds, and get rid of any dead or dying plants.

ALTERNATE USES

Turn old gutters into gorgeous flower boxes

Just hang them from your porch or deck railing. Decide how long you want your flower box to be, then take a pair of tin snips and trim the gutter to size. Run a bead of silicone caulk along the inside edge of each end cap. Fit it onto the gutter and hold it in place for five minutes, until the caulk sets up.

Don't forget about drainage. Drill a hole in the bottom of the gutter every 4 inches with a quarter-inch drill bit. Attach sturdy brackets to the back of the gutters about every 4 feet, then bolt these to the deck railing.

Sprinkle a thin layer of small pebbles or pottery shards in the bottom of the gutter before adding soil to stop the dirt from washing out through the holes.

Quick check for waterproof deck. Test your deck every six months to see if it needs sealing. Sprinkle water on the boards. If the water beads up, the deck is doing fine. If the wood absorbs the water, it's time to reseal it.

Add value to your deck. Adding a wood deck to your home can net you a nearly 73 percent return on your investment – if you take good care of it.

New decks built with pressure-treated wood need to cure for a while before being painted or stained. Old decks, on the other hand, will need a good cleaning.

Sand down splintered areas with 80-grit sandpaper and sweep off your deck. Spray the railings with a cleaning solution, wait 15 minutes, then scrub off dirt with a stiff brush, or rinse it away with a power washer. Be sure to work in the direction of the wood grain. Do the same with the deck boards.

Let the wood dry a few days before staining it. Pick a warm day when the temperature is between 50 and 90 degrees. Sweep the deck again. Stain the railing, balusters, and posts first, then the deck boards. Brush or roll on a thin coat in the direction of the grain. Let it dry, then add a second coat, at least to the boards. Let it dry for at least 24 hours before walking on it.

Seal your deck on an overcast day, not in direct sunlight. Otherwise, the sealer will dry before the wood absorbs it.

Banish stains under plant pots. Stop mildew from forming under the potted plants on your deck. Invest in plant stands to raise them up off the ground.

Best ways to remove grease stains after grilling. For fresh stains on your wood deck, sprinkle baking soda directly on the grease to absorb it. Do it fast, before the grease soaks into the wood. Wait a few minutes, then sweep away the baking soda. Next, scrub the remaining stain with liquid dishwashing detergent and hot water. Rinse and let dry. Clean the deck, if needed, with oxygen bleach – not chlorine bleach – and hot water.

For old grease stains, spritz on an automotive cleaner/degreaser. Let it sit, then wipe away following the cleaner's instructions.

Stop grease stains to begin with. Place an old, rubber-backed welcome mat over the area by your grill that gets the most grease spots.

HANDY HINT

Easy trick for consistent stain color

If you bought more than one gallon of stain for your deck, combine them together in a five-gallon bucket. This ensures you get the same color consistently across the entire deck. Stir the stain thoroughly, but don't shake it, or you'll end up with bubbles in the finish.

Tighten up saggy chair seats. Bring new life to stretched out cane seats. Turn caned chairs upside down and lay a warm, wet cloth on the underside of the seat. Leave it there to dry overnight. This will shrink the natural fibers, forcing the weave to tighten up. Keep sitters off the chair for at least 48 hours. Otherwise, they'll stretch out the seat again.

Don't let bamboo, wicker, and other woven chairs stay saggy for too long. Loose caning puts stress along the edges of the seat frame, making it more likely to break.

Lengthen the life of bamboo and wicker. Vacuum the canes with a soft brush attachment to suck up loose dust and dirt. Then wipe them gently with a mild detergent, warm water, and a wrung-out rag. To banish mildew, wash the piece with three-quarters cup chlorine bleach in one quart water, and rinse well.

Stubborn, set-in dirt may need more work. Hose off the piece, wipe away the extra water, and let it dry for 48 hours in the shade, not direct sunlight. Warm, windy days work best. Never hose down antique pieces.

Bring the luster back to bamboo and wicker by rubbing it with lemon oil furniture polish or boiled, not raw, linseed oil.

Melt wax off wicker furniture. Heat up the wax with a hair dryer, and wipe away the melted wax with a soft, cotton cloth. Keep heating and blotting until the gunk is gone.

Do your own driveway repair. For hairline cracks in concrete, sweep dirt and loose concrete out of the crack with a wire brush. Clean out grease with a special concrete cleaner, if needed. Then grab the tube of concrete crack sealer you bought at the hardware store and squeeze it directly into the crack.

For cracks more than half an inch wide, you'll need a chisel and small sledge hammer. Angle the chisel so it cuts into the concrete at the bottom of the crack. That's called undercutting the edges. Your goal – make the bottom of the crack wider than the top. This shape acts like a key, locking the concrete patch in place so it lasts longer.

Sweep away loose concrete and dirt with your wire brush. Fill the crack with vinyl concrete patch cement. Pack it down with a trowel, then tamp it to get rid of air pockets. Smooth it evenly with the rest of your walkway.

Make moss disappear. Kill the stuff that makes your walkways a slippery hazard. Mix up bleach and water in a one-to-one ratio. Then dab it directly onto the moss with a sponge. You can spray or sprinkle it on, but the bleach may harm nearby plants. Wait a few hours for the moss to die, then hose off the walkway thoroughly.

GRILLS
All set to sizzle

Get those grill grates gleaming. Remove the most stuck-on gunk and set them sparkling in under 15 minutes. Here's how.

- Are the grates still dirty from last time? Let heat do the hard work. Close the lid, turn the heat on high or light a little charcoal, and let the grill warm for 15 minutes. Open the lid and scrub the grates with a stainless steel brush. Burned food should fall right off. Never put grates through the dishwasher or try to clean them in the oven on the self-clean setting.

- Rub half a freshly cut onion onto the grates before putting the food on to cook. The onion residue adds flavor and stops food from sticking. Clean the still-warm grate after grilling using the other half of the onion.

- Grill grates can be made from cast iron, porcelain, or stainless steel. Check your owner's manual for advice on seasoning each type.

Spot signs of fuel leaks. Leaky gas hoses are a recipe for disaster. Spot leaks fast with a little dish soap and warm water. First, find the hose connecting the gas to the burners. Brush on soapy water with a clean baster brush or paint brush, or apply with a spray bottle. Be sure to coat the connections between the hose and gas supply, as well as the hose itself.

Slowly turn on the gas and watch for bubbles, especially at the connections. The soap will start bubbling where there's a leak. If you find leaky connections, turn off the gas and tighten them, then check them again. Be sure to replace cracked or leaky hoses and connectors before you start cooking.

Clever trick to check gas levels

Tired of running out of gas in the middle of grilling? Fill a pitcher with warm water. Turn the propane on and slowly pour warm water down the side of the tank. Run your hand down the tank until you find the place where the water goes from warm to cold. That's the level of propane left in the tank.

Make your grill last longer. Grills take a lot of abuse from sun, rain, freezing temperatures, and burned-on food. Take good care of your grill if you want it to keep on cookin'.

- Clean the inside of the lid when the grill is warm, but not hot. Wipe off light dirt with a damp sponge, or heavy grime with a ball of foil or brass brush. Built-up grease and smoke will flake off like paint.

- Empty drip pans while they're warm, too. Scrape away congealed grease with a plastic putty knife.

- Gas grill won't light? Check the igniter. An electric igniter may simply need a new battery. If that doesn't do it, dip a cotton swab in rubbing alcohol and clean the electrodes attached to each burner.

- Maybe some burners light while others don't. Remove the gummed up burners and scrub them gently with a wire brush to reopen the tiny gas portholes. Flush them out with a garden hose.

- Line the inside of charcoal grills with fresh aluminum foil each time you cook. Wait until the coals are cold, then fold up the foil – coals, ash, and all – and toss in the trash.

- Get rid of light gunk on a stainless steel lid with a Teflon-safe sponge and warm, soapy water. Then clean it weekly with stainless steel cleaner. Wipe with a soft cloth in the direction of the metal's grain. Rub cooking oil onto white spots or corrosion as if you're waxing a car.

- Painted lids are easy to touch up. Scrape off peeling paint with a paint scraper, then sand away corrosion. Wash the lid and let it dry. Spray it with an aerosol can of high-temperature paint.
- Last but not least, invest in a grill cover and use it. You'll stave off rust and other wear and tear from the elements.

SIDING & ROOFS
Spiff-ups for all seasons

Give your vinyl siding a facelift. Spray on a solution of 3 parts vinegar to 7 parts water to remove mold and mildew, say experts at the Vinyl Siding Institute. Your home will look years younger. Scrub textured siding with a long-handled, soft-bristled brush. For nontextured siding, a soft cloth will do.

For more stubborn stains, try cleaning with one-third cup powdered laundry detergent, two-thirds cup powdered household cleaner, one quart liquid bleach, and one gallon water.

Start at the bottom of the house and work your way up. Rinse each section well before the cleaning solution dries. Cover up brick to protect it from the runoff.

#1 thing to never do to your roof. Never, ever pressure wash asphalt shingles. It strips them of their protective granules, the ones that guard against ultraviolet damage from the sun. While your roof may look cleaner afterward, it won't last as long.

Banish those black and brown streaks by safer means. Mix up a solution of one cup trisodium phosphate, one gallon bleach, and five gallons water. Spray it onto the roof, then rinse off gently with a garden hose. Be careful not to spray the solution on nearby plants.

This cleaner will leave the roof slick and slippery. For safety's sake, avoid walking on the roof once you've sprayed it.

HANDY HINT

Lengthen the life of your roof

For a longer-lasting roof, choose lighter-colored shingles. Not only do dark shingles absorb more heat — which can run up your cooling costs — they tend to fail faster, too. The next time you need a roof, consider going with lighter-shade shingles. Better yet, look into metal roofs. They can last twice as long as traditional asphalt.

Best way to beat basement flooding. Clean out your gutters and downspouts to protect your house from water damage. Believe it or not, bad roof drainage is the biggest cause of basement flooding.

Clogged gutters and downspouts can dump water right along the foundation. From there, it seeps through basement walls and under doors. When water freezes inside the walls, it creates cracks, letting in even more moisture.

Keep your gutters clean and free of leaves, dirt, and sticks. Flush clogged gutters and downspouts with a garden hose, and scoop out heavy debris. Hire someone if you must – you'll save thousands of dollars down the road in water damage.

Point downspouts away from your house and make sure they dump water at least 3 to 4 feet from the foundation. You can buy extensions for less than $10 at any home improvement store.

Ladder tricks of the trade. Paying someone else to clean your gutters or fix the siding is by far the safest way to do it. But if you're set on doing it yourself, these tips can help you stay safe on your ladder.

- Invest a few dollars in a ladder standoff. It attaches to the top of your extension ladder and leans against the house siding. This protects the siding and makes the ladder much more stable.

- Keep the ladder from sliding out from under you with this clever trick. Hammer a pry bar into the ground at the base of the ladder Hook the curved end of the bar over the bottom rung and hammer down securely.

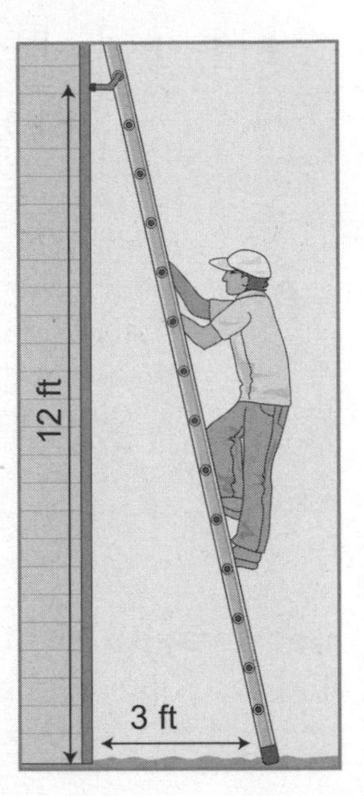

- Stand the ladder back from your house a safe distance, 1 foot away from the house for every 4 feet high. If you plan to rest the ladder against the house 12 feet up, position the base 3 feet away from the house.

Perfect temperature for painting your house. Weather can make the difference between a good-looking exterior paint job and a bad one.

Avoid painting your house when the temperature dips below 50 degrees, unless you are using paint made for cold weather application. Water evaporates from paint as it dries. Too cold outside, and it won't evaporate fast enough. Too hot, and it evaporates too fast. And never paint right after a shower or if rain is on the way.

Also, try to paint each side of the house when it's in the shade. Direct sunlight can force paint to dry too fast, leaving behind blisters and visible brush strokes. Always work from the top down, beginning with gutters and eaves.

Chapter 10

TAKING CARE OF YOU

"The finest clothing made is a person's skin, but, of course, society demands something more than this."

Mark Twain hit the nail on the head with this comment about how important your clothing can be. Paying attention to your appearance lets you project the image you want to show the world — just as Twain did in his famous white linen suits. Learn how to clean and care for clothing, shoes, accessories, jewelry, and more.

LAUNDRY

Get a load of this

7 rules for removing stains. Laundry is not rocket science, but there's a right way and a wrong way to do things. Learn these laundry secrets to be sure your clothes come out clean and looking new – without being damaged.

- Read the garment label. You'll need to know the garment's fiber content along with special instructions for water temperature, whether you can use bleach, and how to dry the item. You won't do yourself any favors if you ruin the garment while getting out the stain.

- Test to see if colors will run. If a fabric is colorfast, the dye won't run or fade when washed. Test by applying the cleaner to a hidden area of the garment, like an inside seam or hem. Wait 15 minutes, then rinse with water and make sure the color doesn't fade or bleed.

- Follow directions on the label of the cleaning product. Learn what fabrics the stain remover can and can't be used on, according to the manufacturer.

- Treat a stain promptly. Don't wait until laundry day. Apply a treatment as soon as you see the spill. Fast action can keep stains from setting and becoming a real challenge to remove.

- Don't combine products. Mixing chlorine bleach or ammonia with stain removal products can cause irritating gases and may even create a deadly concoction.

- Be cautious with bleach. Add bleach and detergent to the wash water before adding the laundry. Dripping bleach directly onto a garment can cause spots. If your washer has a bleach dispenser, follow the manufacturer's directions in using it. For colored clothing, see about using an oxygen bleach instead of regular chlorine bleach.

- Know when to dry-clean. Garments made of natural fibers, like wool or silk, can shrink or become distorted when washed in water. Sometimes it's worth the price of sending an item to the dry cleaner just to avoid the possibility of having it shrink. Dry cleaning – whether the garment is made of natural or synthetic fibers – can also prevent losing color or changing the finish of the fabric.

Tap out a stain

No matter what stain removal product you choose, don't apply it to a stain and then start rubbing. This will only push the stain into the fabric, making it even harder to get out. Instead, place the garment on a hard surface, pick up a metal spoon, and tap the back of the spoon on the stain. Vibrations from the tapping will help lift the material from the fabric.

Turn yellowed cottons to snow white. Your favorite white shirt will eventually start to look dingy, even if you manage to avoid an ink stain or coffee spill. Turn back the clock on your cottons – with or without bleach.

For cotton garments that can handle bleach, try this method. Add one-half cup baking soda and one-half cup bleach to your load. The baking soda helps the bleach work harder for the most sparkling whites ever, and you don't need to use as much bleach.

If you prefer to skip the bleach, try using lemon juice. Soak those dingy socks or even polyester shirts in a bath of hot water and one-half cup lemon juice for an hour or more. When the clothing starts to look whiter, toss it into your washing machine and launder as usual. There's no danger of harming your clothes when you use lemon juice for whitening.

Put an end to ring-around-the-collar. Oh, those dirty rings. You've tried soaking them and scrubbing them, and still – you know the drill. Those perspiration stains on shirt collars are tough to lift. The older the shirt becomes, the darker the inside collar. Pick your favorite of these top tricks to erase ring-around-the-collar.

- Mix together vinegar, water, and a bit of liquid detergent in a spray bottle and spritz it on the ring. Vinegar is an all-purpose laundry spotter that works on a wide variety of stains – including perspiration stains and even stains from deodorant. Vinegar also works to remove detergent residue. You'll certainly save money with a treatment that costs just pennies a batch.

- Dissolve two aspirin tablets in a few tablespoons of warm water. Saturate the stain and let it soak for a few hours. Then launder the shirt.

- Mix up a batch of strong saltwater, and soak away the perspiration stains. Then launder as usual and the stains should be gone.

- Make a paste of cornstarch and water. Apply it to the collar, let it dry, and brush it off.

- Rub these oily perspiration stains with plain white chalk, and the chalk will absorb the oil. The stain should wash out in the laundry.

- Dab the stain with a moist cloth dipped in borax, then wash as usual.

WARNING

Avoid a color-run nightmare

Before you wash that new red shirt with the rest of your clothes, try this amazing test to determine whether the dye will bleed.

Use a steam iron to press a portion of the garment between two layers of a white cotton handkerchief. If the color transfers onto the white fabric, the dye may not have been set properly during manufacturing.

Another testing method is to place a few drops of water on a hidden area of the garment, then blot it with a cotton ball and see if color transfers. If there's a problem, first wash the garment separately in cold water. A dye magnet or color catcher, available where you buy laundry detergent, may also help capture any color that runs in the wash.

Don't let your indigo fade away. Those dark-wash jeans are slimming and fashionable, so don't let the color wash out. Protect them from fading with a simple treatment before their first washing.

Prepare a soak with one-half cup vinegar and a bucket of warm water. Immerse your new jeans and let them soak for 30 minutes. The mild acid in the vinegar helps set the dye so it won't run away in the wash, all for just pennies a treatment. Use white vinegar rather than cider vinegar – unless you want your jeans to have an apple-fresh smell.

ALTERNATE USES

Carpet cleaner cuts laundry stains

Run out of laundry stain remover? Grab a bottle of carpet stain remover and give it a try.

Products like Resolve carpet cleaner and Spot Shot carpet stain remover have good reputations as laundry spot removers. It makes sense. These products are made to cut through tough stains.

But don't try it if your stained garment is made of silk, not colorfast, or labeled "dry-clean only."

Wash away stubborn oily stains. Lipstick, butter, olive oil – they don't belong on your clothing. Even when these greasy stains don't contain much color, they can be tough to remove. You would think a good laundry detergent would do the trick, but sometimes you need more power. Give these three great degreasers a go.

- Shampoo. Dab oily stains on garments with this hair-care product, then let them set before you toss them in the washing machine. Shampoo is made to cut through body oils, and it works on oils on clothing, too. Pick a clear gel shampoo, preferably one made for oily hair.
- Dishwashing detergent. Just as it cuts the grease on your dishes, this mild liquid cleanser works to wash away oils from your favorite shirt. Wildlife rescue groups use Dawn dishwashing liquid to clean off birds coated by oil from an oil spill, so you know it will be both tough and gentle on your clothing. Apply it to the oily spot and scrub gently with an old toothbrush as a pretreatment to get rid of the problem before you launder the garment.

- WD-40. That's right – you can get rid of grease stains with grease. This wonder product, known for lubricating joints of all kinds, also removes grease from fabric. Place a cloth under the stained area of the garment, then spritz on a bit of WD-40 and let it soak in. Cover the stain with some dishwashing liquid, rub it around, then wash as usual.

4 tricks to get out ink spots. Ink stains on your favorite shirt? Not to worry – you don't need to toss it out. Experienced launderers know many ways to get out the ink and get your shirt sparkling white again. Try one of these methods. Be sure to test it on an inconspicuous area of the garment first.

- Spritz on some hair spray. Ink stains, and lipstick stains, are no match for this common hair product. Use enough hair spray to saturate the stain, wait a half hour, then dab out the ink with a wet sponge. This trick should even work on a silk or acetate blouse, but be sure to pretest and rinse out the hair spray afterward.

- Drizzle on some rubbing alcohol. Position the garment with the stain stretched over the mouth of a jar. Slowly drip rubbing alcohol onto the stain, letting it pull the ink into the jar. Another method is to place the garment on an old towel with the stain touching the towel. Dab rubbing alcohol onto the back of the stain, pushing the ink out of the fabric and onto the towel. Continue dabbing until no more ink comes off.

- Blend together lemon juice and salt. Gently rub the paste on the spot, and watch the spot disappear. To whiten whites that can't be bleached, use one-quarter cup of lemon juice in your washing machine. You won't believe how sparkling white your laundry will be.

- Reach in the fridge for some buttermilk. Let the ink-stained garment soak in a pan of buttermilk for a day, then rinse it in cool water and liquid soap. If the stain remains, try it again.

Remember to rinse the garment after the ink stain is gone, then wash as usual.

Sidestep common laundry disasters. Much of the wear and tear to garments comes not from wearing them, but from washing them. You can't avoid the laundry, but you can find ways around causing extra damage in the laundry room. Follow these steps each time you prepare to do the wash.

- Zip and button. Before you toss a garment into your washing machine, button all the buttons and zip up the zippers. Securing these closures can keep them from snagging other items in the wash cycle.
- Be careful with stains. Pretreating stains is a great idea, but don't put those garments into the dryer. If the pretreatment didn't work, the dryer heat can set the stain for good. Same thing goes with the heat of an iron. This little bit of caution is the best trick to keep stains from ruining your clothes.
- Use your laundry bag. Even if a delicate item can go through the wash cycle, it may still need to line dry rather than suffer the heat of the dryer. Be sure you remember to separate these items by securing them in a mesh laundry bag before putting them into the washing machine. You'll avoid an accidental run through the hot dryer.
- Don't overdry. Leaving clothes in the dryer too long can cause them to get old before their time. Use the moisture-sensor feature on your dryer if it has one.
- Mend first, wash second. It may seem obvious – until you forget this rule. Stitch up a hole or tear in a garment before you toss it in your washing machine. Agitation during the washing process can cause unraveling, making the damage worse.

ALTERNATE USES

WD-40 works to get the gum out

Grab that can of WD-40 from the garage, and use it in your laundry room to remove caked-on messes from clothing and linens. With a little finesse, you can use this wonder treatment to get out rubber cement, gum, even roofing tar stains from clothing. Test the WD-40 on an inconspicuous area of the clothing to be sure it won't cause damage.

Here's how to handle waxy substances, like chewing gum, dried crayon, and Silly Putty.

- First, take a piece of ice, and rub it on the chewing gum stuck to the fabric to harden the mess.
- With a dull-edged knife, like a butter knife, scrape off as much gum as you can from the fabric. Be careful you don't damage the fabric.
- Apply a few drops of WD-40 to the remaining gum.
- Launder immediately.

Lemon spritzer gets the best of rust. Rust stains on a garment don't have to mean it's headed for the rag bag. Call out the power of citrus to mildly bleach a white garment. Follow these steps.

- Saturate the rust stain with lemon juice, and sprinkle on some salt. Citric acid in the lemon cuts through the rust.
- Lay the garment out in the sun.
- If the stain remains, pour very hot water through the stain. If the fabric is tough, you can even use boiling water.

You can also try combining lemon juice and cream of tartar, spreading it on the stain, then waiting a half hour or so for the mixture to remove the rust.

If the rust remains, you may need to head to the store for a specialty product made to remove rust. Products like Whink Rust Remover and Rust Magic can do wonders if the lemon juice treatment fails. Read the directions to be sure you can use the product on your garment.

HANDY HINT

Protect your delicates

An old pillowcase makes a great laundry bag for your delicate washables when you add a drawstring closure. Items like scarves, nylons, and lace tops won't get tangled, stretched, or snagged when you place them in the bag before tossing it all in your washing machine. Be sure to use the proper cycle and temperature for these items.

Egg-cellent way to make egg stains vanish. Egg spilled on your clothing should bring up a yellow caution flag. Don't dab the stain with hot or warm water, since that will basically cook the egg onto the fabric. Then you're stuck with a crusty mess. Instead, follow these steps.

- Scrape off as much of the egg as possible, being careful not to damage the fabric.
- Run cold water over the stain. Pay close attention to the water temperature.

- Pretreat the stain with a laundry detergent that contains enzymes. This kind of product can help break up the egg protein so it will wash away. Soak in the cold water and pretreatment for a half hour.
- Wash the garment as usual. Be sure the stain is completely gone before you toss it into the dryer. If not, wash it again, possibly after another round of pretreatment.

3 ways to mow down grass stains. Grass stains may seem to be taking over your casual clothes whenever you get down and dirty in your garden. Try these top three methods to get out the grunge.

- Apply a bit of dishwashing detergent directly to the spot, then add a few drops of distilled vinegar. Don't rub the spot vigorously – you don't want to grind it into the fabric.
- A second technique is to spritz on some hydrogen peroxide. Keep a spray bottle of this handy product in your laundry room for just such purposes.
- For grass or blood stains on fabric that is washable and colorfast, wet the item thoroughly. Then apply a few drops of Murphy Oil Soap as a pretreatment, and wash as usual. This handy, all-purpose cleaner works on materials of all kinds – not just wood.

Of course, you'll want to test the stain removal product on a hidden area of your garment first.

Save with homemade fabric softener. A bottle of liquid fabric softener can run about $5 for enough to do 21 loads. Cut the cost by two-thirds and use a natural alternative when you make your own fabric softener. You don't need to buy specialty ingredients, since you probably have these items in your pantry already. Here's how.

In a plastic bottle, mix together one cup each of baking soda and white vinegar, then add two cups water. Don't worry when the soda and vinegar start to fizz. Cover the bottle and shake it up.

Use about one-quarter cup in the final rinse of the wash cycle. You may really appreciate this blend if the strong perfumes of some fabric softeners bother you.

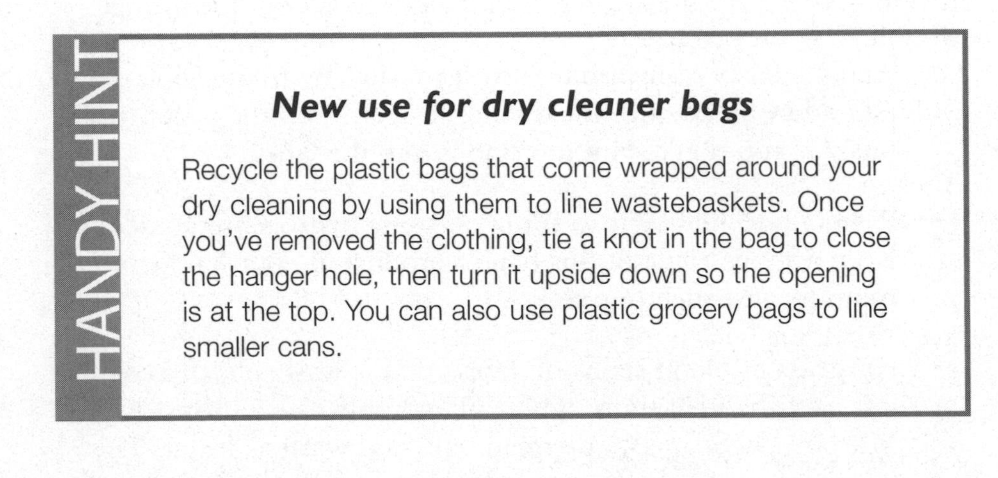

HANDY HINT

New use for dry cleaner bags

Recycle the plastic bags that come wrapped around your dry cleaning by using them to line wastebaskets. Once you've removed the clothing, tie a knot in the bag to close the hanger hole, then turn it upside down so the opening is at the top. You can also use plastic grocery bags to line smaller cans.

CLOTHES
Wardrobe wonders

De-fuzz your favorite sweaters. You can tell a sweater's age by the volume of fuzz and fluff balls it carries. Luckily, it's easy to make your sweaters look young again.

You can use a disposable, single-blade razor to shave off the pills, or wrap a length of packing tape around your hand and use it to pick up fuzz. A battery-powered sweater shaver may also do the trick on large balls.

A simpler solution may be to invest in a pumice stone. A good choice is the Sweater Stone, available online and in some clothing stores for around $10. It's a natural pumice stone made to detach pills and fuzz when rubbed against knit fabric. Just smooth it over your sweater, and ugly pills collect into balls of fluff that fall right off. Good news – the Sweater Stone should last a decade.

Unstick sticky zippers. End the frustration of fighting with zippers that won't do their job. Put the zip back into a sticky zipper with just a bit of lubricant.

Apply a drop of oil to the teeth of a zipper, and it'll run smoothly. Try dabbing a bit of olive oil on the zipper using a cotton swab. If you're out of olive oil, use a drop of WD-40. You can also try a bar of soap, or carefully rub pencil lead across the zipper to apply a layer of graphite to the metal.

2 dozen uses for an old T-shirt. Don't throw out your favorite tattered T-shirt. Give it new life with one of these thrifty recycling ideas.

- Take several to your local veterinarian or animal shelter to be used as bedding for animals that board overnight.
- Use them as stuffing for homemade floor pillows.
- Wrap around fragile items for storage or moving.
- Cover plants in the garden to protect from frost.
- Rip into strips, and use as plant ties during the growing season.

- Sew shut the neck and armholes to make seat cushions for your patio or boat.
- Cut into strips and knit or braid into a scarf.
- Use the decorative portion to make a tote bag.
- Wrap gifts.
- Cut out the picture from several, and combine to make a memory quilt.
- Make headbands to match your workout outfits.
- Use as painting frocks for your grandchildren.
- Create dust jackets to protect your favorite books.
- Line the inside of a plant pot to keep the soil from leaking out.
- Dust your furniture without scratching it.
- Sew into small bags and fill with tiny beans or rice for homemade toys.
- Polish jewelry or flatware.
- Clean your eyeglasses.
- Make a washable seat cover for your bicycle or bucket seats in your car.
- Wash and wax your car.
- Stretch over a canvas for unique wall art.

- Cut into squares, add a bit of liquid fabric softener, and use as dryer sheets.
- Give your dog a security blanket when he's away from home.
- Wrap around out-of-season shoes to keep off the dust.

Tricks to keep from popping your buttons. Secure buttons on your clothing so you can hop off the button-replacement treadmill.

- Before you wear a new blouse, pull out some clear nail polish and place a dot on the threads of the buttons. This trick keeps the thread from fraying.
- Use fishing line, embroidery floss, or dental floss to sew on buttons that will get heavy wear, like those on a bulky winter coat or children's clothing.
- When sewing on a four-hole button, sew through two holes, then knot and cut the thread. Use a separate piece of thread to sew through the other two holes. Even if one thread breaks, the button won't fall off.
- To keep from sewing on a button too tightly, causing it to fall off from the strain, place a straight pin on top of the button while you stitch through the holes. When you're done sewing, pull out the pin.

Bring water-repellent clothing back to life. Jackets, hats, pants, and other items of clothing with fabric that beads up the rain can make life easier when you're out in bad weather. That's because of the magic of durable water repellent (DWR) fabric treatments.

You may know DWR chemical treatments by brand names like ReviveX or Scotchgard. They're commonly used to coat the outer layer of raincoat materials, making your Gore-Tex jacket even more water resistant. But the DWR can lose its power over time because of dirt on your jacket, washing it too many times, or rubbing against part of the fabric. Don't throw away the jacket. You can renew a DWR to bring back its water-shedding potential. Here's how.

- First, wash your garment according to the manufacturer's instructions to remove dirt and body oil. Getting rid of the grime can do a lot to restore a water-repellent fabric treatment.

- Next, apply heat, which works to "fluff up" the DWR, creating enough surface tension on the fabric to force water droplets to roll off rather than soaking in. Again, check the manufacturer's instructions, but the simplest method is to toss your jacket in the clothes dryer on medium heat for about 15 minutes. You may also apply heat using an iron at a warm setting, but protect the fabric with a towel. Or use the heat of a blow dryer to achieve the same goal. Set the dryer on high heat, then move it slowly over the surface of the jacket.

- Finally, reapply more DWR if excess rubbing has removed the protection in a certain area. Use ReviveX or a similar spray-on product.

Roll up scarves to keep out wrinkles.
Save cardboard tubes that hold paper towels or wrapping paper. You can use them to keep scarves wrinkle-free. Just roll the scarf around the tube, smoothing out any creases. Add another scarf for a second layer.

Wrinkle-free clothing, no iron required.
Wrinkle-releasing sprays work to smooth out fabric without the heat

of an iron. They can be helpful when you're traveling or if you just don't want to set up your ironing board.

Mix up your own wrinkle-release formula with a cup of distilled water and a teaspoon of liquid fabric softener. Put it in a spray bottle that sends out a fine mist. Spray it on your wrinkled garment, then pull and smooth the fabric to remove wrinkles. Hang the garment or lay it flat to dry. It's probably best to test this formula on the fabric first to be sure it won't leave a stain.

If you're out of fabric softener, just spritz on a bit of plain water, then smooth the fabric and use a hair dryer to remove wrinkles while the garment dries.

SHOES & PURSES
Fabulous finishing touches

Stretch tight shoes for just-right fit. Stop the pinch. Try this homegrown method of stretching shoes, and soon they'll be just right.

First, prepare the shoes if they're leather by applying a leather moisturizer. Then fill a small, sturdy, plastic zip-close bag nearly full with water, seal it, then stuff it into your shoe. Be sure it fills the shoe completely in the area you want to stretch. Put the shoe in the freezer, and leave it there overnight. Water expands as it freezes, so you're molding your shoe from the inside out.

If your shoe pinches because of a bunion, you'll need to get the shoe stretched in just that area. Have it done by a professional repairman, who has the tools to do the job for around $12 to $15.

Stop your pet from chewing your shoes. You love your dog – and you love your new pair of leather loafers. You can keep both of them safe with these tips.

- End the boredom. Dogs often resort to chewing to keep themselves busy when they're bored – kind of like people biting their nails. Give your dog the right amount of exercise, probably 30 minutes twice a day, and he should leave your shoes alone.

- Give him a routine. Your dog likes to know what's coming – dinner at a certain time of day, a walk when he expects it. Disruption can lead to anxiety and nervousness, making him prone to chewing.

- Provide a replacement. Dogs are made to use their teeth, so buy your pet a Nylabone, Kong toy, or tennis ball and urge him to stick to that. Don't give your dog all his chew toys at once, but rotate them in and out, so he'll be happy with a "new" item once in a while. And don't leave your expensive shoes within his reach. He'll choose the shoes because they smell like you.

- Pick a repellant. Spray a bit of watered-down perfume or cologne on your shoes, since most dogs don't like the smell of colognes. Or mix up a batch of one part water and one part vinegar in a spray bottle and use that to keep Rover away from your loafers.

Keep your white shoes looking brilliant. Protect white sneakers with a spray-on fabric protector before they have a chance to get grimy. Or apply a light coating of spray laundry starch when they're new. But once white shoes pick up dirt, you'll need to use some elbow grease to get them looking fresh again.

It's best to avoid the washing machine and dryer, which can put extra wear-and-tear on your shoes. Instead, use a soft toothbrush and some soap to scrub off the dirt by hand. Applying toothpaste – the plain old white kind – with a cloth can do wonders to remove scuff marks from white leather sneakers.

To help them dry, stuff your damp shoes with newspaper. The paper will absorb moisture while it helps your shoes keep their shape.

HANDY HINT

Cheap fix for worn stitching

As strong as dental floss is, you can put it to work to temporarily repair your shoes. Use a tapestry needle and a long piece of dental floss to sew through stitches that have come undone. Hide the knots inside, and the repair will be invisible.

Brew up a batch of nontoxic shoe polish. Many types of shoe polish contain ingredients that can irritate your skin and eyes or cause an allergic reaction. But even if you swear off commercial shoe polish, you still want to protect your leather shoes from water – and you want them to look good. Brew up a batch of leather-protecting shoe polish that takes just two ingredients.

Here's what you'll need – 1 ounce beeswax and one-half cup olive oil. Melt the beeswax in the top of a double boiler. Stir in the olive oil, remove from the heat, and let the mixture cool. Pour it into a glass jar that seals tightly.

Apply the polish to leather shoes using a soft cloth. You may want to warm it slightly with a hair dryer so it's easier to apply.

Keep shoelaces from unraveling. When your shoelace tips begin to fray, mend them with a bit of clear fingernail polish. Just dip the shoelace ends in polish, then squeeze and twist them together tightly. Wear a disposable latex glove or put your hand inside a small plastic bag while you do this to keep polish off your fingers.

You can do this repair without removing the laces from your shoes, but take care to avoid getting polish on your shoes. Set the shoes on your bathroom counter with the laces hanging off the edge while the polish dries overnight.

3 ways to take the smell out of shoes. Once you've broken in those comfortable shoes, keep them in good condition – including fighting off bad odors. Here are three methods worth trying.

- Sprinkle some baking soda in your shoes to absorb odors. Leave it overnight, then tap out the excess baking soda before you wear the shoes.

- Save used dryer sheets, and tuck one into each shoe to fight odors.

- Open up the shoes completely and place a piece of plastic wrap inside. Put a cotton ball with several drops of clove oil on the plastic to remove bad odors. Toss the plastic wrap and cotton ball before you wear the shoes.

Make your handbag last a lifetime. Your favorite handbag has all the right pockets, feels comfortable on your shoulder, and looks great. Keep it that way by caring for it like an old friend.

- Safeguard the outside. Pick up a leather protector spray at a cobbler or the store where you bought your leather handbag, and follow the instructions on the label. Doing this will protect the leather from water and spills.

- Take care of the insides. Avoid danger to your bag by carrying ink pens and other risky items sealed in a zip-close plastic bag. Ink quickly soaks into leather and may require professional help to remove.

- Keep it safe from dangers. If you truly love your bag, don't take it to places where it's bound to come into contact with damaging substances. The hairdresser and grocery store are two great examples. Also, rely on the hook on the back of the restroom stall door to avoid placing your bag in filth.

- Clean the outside. You can safely use watered-down dishwashing liquid to wipe the outside of your vinyl or cloth bag. You'll probably need to do this about twice a year if you use the bag every day. Consider having your handbag professionally cleaned if it's an expensive leather bag.

JEWELRY

Keep the bling in your life

2 ways to clean a girl's best friend. Remember how your diamond earrings sparkled when you first saw them in the jewelry store? They were really something to see when they were new. Get that like-new sparkle again by cleaning your diamonds like the jewelers do. Skip the $50 jewelry-cleaning products, and pick one of these top two methods.

- Dip diamond jewelry in ammonia and water. Mix together three parts water with one part ammonia, then immerse your diamond jewelry in the potion. Gently scrub around the diamonds with a small brush, like an old toothbrush or makeup brush. Rinse off the piece and let it air dry. Don't use ammonia if your jewelry has other gems, like emeralds or sapphires, set along with the diamonds. Instead, soak these pieces in a mixture of mild dishwashing liquid and warm water.

- Polish them with toothpaste. Use a dab of toothpaste – regular paste, not a gel – and an old toothbrush to gently clean around your diamonds. Stick with jewelry that contains gold and diamonds. Avoid using toothpaste on more fragile stones, like pearls.

Make your costume jewelry sparkle. A little clear fingernail polish can go a long way toward keeping your costume jewelry looking great.

First, protect the finish of silver-tone or gold-tone jewelry with a layer of clear polish. Coat the inside of the jewelry – the side that rests against your skin – before you wear it, and it won't lose its sparkle and shine. The polish will also keep your skin from turning black or green from the tarnish. You can also use this trick to protect a shiny belt buckle.

Here's another clever idea. Use clear nail polish to temporarily reset a stone that's come loose from a costume ring or pendant. Use it like glue for an invisible fix.

Tricks to remove a tight ring. Avoid the pain of removing a ring from a swollen finger. When your ring starts feeling tight and you can't get it off your finger easily, grab one of these items and get the job done quickly.

- Ice, ice pack, or ice water. Cool your fingers to shrink the swelling, and your problem may be solved.

- Soap lather, dishwashing liquid, or soapy water. All these provide a bit of lubrication to help the metal slide along your skin.
- Vegetable oil, butter, baby oil, or WD-40 – anything that lubricates your finger will help.

Keep your favorite trinkets at your fingertips. Store jewelry so it's easy to find and easy to handle with stiff or sore fingers. These bauble-sorting tricks will let you continue to enjoy dressing up even if arthritis robs your fingers of some agility. Separate items into categories for greatest efficiency.

- Rings. Save an egg carton, or repurpose an ice cube tray. Either will fit flat into your dresser drawer, and you can store a ring in each compartment.
- Necklaces. Save space and keep your necklaces in view by hanging them on hooks. Use small hooks that attach by suction cups to a bathroom or bedroom mirror. If you want to splurge, pick up a jewelry stand with hooks to hang your necklaces to prevent tangles.
- Bracelets. Once you clear out those bulky necklaces from your jewelry box, your bracelets will be easy to find in their spacious resting place. Or pick up a two-sided hanging jewelry organizer with pockets to hold items of various sizes so they won't damage each other. You can hang it in your closet or behind the bathroom door.
- Clips and pins. Set up a three-ring binder with clear plastic pockets, and keep small pins from scratching each other. It's easy to flip through the pages to find the piece you want to wear.
- Earrings. Keep pairs together and accessible in a weekly pill box. Open the lid of the pair you want to wear, and shake them into your hand.

Untangle a knotty necklace. Avoid the frustration of getting knots out of a necklace chain by following this sure-fire method.

- Unclasp the knotted chain and lay it out on a piece of waxed paper or a wooden cutting board. These surfaces keep the chain from sliding around.
- Add a drop of baby oil to the knot or sprinkle on some baby powder to help the chain links slide easily.
- Take two straight pins and use them as tools to pry apart the knot. Place the points in the center of the knot, then gently pull it apart until it loosens enough to use your fingers.

Keep your delicate chains from getting knotted again by storing them with their clasps connected.

Smart necklace keeper. Screw several tiny cup hooks into a wooden clothes hanger and use it to store necklaces. Hang one chain on each hook, and you'll never have to deal with tangles again.

WARNING

Surprising enemy of silver

Zip-close plastic bags may seem like the ideal containers to keep silver clean and dry, but they are actually a poor choice. Sealing in the air means condensation can develop inside the bag, leading to tarnishing. For the same reason, don't cover silver in plastic wrap.

Little-known danger to precious metals. Leave your jewelry at home when you swim in a pool or the ocean. Chlorine and heat can cause discoloring and corrode the finish of precious metals like gold and platinum. Add in salt and sand, and your delicate gemstones – opals and pearls – can change color, while soft gold can be scratched.

6 ways to clean silver. There's more than one way to skin a cat. Same thing goes with keeping your silver flatware and jewelry tarnish-free and full of sparkle. See what ingredients you have on hand, then get polishing.

- Soak it in sour milk. Soak your silver in a pan of sour milk overnight, making sure the silver is completely submerged. If you don't have any sour milk, you can make it by mixing a cup of milk with a tablespoon of lemon juice or vinegar. Or mix together one-third cup of powdered, nonfat milk with a cup of water, then stir in a tablespoon of lemon juice or vinegar.

- Foil away tarnish. Line a baking pan with aluminum foil – shiny side up – and make sure it covers the pan completely. Add your silver pieces and cover with warm water and several tablespoons of baking soda. Wait 10 minutes, and the tarnish will be gone without any effort.

- Mix up homemade polish. Blend together equal parts of baking soda and vinegar into a paste, then use a soft cloth to rub tarnish off your silver. Rinse off the polish when you're done.

- Try some toothpaste. Toothpaste works well to remove spots of tarnish, but it's too abrasive to use as your main silver cleaner. To clean a small area of tarnish, wet the silver, then rub on a tiny bit of toothpaste with your finger. Rinse the silver and dry with a soft cloth. Avoid toothpaste with extra ingredients, like whiteners.

- Get a lemon-fresh shine. Clean silver in plain lemon juice or a paste of lemon juice blended with salt.
- Make your own polishing gloves. Dig out those old Sunday cotton gloves and use them to polish silver – without getting any fingerprints on the metal as you work. Mix together two cups cold water with one-half cup ammonia and a quarter cup liquid silver polish. One by one, dip and saturate each glove in the solution, then hang to dry. You'll have enough solution to make several pairs of polishing gloves.

WARNING

Take action when serving these foods

All food is not created equal. Some foods actually speed up tarnishing when they come in contact with your silver. If you serve some of these problem foods, be sure to clean your silver soon after the meal to avoid excessive tarnishing. Wash your flatware using a mild dishwashing liquid and dry it immediately with a soft cloth.

- fish
- fruit juice
- salt and salty foods like butter
- eggs, especially egg yolk
- broccoli and onions
- tomatoes, tomato sauce, and ketchup
- mayonnaise, mustard, salad dressing, and vinegar

In addition to foods, materials like wool, felt, rubber, latex, newspaper, and residue from your fingers can also speed up tarnishing.

Sneaky trick to prevent tarnish. You love using your grandmother's good silver when company comes, but you hate polishing it every time. Try putting a piece of chalk in the drawer with the silver. The chalk will absorb moisture and prevent tarnish. White chalk costs pennies, so put some in your jewelry box, too.

GLASSES
Worth a second look

Extend the life of your glasses. Your eyeglasses are your friend. You need them every day to help you read the newspaper, thread a needle, and drive to the store. Take good care of them by following this schedule for care.

Every day.

- Inspect your eyeglasses before you put them on in the morning. Look for signs of wear and loose hinges.
- If you use hair spray, apply it before you put on your glasses. Overspray can damage lens coatings.
- Put on your eyeglasses and look at them in the mirror. If they seem crooked, head to the optical shop for an adjustment.
- Use both hands when you remove your glasses to avoid pulling and stretching the frames.

Every week.

- Clean your eyeglasses to remove dirt and grime that could scratch the lenses along with perspiration that can damage the frames. Start by rinsing them under water, then use a spray lens cleaner and microfiber cloth. Cleaning your lenses with a solution made for other purposes may damage lens coatings.

- Don't wipe the lenses while they are dry. That can cause scratches. Add a bit of water first, then wipe clean with a cleaning cloth made for eyeglasses. Using a napkin or towel that's not made for the purpose can scratch the lenses.

Every year.

- Take your glasses to the optician for an inspection. She may be able to make small adjustments to the frames to help them fit properly.

- While you're there, look around at new frames. Sometimes a new activity calls for a special type of eye wear, and it's always handy to have a spare pair.

- Consider having an annual eye exam, which will tell you if your prescription has changed. The American Optometric Association suggests annual exams for people age 61 and older and those with certain risk factors, like diabetes, previous eye surgery, and a family history of eye disease.

Wise ways to protect your sunglasses. You invested good money to protect your eyes with quality sunglasses. Keep that perfect pair in tiptop condition by steering clear of these damaging bad habits.

- Never leave your sunglasses on the car dashboard. Excess heat and direct sunlight will damage the coating on the lenses, making it difficult to see clearly.

- Stop tossing your sunglasses into your purse or bag without first putting them in a case. Pick a hard-shell case for the best protection from scratches and smashes.

- Don't fold up your sunglasses and set them down on their lenses. This can scratch or damage the lenses. Instead, place them so the lenses face upward.

- Get out of the habit of putting your sunglasses on top of your head when you walk indoors. Hold back your hair with a headband instead. Wearing glasses on your head stretches the frames so they don't fit well.

Fast fix for a broken frame. You don't even notice it's getting loose, then the tiny screw that holds together your frames is gone. You're left holding the pieces – and you sure can't see well enough to locate a screw on the floor.

Give your frames a temporary fix by using a short length of dental floss. Just thread it through the holes in the hinge, tie it tightly, then snip off the long ends. Strong dental floss will keep the pieces together until you can get to the repair shop. Plus, a little thread is less noticeable than having a straight pin or paper clip sticking out of your frames.

5 ways olive oil keeps you beautiful. Don't toss out the cheaper stuff when you upgrade your culinary olive oil to the extra virgin variety. Put it to good use in your bathroom to pamper your hair, skin, lips – nearly every part of you. Olive oil can replace expensive beauty products as a cheap and effective moisturizer and conditioner. Here's what you can do.

- Condition your hair with a tablespoon of olive oil. Massage it into your hair and scalp, leave it on for 20 minutes, then rinse and shampoo. You can also mix up a batch of thick conditioner from one-half cup olive oil and a mashed avocado, or blend equal parts olive oil and mayonnaise. Work the deep conditioner through dry hair, then wrap your head in plastic for 20 minutes before you rinse and shampoo.

- Exfoliate with a simple scrub made from olive oil and a bit of granulated sugar. Add enough sugar so the consistency feels good, but not too gritty. Massage it on your face gently, then rinse off.

- Try the secret of European women for keeping their skin youthful by substituting olive oil for a daily moisturizer. You can even add a spoonful of olive oil to your bath for a soak that will leave your skin moisturized and refreshed.

- Skip the expensive medicated lip balm, and rub a bit of olive oil on your lips.

- Rub a few drops around your nails and gently push back the cuticles. Olive oil makes a great hand and cuticle cream.

Unbeatable way to clean combs and brushes. Brushing your hair does more than simply give it style. It also removes dirt and oil from your hair and scalp. But that means the dirt and oil end up on your brush. That's why hair-care tools need regular cleaning.

Paul Borland, a hairstylist since 1988 and owner of KelliPaul Salon & Spa in Peachtree City, Ga., suggests using a different cleaning solution depending on what you need to remove from your brushes and combs.

"A solution of baking soda mixed with shampoo and water helps remove the residue of hair spray and styling products," Borland says.

Otherwise, warm water and mild soap – especially one with an antibacterial agent – do a great job of removing hair oils and body waste, he says. You can also mix up ammonia in warm water.

"Keep it mild," Borland warns. And clean your brushes – don't soak them. "I'm not a big proponent of soaking combs and brushes," Borland says, noting that both wooden and plastic handles can be damaged from spending too much time in water and chemicals. That's why it's important to dry your brush soon after cleaning. "Use a hair dryer to dry the brush if it has a wooden handle, or lay it out on a towel if it's plastic," he says.

Whichever cleaning ingredients you choose, clean your brushes about once a week following these steps.

- Mix up the cleaning solution in warm water and coat your brushes with it.
- Use one brush or comb to scrub up another one.
- Rinse off the cleaning solution.
- Dry the brushes thoroughly.

If you paid a lot for your hairbrushes, Borland suggests contacting the manufacturer to find the best way to clean them.

Get more mileage out of your makeup brushes. Keeping your makeup brushes clean does more than just keep your face clean. Washing them regularly also keeps your makeup clean and free of oils that can be transferred from your skin to the brush. That means your powder won't cake and eye shadows won't harden.

Some experts say to wash your makeup brushes twice a week and use hair conditioner on them monthly. Clean them with water and a good brush cleaner. You can also wash them in your daily skin cleanser, which is usually milder than brush cleaners. Or mix up your own brush cleanser from warm water and a bit of Woolite. Then mold the brush back to its original shape, and let it dry overnight.

But brushes don't last forever. When the bristles look frizzy and develop split ends, it's time to replace the brush.

Beauty tricks for frugal people

Try these tricks to use up every last bit of your favorite beauty products without wasting a drop.

Product	Tricks to get it all out
lotion in bottle	Store bottle upside down so the remaining lotion is near the opening when you're ready to use it.
lotion in pump dispenser	Lay bottle on its side, remove pump, use a cotton swab to dig out the last drops.
shampoo and conditioner	Add a few drops of water, shake bottle, pour into your hand to use.
toothpaste	Pull tube along edge of bathroom counter to scrape remains toward the opening. When that doesn't work anymore, cut tube in half and squeeze out the rest.
lipstick	Use a lip brush to reach the last bits.
hair spray	Once the level of hair spray is below the reach of the pump sprayer in a nonaerosol dispenser, take off the top and pour the remains into the new bottle.
cream	Squeeze remaining cream toward the cap, cut tube into thirds, and discard middle section. Place end of tube over section with opening to keep it fresh, or store in plastic bag. 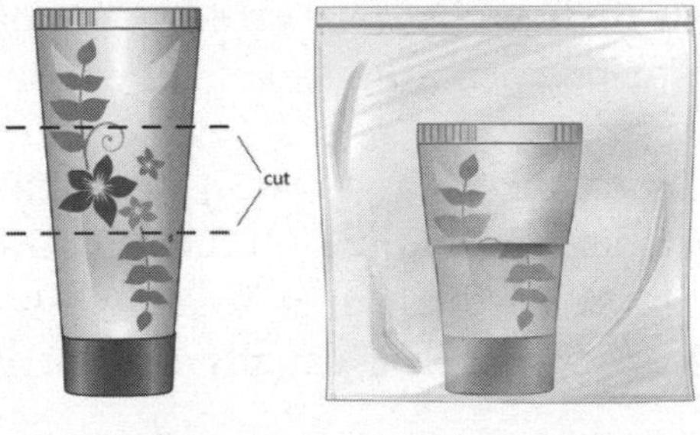

cut

Extend the life of razor blades. What's the greatest threat to the sharpness of your razor blades? It's not your hair – it's water.

Moisture that stays on the metal blades brings on microscopic rusting that causes flakes of metal to come off, so the edge of the blade becomes blunt and jagged. Then the blade ends up pulling at hairs rather than cutting them cleanly.

You can buy a handy razor dryer like the RazorPro, which sells for around $15. It uses a tiny fan to dry off your blade each day, but then you'll have to replace the batteries in the gadget every so often.

A simpler method is to dry off your razor on an old towel each day to keep moisture from damaging the blade. Or aim your hairdryer at the razor for a few seconds to get rid of moisture. Always store your razor outside the bathroom, which tends to be humid. Your razor blades will last longer, and you'll still enjoy a clean, comfortable shave.

Protect your pearly whites

Nothing makes you look older than dingy, stained teeth. Whitening strips can help, but the jury's still out about how safe they are to use frequently.

Instead, prevent stains from coffee, tea, or red wine by rubbing a thin layer of petroleum jelly on your teeth before you take a sip. The thin coating serves as a barrier, and it'll keep lipstick off your teeth, too. What's more, a small tub of petroleum jelly is cheaper than teeth-whitening strips.

Free liquid hand soap. Save those empty liquid hand soap dispensers, and refill them with your own homemade brew. It's easy and free.

When bars of soap get too small to use, dry them off and keep in a plastic bag. Once you've saved a half cup or more, chop the pieces into smaller bits. Bring two to three cups of water to a boil, pour in the soap, and stir until it dissolves. Let the mixture simmer for a few minutes.

After it cools, pour it into your recycled soap dispensers. You can make the mixture thicker by using less water, but it will work just fine even if it's thinner than store-bought liquid soap.

HANDY HINT

Soothe dry, chapped hands while you sleep

Wash your hands at bedtime, toweling them off but leaving them damp. Spread on a rich moisturizing cream while they're damp to trap in your skin's natural oils. Be sure the moisturizer is thick enough to stay in place. Put a dab on your hand, then turn it over. If it drips off, it's not thick enough.

Next, slip on a pair of cotton gloves and hit the hay. In the morning, your hands will feel soft. Repeat for another night or two for the best effect.

Moisturize with mayo. Oil, egg yolk, and lemon juice or vinegar. Those ingredients in mayonnaise can do great things to add moisture to both your skin and hair.

Use mayonnaise – the real kind, not salad dressing – as a night or day moisturizing cream. With a clean spatula, take one-half teaspoon or so from the jar and rub it gently onto your face and neck.

And next time your hair needs deep conditioning, pull out the mayo jar. First shampoo and rinse your hair, then generously apply real mayonnaise. Wrap your head in plastic and leave it in for about 15 minutes. Rinse and shampoo again.

Ice away pain for less. Headache, sinus pain, tennis injury – there's always a reason to have an ice pack nearby. Don't pay for an expensive reusable ice pack that may start to leak after a few uses. You can safely make your own soothing ice packs at home from these fillings and a good-quality zip-close plastic bag. Double-bag to ensure no leaks.

- Mix two parts water with one part rubbing alcohol. Add a bit of blue food coloring so nobody mistakes the bag for water. Pour into a zip-close bag, seal, and freeze. The alcohol keeps the pack from freezing solid, so it stays slushy and molds comfortably to your body.

- Fill a bag nearly full with liquid dishwashing soap like Dawn or Palmolive, freeze it, and enjoy a mess-free, slushy cool pack. This option is basically free, since you can thaw and use the dish soap when you need it.

- Use up that bottle of clear corn syrup by filling a bag nearly full. Freeze it, and you have another variety of soft ice pack.

Go herbal for great hair color. Using an herbal rinse is a traditional way to color your hair and cover the gray. You can cut down on using chemicals and save money by mixing up a rinse that works with your natural hair color.

To prepare an herbal rinse, bring two cups water to a boil, then pour the water over the herbs in a bowl. Let the mixture steep for several hours. Strain out the solids using a paper coffee filter, and the rinse is ready to use.

- Rosemary is an old-fashioned rinse to make your hair shiny and healthy looking. Use about 1 ounce of dried rosemary.

- Sage works to darken brunette hair and cover gray. Use about one-quarter cup dried or fresh sage leaves in the infusion, pour onto your hair after shampooing, and don't rinse it out.
- Chamomile or calendula petals will lighten blonde hair. Use a quarter cup of either to make an infusion. If you don't want to brew an infusion to lighten your blonde, simply mix one part lemon juice with three parts water for a simple rinse. Be sure to rinse out the lemon juice with cold water.
- Coffee grounds can darken brunette and red hair. Take used coffee grounds, steep in hot water for 20 minutes, then strain and rinse your hair.

HANDY HINT

Save your hair from pool damage

Swimming and water aerobics are great forms of exercise. Doing them in a chlorinated pool, however, can take a toll on your hair. Chemicals that keep the water clean can leave your hair damaged, dry — even green — over time. Don't let that happen.

- Wet your hair before you swim. When porous hair strands soak up fresh water, they can't quickly soak up chlorinated pool water.
- Block the water with oil. Apply some conditioner or hair oil to your hair before you swim. Keep it light to avoid creating a mess in the pool.
- Keep your hair dry. Consider wearing a swim cap or tying up your hair while in the pool, especially if you don't plan to swim underwater.
- Shampoo as soon as you're done. Washing the pool's chemicals out of your hair — especially using a clarifying shampoo — can help minimize the damage.

Go shabby-chic for a vintage look. Take a hint from pioneer women, and use black tea to dye fabric, drapes, or clothing. You can make a new quilt look antique by bathing it in a tea-dye bath. Or hide a stain on your favorite curtains or dish towels while you create a vintage look. Here's how.

Brew up a large batch of black tea, letting the bags steep until the tea is darker than the finished color you want. Wet your prewashed fabric – or quilt, clothing, or drapes – and wring it dry. Then immerse the fabric into the tea bath, swirling it to be sure the tea is evenly distributed. Let the fabric soak for at least 30 minutes, moving the fabric around occasionally so it colors evenly. When it's the shade you want, pour off the tea, dry the fabric in the dryer, and rinse in cold water.

The same trick also works with coffee. Just place used coffee grounds in a hot water bath to get the right color. Then soak your fabric until it's as dark as you want and rinse in cold water.

Never deal with tangled yarn again. No need to buy a yarn bra. Recycle plastic mesh vegetable bags and use them to keep yarn from tangling.

When crocheting or knitting with two colors of yarn at once, place both skeins or balls in the bag. Then thread the ends of each color yarn through different holes in the bag. No more tangles.

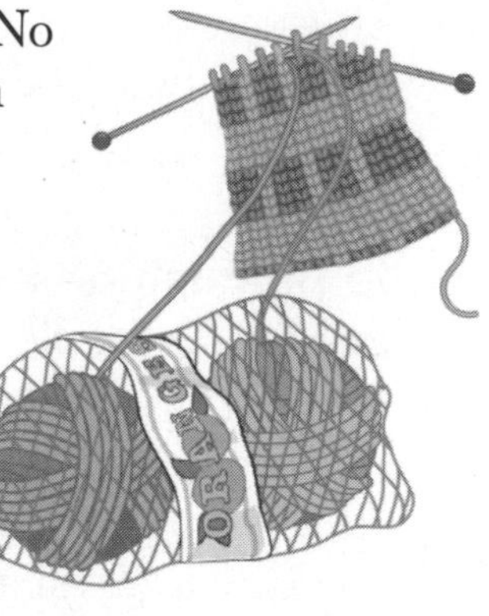

Put a lid on yarn for free. Keep your skein of yarn clean, dry, and free of tangles. Save the plastic container from a cylinder of pop-up wipes and use it as your yarn caddy. Be sure to rinse it out and let it dry first. Then place your ball or skein of yarn in the cylinder, thread the end of the yarn through the top hole, and replace the lid. You can pull yarn out as you need it while knitting or crocheting without having to chase a rolling ball.

Cheap yarn for the asking. Recycle old sweaters your family won't wear anymore or treasures from your local thrift store. Choose a sweater that's large, containing lots of yarn in a color you want to use for knitting or crocheting. Avoid acrylic and look for wool or cashmere on the label. Unravel the yarn starting at the shoulders, rolling it into balls. You'll need to wind the yarn into loose hanks so you can wash it by hand in hot water. When the water cools, rinse the yarn in more cool water and drip dry. Once the yarn is dry, it's ready for your handiwork.

Or try felting a 100-percent wool sweater into something great. Be sure the sweater's tag does not say "washable," since the process won't work. Wash the sweater in your machine in hot water using a cycle that creates lots of agitation. You may need to do this several times, letting the garment shrink and tighten up. The idea is to shrink the sweater while the fibers lock together, creating a kind of dense fabric that can be cut without raveling. Cut the sweater apart and use this thick felt to make place mats, mittens, eyeglass cases, purses – whatever you're in the mood to create.

Candle pincushion keeps needles shipshape. Avoid wasting the remains of a candle while you give needles and pins new life. Place the stump of a fat candle near your sewing chair and use it as a pincushion. Your pins won't get lost or rusty, and your needles will slide through fabric like butter after spending time in their waxy home. Be sure to clean any wax residue from the eye of your needle before you try to thread it.

ALTERNATE USES

Organize craft supplies with recycled containers

You can spend a lot of money on fancy, plastic storage bins, which may not even hold all your fabric, yarn, and other craft supplies. Reuse containers hanging around your house in clever ways to help corral items in the craft room.

- Store ribbons, trim, thread, and embroidery floss in clean cookie tins. The large popcorn tins work great for yarn.
- File sewing patterns in accordion folders, organizing by article of clothing or size.
- Use medicine bottles for tiny beads and snaps.
- Sort buttons by color into baby food jars.
- Put books of needles, pins, scissors, thimbles, and other small tools into an old toolbox.
- Keep large, zippered plastic bags, that come with sets of sheets or other bedding, to hold all parts of a project — pattern, fabric, and accessories.

Wash out any food containers in hot, soapy water before you repurpose them for craft supplies.

Cover your books in style. Use leftover fabric to make book dust jackets that let you decorate your bookshelves for free. You can even give a coffee table book extra sparkle when you use it as a showplace for vintage textiles.

You don't even need to buy fabric. Dig out some old cloth napkins, cut up a blouse that's gone out of style, or trim down a quilt block that never made it into a project. If you saved those sample pieces of upholstery fabric from your last redecorating spree, now is the time to use them. When you run out of textiles, head to the fabric store for colors and patterns you love.

Start by cutting the fabric several inches larger than needed to cover the book. Fold and press a quarter-inch to the wrong side along the top and bottom edges of fabric. Secure it with fabric glue or a narrow hem. Fold and press down the top and bottom to the wrong sides so the fabric is the same size as the height of the book. Finally, fold in the sides to fit the book and press to crease. Slip the front and back covers into the folded pockets.

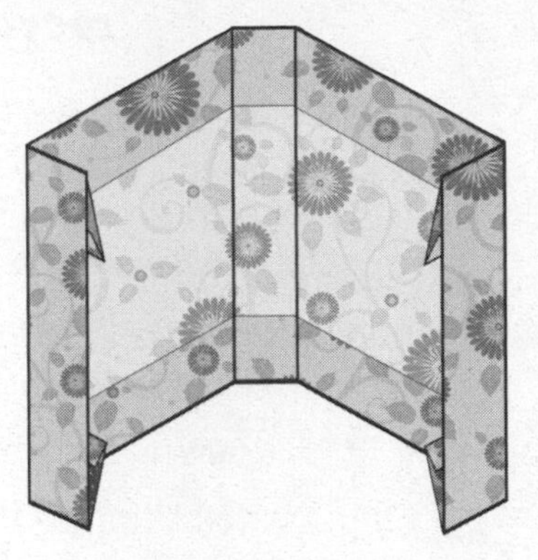

New life for used wrapping paper. Let your beautiful gift wrap have a second life by running it through your paper shredder. Colorful shredded paper becomes great filler for gift bags, saving you the cost of buying tissue paper. Shredded wrapping paper also does a good job of protecting a fragile item in a bag or shipping box. Keep different colors of shredded paper in separate bags, so you can coordinate the paper to your gift bag. You'll also cut down on household waste around the holidays.

Live safely on your own. Stay in your own home with no fear, even if you live alone. Follow these top 12 home safety tips, and you can feel safer in every room.

- Install smoke detectors and carbon monoxide alarms. Be sure to change the batteries twice a year.

- Think about how you would get out of your home in case of a fire. Make a detailed plan.
- Be sure there's a working fire extinguisher in your kitchen, and know how to use it.
- Pay attention when you're cooking, and have baking soda nearby in case of a fire.
- Scout out and get rid of falling hazards. Don't put down slippery area rugs or store items on the stairs.
- Call a professional to inspect and clean your chimney.
- Don't overload electrical outlets or run too many extension cords through the house.
- Never leave a space heater unattended.
- Make sure your water heater is set no higher than 120 degrees Fahrenheit.
- Add nonslip treads or a rubber mat to your tub or shower floor.
- Install telephones in various locations around the house so you'll always be close to one.
- Look into buying a personal emergency response system, an electronic device you can wear that lets you call for help in case of an emergency.

Simplify your life with nail polish. Skip the specialty products, and put this $3 item to work. Try these tricks to see how a simple little bottle of nail polish can keep you safe and comfortable at home while it saves you money.

- Place a drop of clear polish on tiny eyeglass screws before you tighten them. No need to worry about the screws coming loose and getting lost.

- Keep instructions on your medicine bottles from smudging by covering the print with clear polish.
- Coat the inside of your nickel-containing ring with clear polish if you get a rash when you wear it. The polish forms a temporary barrier to protect you if you're sensitive to the nickel.
- Mark each key on your ring using dots of different colors of polish. Your keys will be color-coded and you didn't have to spend money on colored key markers.
- Shrink an ugly wart by coating it with clear nail polish to block out air.
- Mark measurement levels on your glass or plastic measuring and medicine cups. Use a bright color that's easy to see and you won't waste ingredients or take the wrong dose of medicine.

Survive a power outage. Next time the power goes out in your house, follow this advice from the American Red Cross. You'll be comfortable and safe until the lights come back on.

- Use flashlights to provide light. Steer clear of lighting candles or oil-burning lamps, and you'll avoid the risk of a fire.
- Try to switch off any appliances and lights that were on when the power went out. Leave on a single lamp to alert you that the power has come back on.
- Unplug delicate electrical equipment such as computers and turn off equipment like air conditioners so power surges don't damage their insides.
- Keep the refrigerator and freezer closed as much as possible, so the cold air stays inside. This precaution can help save food from spoiling.
- Have a battery-powered radio ready, and use it to follow local news for updated information on the cause of the outage.

- Never run a generator indoors, including in the basement or in an attached garage. Dangerous carbon monoxide can collect in your home.
- Do not connect a generator to your home's electrical system. Instead, plug electrical devices directly into the outlets on the generator.
- Avoid driving if possible, since traffic lights may not be working.

HANDY HINT

Fill emergency kit for free

Stock a disaster supply kit with water, canned food, matches, batteries, a first aid kit — everything you might need if a hurricane, flood, or power outage hits your neighborhood.

Some items you can get for free. Save the sample-size bottles of shampoo, toothpaste, shower gel, and sunscreen you get from hotels and airlines. These are usually large enough to last a couple days. And why not stockpile the individually wrapped plastic cutlery and napkins you often get with takeout food?

The same with packets of sugar, salt, pepper, mustard, ketchup, mayonnaise, and creamer. You'll also find hundreds of ways to use plastic grocery bags, so make sure your disaster kit has a good supply.

18 steps to crime-proof your home. Stop losing sleep worrying about intruders in your home. Instead, take action by following these simple safety guidelines.

- Trim trees and shrubs near your doors and windows so there's nowhere to hide.

- If you must have bushes near the house, pick a variety with thorny, thick branches.
- Put down loose gravel or pebbles between the bushes so footsteps there will be noisy.
- Install lights and motion detectors outdoors.
- Be sure no valuables inside your home are visible from the outside.
- Look into installing grates, bars, padlocks, or bolts on your windows and doors.
- Be sure your exterior doors are either metal or solid hardwood, at least 1 3/4 inches thick.
- Install a peephole in your door, so you can see who's knocking.
- Put deadbolt locks on exterior doors.
- Be sure your double-hung windows are locked with either key locks or nails.
- Keep your fence gates locked at all times.
- Check to see that your pet door can be locked when you are out of town.
- Don't hide a key outside your house. Have a trusted neighbor keep it for you.
- Don't put valuables in the obvious places burglars will check first.
- Put away ladders and tools rather than leaving them out in the yard.
- Secure your shed and garage with padlocks.

- Install vertical bolts on sliding glass doors.
- Get help from your friends by organizing a neighborhood watch program.

Keep valuables safe without a safe. Don't make the mistake of hiding your goods in obvious places burglars will search first. These include:

- under the mattress
- in the cookie jar
- in the bathroom, where thieves look for prescription drugs
- at the back of your sock drawer
- out in plain view

Instead, hide your valuables where burglars rarely go – places full of clutter, like the basement or the garage. These rooms may be the safest spots in the house for valuables since they look too messy to bother searching through.

Whichever room you choose, camouflage your treasures by hiding them inside an ordinary looking object. You can buy fake soup cans, for instance, but some of these purchased "diversion safes" are so common they won't fool anyone. Try making your own ingenious hiding place from an item that blends into your decor. Think about using an empty baking soda box in the pantry, or hiding items inside a tennis ball you store with other sports equipment.

On the other hand, heirloom jewelry or other valuables that can't be replaced belong in a safety deposit box at the bank. You can store cash and other items you want at home in a safe, but be sure it's fireproof and hard to remove – possibly even bolted down.

Make your own diversion safe. A hardcover book with a secret compartment is a clever way to hide money, a passport, or small pieces of jewelry. Here's how to make one for little or no cost.

- Pick a title that will blend in with the other books on your shelf.
- Remove the book's dust jacket.
- Isolate the first dozen or so pages of the book by placing a sheet of plastic wrap behind them. You want to leave these pages as they are.
- Use a paintbrush to spread a solution of equal parts water and white glue onto the outside edges of the remaining pages in the book. You want them all to stick together.
- Place the book face down and set a stack of heavy books on top to keep the pages flat while the glue dries.
- With a sharp utility knife, carefully cut a rectangle from the inside of the glued-together pages, creating a hole in the book. Leave the outside glued edges uncut, so the book looks intact when it's closed.

- Spread more glue along the inside and outside edges of the book's secret space, and let it dry.

Get wise to handling kitchen grease fires. Seniors are three times as likely to be injured in a home fire as younger folks. Make sure that's not you by learning how to handle a small kitchen grease fire. Just remember, when in doubt, leave the building and call 911.

First, avoid doing things that can make a grease fire spread, like pouring water on it or trying to move the burning pan. Instead, smother the flames by either putting a lid on the pan or dousing the fire with handfuls of baking soda. As soon as it is safe to do so, turn off the stove and wait until the pan is completely cooled before you touch it.

Baking soda is your best friend in this situation. In fact, some fire extinguishers made for flammable liquids and electrical fires are actually just cans of pressurized sodium bicarbonate – baking soda. So don't throw away that out-of-date box of baking soda, but place it near the stove.

Two final notes of warning. Be sure you don't accidentally grab baking powder, which contains flour or starch and can make a fire spread. And keep your kitchen exhaust hood clean of grease, so there will be less fuel if a fire does start.

Put out fires like a pro. Don't be afraid to use your home fire extinguisher to put out a small fire that's contained to a single area. You can't practice using the device, since the pressurized contents are good for a single use only, but you can read the instructions and get to know your fire extinguisher beforehand, so you'll be ready when you need it.

Remember the word PASS, and you'll know the steps to follow.

P – Pull the safety pin, located where the trigger meets the top of the tank.

A – Aim low. Point the spray at the base of the fire.

S – Squeeze the lever slowly and smoothly.

S – Sweep the device from side to side, continuing to spray until the fire is completely out.

Your main goal is to get away from a fire safely, so know when to stop fighting the fire and leave.

HANDY HINT

Smart tool saves energy

An automatic controller can turn on the lights when you enter a room, then turn them off again when you leave. You'll save energy and money without having to roam around in the dark.

Consider the Sentina uSwitch Motion Sensor switch, available for around $35. Plug it into the wall socket, then connect a lamp. You decide how long you want the lamp to remain on after you leave a room — one minute, five minutes, or 10 minutes. You can order this product online at *www.datexx.com*.

2 tips for cleaning up glass shards. Oops – there goes another water glass, broken on the floor. Now you have both a mess and a safety hazard. Here's how to clean it up easily.

First, get out the flashlight. Turn off the overhead lights in the room, shut the curtains, and shine your flashlight where the glass is. Keep it aimed low, so the glass sparkles.

Once you see the glass pieces, pick up larger ones carefully with your fingers. Then use a slice or two of bread to pick up the tiny slivers. They'll get lodged in the bread when you press it on the glass shards, and your hand will stay safe. Toss out the bread immediately so nobody thinks it's good to eat. Sticky tape also works to pick up the shards.

INDEX

A

B

C

D

E

F

G

H

N

O

P

Q

R

S

T

U

V

W

Y

Z